9/92

# An
# Intimation
# of
# Things
# Distant

Anchor Books
Doubleday
New York · London · Toronto · Sydney · Auckland

# An Intimation of Things Distant

The Collected Fiction of Nella Larsen

Edited and with an Introduction by Charles R. Larson

With a Foreword by Marita Golden

AN ANCHOR BOOK
PUBLISHED BY DOUBLEDAY
a division of Bantam Doubleday Dell
Publishing Group, Inc.
666 Fifth Avenue, New York, New York 10103

ANCHOR BOOKS, DOUBLEDAY,
and the portrayal of an anchor
are trademarks of Doubleday,
a division of Bantam Doubleday
Dell Publishing Group, Inc.

The Anchor Books edition is the first publication of *An Intimation
of Things Distant*

An earlier version of Charles R. Larson's Introduction appeared in
the Spring 1989 edition of *Belles Lettres*.

Book design by Guenet Abraham

Library of Congress Cataloging-in-Publication Data

Larsen, Nella.
     *An Intimation of Things Distant: the collected fiction of Nella
  Larsen* / edited and with an Introduction by Charles R. Larson ;
  with a Foreword by Marita Golden.—1st Anchor Books ed.
        p.      cm.
     I. Larson, Charles R.   II. Title.
  PS3523.A7225A6   1992
  813'.52—dc20      91-3374
                       CIP

ISBN 0-385-42149-4
Introduction copyright © 1992 by Charles R. Larson
Foreword by Marita Golden copyright © 1992 by Anchor Books

10 9 8 7 6 5 4 3 2 1

# Contents

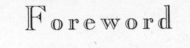

# Foreword

Nella Larsen's heroines are emotional nomads, women whose intelligence and genius for rebellion make them ill suited for the proscribed existence ordained by whites for blacks in 1920s and '30s segregated America. No tragic mulattoes here. These prim, proper colored ladies bristle with discontent and yearning. But, most important, they are driven by the impulse to shape their lives rather than suffer them, even when their grasp is unsure and they are careening full tilt towards disaster.

In Helga Crane and Clare Kendry, Nella Larsen has created two characters that are rich, complex, and contradictory. *Quicksand* and *Passing* launch each woman on a quest for self that predicts the themes of much of the most important writing in American literature of the last twenty years. Inevitably, any writer whose female protagonists resist the expected, the traditional, the "correct," is dialoguing with the literary legacy of Nella Larsen.

I initially discovered Nella Larsen as an undergraduate enrolled in a Black American Literature course taught by Charles Larson at American University. Even now I recall quite vividly the breath-snatching shudder that gripped me as I read the final pages of *Quicksand*. I can't remember any ending to a novel which frightened or warned me more effectively. I had not even become at that point the apprentice writer I would evolve into a few years later, but was a young woman reading everything I could find, questioning it and struggling to dredge up my own voice—a voice that, luckily for me, was nurtured and encouraged by parents who taught me that honesty and justice were more important than peace and quiet. I shuddered when I closed the final pages of *Quicksand* in 1970 because the cloistered world of academia allowed me on some level to intellectualize the bleak portrait of female destiny Larsen so deftly painted. And the powerful hold of the book for me sprang largely from the elegant timbre, the poise and remarkable beauty of Larsen's style.

In 1990, having weathered the Reagan years, witnessed the feminization of poverty in America, the retrenchment of the nation's commitment to social equality, having been married, become a mother, divorced, been a single parent, and remarried; having taught university courses disguised, I hope, as an intellectual agent provocateur, and told some of the still untold stories of my people in my own writing, now I shudder when I reach the conclusion of *Quicksand* for its eternal relevance.

At more moments in my life than I care to admit, I have been Helga Crane. Any woman who has searched for a metaphorical place in the sun, a job where she could be paid what she deserved (despite her ovaries), or sought to fashion a love, an affair, or a marriage based on respect and honor for self and partner, has been Helga Crane too. The angst, the tension that rivets the lives of Larsen's heroines makes their dilemmas completely contemporary and timeless.

The tension between the individual and society, the yoke-like manner in which society encroaches, and the courage Larsen's women find to resist predict writers as diverse as Ellison, Wright, Shange, and Walker. While the social milieu that Larsen explores is fairly insular, the black bourgeois, a thin sliver of 1920s black America, her vision is broad. The political and social debates of the period, the texture of the Harlem Renaissance, the specific fabric of Negro life, be it urban or rural, are captured with an eye for detail that is nearly surgical. While always delicate and often poetic, Larsen is tough-minded and withering in her critique of black bourgeois manners and obsessions.

The geography of the soul, the rocky, rich terrain of dreams, is in reality the setting for *Quicksand* and *Passing*. Helga Crane and Clare Kendry are women of enormous energy, talent, and sensitivity who find no release for or realization of those gifts in either black or white society. The real tragedy for both women is that there is literally no place for them to be somebody except in the arms of a man. Marriage is their only legitimate option. The worlds that created and confined them were neither large enough nor good enough for them. For these restless, spirited souls were hampered as much by the failure of imagination of those around them as by their own weaknesses. Both women could imagine themselves free from racial prejudice and, by extension, from sexual oppression—unfettered, whole; they just couldn't make themselves that way.

I have often thought that Helga Crane could have been, in another time zone/reality/universe, a better painter than Axel Olsen. Her keen eye for observation, her sensuality, idealism, her hunger for life, wedded to the largeness and breadth of her female vision, would have created works to drench the eye and salvage the soul. At other times I have imagined Helga Crane as a dancer or, like Larsen herself, a writer, but one who would find a way to devise a more satisfying ending than the script the world had handed her. That's what I have dreamed.

Literature at its best is a prescription. And the best writers imagine us all free. With Nella Larsen, I wait for the world to finally, one day, listen to its scribes, the only conscience it sanctions and steadfastly ignores. And like Nella Larsen, I try to nudge the world closer to beauty and farther away from madness with every word I write.

*Marita Golden*

# Introduction

The erroneous "facts" concerning the life and career of Nella Larsen are nothing less than legion. Her brief literary career is said to have come to an abrupt halt because of the charges of plagiarism concerning her only published short story. After that awkward incident in 1930, she is said to have ceased her creative efforts and disappeared not only from the Harlem artistic scene but from the consciousness of her many friends as well. Larsen's readers have speculated that she passed for white—in the manner of the heroine of her 1929 novel, *Passing*. At the time of her death, there were no published obituaries. Her childhood, her parentage, and the date of her birth have all been incorrectly recorded—as have virtually all of the other details of her life. Worse, critics have been content to accept hearsay instead of researching the actual facts, thereby perpetuating the distortions that Larsen herself often generated in order to conceal the painful events of her private life. One fact, however, is indisputable. If one classifies Jean Toomer's *Cane* (1923) as a collection of his works—as do many critics—then Nella Larsen is the major novelist of that coalescence of African–American aesthetic expression during the 1920s known as the Harlem Renaissance.

In the early part of that fabulous decade, Larsen and her husband, Elmer Imes, were part of the Harlem elite, hobnobbing with some of the most famous people of the era: W. E. B. DuBois, Walter White, Jessie and Arthur Fauset, Charles S. Johnson (the editor of *Opportunity*), James Weldon Johnson, and Carl Van Vechten. When Nella married Elmer in 1919, she must have been the envy of many of her friends. Elmer had a Ph.D. in Physics from the University of Michigan at a time when most black Americans had not graduated from high school. Nella herself, a graduate of the Lincoln Hospital of Nursing, would shortly embark upon a second career. As a librarian at the Harlem branch of the New York City Public Library, she was clearly in the eye of the storm—the explosion in black artistic creativity that created what Alain Locke, in 1925, called the New Negro. Parties, cabarets, literary soirees. Harlem was the place to be, and Nella was very much a part of it. Her letters written during the early part of the 1920s illustrate that she derived a great amount of satisfaction from being one of Harlem's intellectuals.

Exactly when and why Larsen decided to become a writer, it is difficult to tell. In an interview she gave to the *Amsterdam News* (May 23, 1928), she claimed that she had begun writing because of complications with her health. In that interview, Larsen is described as a "modern" woman who

> smokes, wears her dresses short, does not believe in religion, churches and the like, and feels that people of the artistic type have a definite chance to help solve the race problem.

Her hobbies are doing her own housework, and there is much to do to keep a five-room apartment so clean (and from the smell from the kitchen door she must be an excellent cook), sewing and playing bridge.

Nella's first publications, in 1920, were in *The Brownies' Book*, a magazine for black children edited by Jessie Fauset. For those two works, she used the by-line Nella Larsen Imes, and she claimed in the introductory remarks to each piece that she had spent her childhood days in Denmark. Thereafter, she worked on fiction for the adult reader, in time publishing two short stories in *Young's Magazine*: "The Wrong Man," January 1926, and "Freedom," in April of the same year. In later years, she would refer to these stories as "hack writing," as she must have felt in part when she wrote them, since they were published under the pseudonymous anagram: Allen Semi. Most of the stories that appeared in *Young's Magazine* at the time would be called pulp fiction; the writers of these stories have become as forgotten as the magazine itself.

Both of these stories were probably thrown up as warning signs for Elmer, who was a notorious womanizer and, by 1926, well on his way to contributing to the demise of their relationship. Under the surface narrative, both stories tell us that marriage is often a precarious balancing act, especially when spouses have not been honest with each other and have concealed aspects of their former selves. Both stories are free of any racial commentary—no doubt because of the magazine in which they appeared, though Nella herself at this early stage in her artistic career was known to waffle a bit about her racial origins.

By the time Nella's first novel, *Quicksand*, was published, in March of 1928, she had stopped working as a librarian. She had also decided to use her maiden name for her work, a decision which was probably interpreted by her friends as a clear indication that her marriage was in trouble. Though the Harlem Renaissance was in full swing, Nella could not have helped but be disappointed that it was not *Quicksand* that became a best seller that year but Claude McKay's much more sensational *Home to Harlem*. Still, she could take comfort in the fact that her novel received the better reviews, as well as an award from the Harmon Foundation. The enthusiasm for *Quicksand* has only increased with the passing years.

*Quicksand* is the story of an educated black woman's inability to find her niche in the contemporary world. The scope of Helga Crane's search is international (America and Europe) and is exacerbated by the fact that she is not only middle-class but mulatto. What separates Larsen's novel from earlier works concerned with the plight of the tragic mulatto (Frances Harper's *Iola Leroy*, 1892, or Charles Chesnutt's *The House Behind the Cedars*, 1900, for example) is the depth of her characterization, as well as her superior narrative technique. Helga Crane is the most fully realized and convincing black woman depicted in American fiction to that date. Above all, hers is a portrait of loneliness and pain, despair and sorrow—qualities which bind her to the heroines of any number of later works by black women writers: Zora Neale Hurston, Ann Petry, Toni Morrison, Gayl Jones, Alice Walker, Gloria Naylor.

The novel clearly draws upon autobiographical details from Larsen's own troubled past, converting the raw materials of her life into an often spellbinding psychological portrait of her heroine. As a child, Helga is taught to regard her color with hatred and self-loathing. Like Larsen herself, Helga's mother is white, her father black. The story describes a number of painful incidents in her adolescence when Helga is separated from the rest of her family. The eventual reality of her mixed heritage and subsequent loneliness follows her all of her life (both in the South and in the North in the United States, as well as in Europe) and destroys most of her relationships with other people once she becomes an adult. The novel's grim ending implies that educated black women (sophisticated and cultured black women, middle-class black women) are trapped in a life with few if any satisfactory alternatives. Intellect is a dangerous commodity; thinking leads to unhappiness and misery. The only possible escape is into emotion—abandonment of the mind. Larsen suggests that there can be no other escape from racism, and even a return to one's roots, for a woman like Helga Crane, may offer only temporary solace.

*Passing*, published the following year, was equally despairing in its depiction of the lives of middle-class black women. The story has frequently been misconstrued as Clare Kendry's tragedy, since she is the character who has crossed over the color line, concealed her racial origins, and whose past is eventually discovered by her bigoted white husband. Larsen's superior craft added new meaning to the subject implied by her title. No passing novel can be regarded as anything other than a strong indictment of American life; people are driven to such drastic measures because of American racism and the need for economic survival. When Irene first muses over Clare's boldness, Larsen states, "She wished to find out about this hazardous business of 'passing,' this breaking away from all that was familiar and friendly to take one's chance in another environment, not entirely strange, perhaps, but certainly not entirely friendly. What, for example, one did about background, how one accounted for oneself. And how one felt when one came into contact with other Negroes." Yet the central story—for all of the realities of Clare's unhappy life—is what happens to her childhood friend, Irene.

After several encounters between the two women, Irene Redfield's almost morbid fascination with Clare Kendry's fate becomes the novel's main focus. It is Irene who cannot control her curiosity and thrusts her hand into the tar baby (Clare) and thereby finds herself trapped in a situation she never foresaw. Thus, the primary theme is not race (as has usually been interpreted) but marital stability. *Passing* describes Irene's attempts to keep her marriage intact in the face of her husband's possible adultery with Clare. In many ways, Larsen has written an old-fashioned tale of jealousy, infidelity, and marital disintegration. Although at the end Irene may believe that her "sudden moment of action" has released her from the threat of losing her husband, one cannot help pondering about Brian's absence in the final pages of the novel. In a strange transference of conditions, Irene has inherited Clare's life of duplicity and isolation.

By the time *Passing* was published, the fault lines in Nella Larsen's own marriage were so unstable that it was only a matter of time before the relationship would end. Clearly aware of this, she began making preparations for her future, since her writing had not brought her economic security. She applied for and was awarded a Guggenheim in 1930, distinguishing herself as the first black woman to be so honored. Yet some of the glory was already diminished by charges that her story, "Sanctuary," published in *Forum* in January of that year, had been plagiarized. (The accusations, published in a letter to the editor in the April issue, stated that "Sanctuary" bore a "striking resemblance" to Sheila Kaye-Smith's short story "Mrs. Adis.")

The power of Larsen's story is undeniable. Race is the strongest tie that binds people together. Even though Jim killed her son, Annie will protect him because he is black. Nowhere else in her published work had Nella Larsen made such an emphatic statement about blackness. The story is terse, direct—totally convincing in its use of character and motivation, as well as in its successful employment of dialect (the sole piece of dialect fiction Larsen published during her career). Followers of her work coming upon "Sanctuary" must have been surprised. Did the story herald a shift in her attentions away from middle-class blacks to that of the folk?

The Guggenheim year, which was spent mostly in southern Europe, permitted Larsen to gain new perspectives on her writing and her marriage, though not exactly the ones she may have expected. By the time she returned to the United States, early in 1932, both were essentially at a dead end. Still, she made one final attempt to patch up the relationship with Elmer, even to the extent of spending some months with him at Fisk University in Nashville (where Dr. Imes had been installed as a kind of one-man Physics Department). But the rift was apparently too wide for them to repair. Their divorce, which became official on August 30 of the following year, was described in scandalous headlines in three articles in the *Baltimore Afro–American*:

FISK PROFESSOR
IS DIVORCED BY
N.Y. NOVELIST

Friends Think Love
Cooled While Wife
Wintered in Europe

RECALL "JUMP"
FROM WINDOW

Elmer's mistress was referred to as "a white member of Fisk University's administrative staff," and Nella herself was said to have jumped out of a window and broken her leg.

Larsen's withdrawal (her so-called disappearance) can be pinpointed to several of these congruent events in her life. Certainly, the negative publicity about her divorce (front-page headlines) must have been a bitter pill to swallow—even worse because Elmer's mistress was a white woman. As she said of Imes years later to one of her co-workers, "He broke my heart." So total was her sense of rejection that she lived for several years in a state of depression. One particularly revealing fact about her later life is that she identified herself as *Mrs. Imes* and not as Nella Larsen. (This is also the reason why critics failed for so long to locate her death certificate.)

Nella's rejection by Elmer came almost simultaneously with the difficulties she was encountering with her writing. The charges of plagiarism after the publication of "Sanctuary" were seconded by intense backbiting by a number of her so-called writer friends, who were jealous of her recent successes. The similarities between the two stories are embarrassing. Yet she was too much of a consummate artist to have attempted such a deliberate borrowing. Furthermore, as a librarian she would have understood the consequences of such an act more clearly than almost anyone else. It seems much more likely that she possessed something akin to a photographic memory, and for that reason "Sanctuary" contains those telling similarities to "Mrs. Adis." Perhaps, also, "Sanctuary" was written out of a need to prove to herself that she could survive as a writer, support herself between novels. When she submitted it to *Forum*, it was still months before she would learn the results of her application for a Guggenheim.

She could probably have lived with the public humiliation if her subsequent work had not met with such total rejection. *Mirage*, the novel that she wrote on her Guggenheim, was quickly rejected by

Alfred A. Knopf, the publisher of her first two books. Two other novels that she wrote after her return to the United States met with similar disapproval. Thus, there was a series of rejections that thwarted her career (both as artist and as wife) in the early 1930s— at the same time that the Depression had slammed a door on the Harlem Renaissance and the New Negro was no longer in fashion.

The alimony that Elmer paid her ($150 a month) until his death in 1941 was apparently adequate for Nella's well-being and may possibly have been her only source of livelihood during the 1930s. About the time of his death, however, she returned to her earlier profession: nursing. By February 14, 1944, she had worked herself up to Chief Nurse at Gouverneur Hospital, in New York City. She lived nearby on Second Avenue, more at a geographical distance from Harlem than an emotional one. Beginning with the Manhattan telephone directory for 1955/1956, she is listed as "Imes, Nella L. Mrs." In all of her nursing positions, she was known as Nella Imes. In September of 1954, her position at Gouverneur was changed to Night Supervisor. Then in 1962, some months after she was mugged, she transferred to Metropolitan Hospital, as a Supervisor of Nurses, a position she held until her retirement. She was found dead in her apartment the following year: March 30, 1964.

The mysteries of Nella Larsen's life after the Harlem Renaissance —a series of responses to repeated rejection—are all the more revealing when juxtaposed to a number of events of her childhood. Yet many of these details are difficult to access because she rewrote her early life as if it were one of her novels. The dust jacket for *Passing*, for example, informed readers that

> Nella Larsen's mother was Danish, her father a Negro from the Virgin Islands, formerly the Danish West Indies. When she was two years old her father died and shortly afterwards her mother married a man of her own race and nationality. At eight she and her half-sister attended a small private

school whose pupils were mostly the children of German or Scandinavian parents. When she was sixteen she went to Denmark to visit relatives of her mother and remained there for three years.

Some of this information is true, but much of it is simple fabrication. Although she always claimed that April 13, 1893, was the date of her birth, the year in fact was 1891. There is no birth certificate to verify this date, but the earlier year is easy to establish because of documents pertaining to Anna, Nella's half-sister, whose father was white. The place of Nella's birth—which she claimed as Chicago—is much more problematic. A close friend of the Larsen family for nearly fifty years claimed that Nella's mother told her on several occasions that Nella was born in New York and that her father was an African-American chauffeur for the family for whom she (Mary Hanson) worked. Thus, the question of Nella's biological father remains conjectural.

When Mary Hanson married Peter Larsen, February 7, 1894, their child (Anna) was already a year and a half old. Census documents and the death certificates of these three people help establish some of the details concerning the Larsen household. The most revealing fact (from the 1910 census) helps us speculate about what had already happened. In the category listing family information ("Mother of How Many Children"; "Number Here"), a "1" has been written. "Number Now Living" also indicates only one. Thus, not only was Nella no longer living with them (she would have been nineteen) but she had also been written out of their lives.

Something traumatic happened to Nella between the years 1894 (when her mother married Peter Larsen) and the time of the 1910 census. Exactly what that event was we may never know, but there are certainly clues in *Quicksand*. Early in the novel, Helga is described as a "solitary girl with no family connections." When Helga declines her Danish suitor's proposal, she informs him, " 'If we were married, you might come to be ashamed of me, to hate me, to hate all dark people. My mother did that.' " Other comments (such as "her unloved, unloving, and unhappy childhood") scattered throughout the narrative support the thesis that Helga Crane is a thinly disguised portrait of Larsen herself. Perhaps the most revealing support of this conjecture, however, comes from Anna, who not only inherited all of her half-sister's estate when Nella died, but remarked to a family friend, " 'Why, I didn't know that I had a sister.' "

My speculation is that Nella was removed from the Larsen household sometime around the age of nine or ten, though it may have been later. It had to have been early enough for her sister, Anna, to have completely forgotten about her. Nella's pain may have been alleviated by her eventual repression of her past, the reason for rewriting her childhood when she became an adult. Why not embroider it in *Quicksand* by placing Helga Crane in a culture (Copenhagen) free of racial prejudice—the exact opposite of the one in which she had grown up in America? If she could not escape the trauma of her own childhood, she could at least escape it symbolically through her art. What a pathetic irony that her writing career was snuffed out so abruptly.

Other relevant facts concerning Nella Larsen's childhood and years during the Harlem Renaissance tell us that she never traveled to Denmark and attended school there as she repeatedly claimed (Department of State passport records); that she did not earn a degree in Library Science as she stated a number of times (Columbia University records); and that she did not pass for white after the decline of the New Negro. Such a radical move would have been totally inconsistent with her sense of pride and justice. She was proud of her race and her own accomplishments.

The fact is that after returning to her earlier nursing profession—which I do not believe can be looked at as a negative act—she excelled. In the eyes of her peers at Gouverneur Hospital, Nella became an exemplary worker, who instilled in others a sense of respect and admiration. "She really loved people," one of them told me, "especially the sick. She would see that anything could be done to help them." She was dedicated to her career and frequently rewarded for her superior efforts. Though reclusive and lonely when away from the hospital, at work she accepted the mandate of her profession. That there was no obituary to record her death hardly mattered. Her funeral was attended by forty or fifty of her co-workers.

Nella Larsen Imes was a sad, beautiful, lonely woman—elegant (as her pictures show us), sophisticated, witty, cultured, urbane. Tragedy and disappointment were constants in her life, yet she ultimately worked out a pattern of survival that permitted her to administer to the sick and the downcast, as she inched along her own lonely pathway toward obscurity and oblivion. As she effaced herself and became more reclusive, her professional life soared. She knew, even if she was not rewarded in kind, that the pain of the inner soul can be mitigated by others and that invisibility is often one's only guarantee of survival.

*Charles R. Larson*

## A Note on the Texts

To make these texts from the 1920s more accessible to the contemporary reader, minor changes have been made with spelling, punctuation, capitalization, and spacing. British spellings ("colour" instead of "color") have been altered throughout. Obvious typographical errors in the original texts have been corrected.

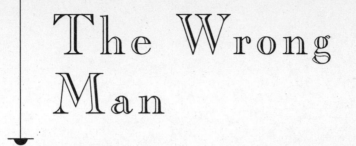

# The Wrong Man

The room blazed with color. It seemed that the gorgeous things which the women were wearing had for this once managed to subdue the strident tones of the inevitable black and white of the men's costumes. Tonight they lent just enough of preciseness to add interest to the riotously hued scene. The place was crowded but cool, for a gentle breeze blew from the Sound through the large open windows and doors, now and then stirring some group of flowers.

Julia Romley, in spite of the smoke-colored chiffon gown (ordered specially for the occasion) which she was wearing, seemed even more flamingly clad than the rest. The pale indefinite gray but increased the flaring mop of her hair; scarlet, a poet had called it. The satiny texture of her skin seemed also to reflect in her cheeks a cozy tinge of that red mass.

Julia, however, was not happy tonight. A close observer would have said that she was actively disturbed. Faint abstraction, trite remarks nervously offered, and uncontrolled restlessness marred her customary perfect composure. Her dreamy gray eyes stole frequently in the direction of Myra Redmon's party. Myra always had a lion in tow, but why that particular man? She shook a little as she wondered.

Suddenly, the orchestra blared into something wild and impressionistic, with a primitive staccato understrain of jazz. The buzz of conversation died, strangled by the savage strains of the music. The crowd stirred, broke, coalesced into twos, and became a whirling mass. A partner claimed Julia and they became part of the swaying mob.

"Some show, what?" George Hill's drawling voice was saying, while he secretly wondered what had got into Julia; she was so quiet, not like herself at all.

Julia let her eyes wander over the moving crowd. Young men, old men, young women, older women, slim girls, fat women, thin men, stout men, glided by. The old nursery rhyme came into her mind. She repeated it to George in a singsong tone:

> *"Rich man, poor man,*
> *Beggar man, thief,*
> *Doctor, lawyer,*
> *Indian chief."*

George nodded. "Yes, that's it. Everybody's here and a few more. And look, look! There's the 'Indian chief.' Wonder who he is? He certainly looks the part."

Julia didn't look; she knew what she would see. A tall, thin man, his lean face yellowed and hardened as if by years in the tropics; a man, perhaps, a bit unused to scenes of this kind, purposely a little aloof and, one suspected, more than a little contemptuous.

She felt a flash of resentful anger against Myra. Why was she always carting about impossible people? It was disgusting. It was worse—it was dangerous. Certainly it was about to become dangerous to her, Julia Romley, erstwhile . . . She let the thought die unfinished, it was too unpleasant.

She had been so happy, so secure, and now this: Ralph Tyler, risen from the past to shatter the happiness which she had grasped for herself. Must she begin all over again? She made a hasty review of her life since San Francisco days: Chicago and the art school where she had studied interior decorating with the money that Ralph Tyler had given her; New York, her studio and success; Boston, and marriage to Jim Romley. And now this envied gay life in one of Long Island's most exclusive sets. Yes, life had been good to her at last, better than she had ever dreamed. Was she about to lose everything—love, wealth, and position? She shivered.

"Cold?" Again George's drawling voice dragging her back to the uncertain present.

"No, not cold. Just someone walking over my grave," she answered laughingly. "I'm rotten company tonight, George. I'm sorry; I'll do better. It's the crowd, I guess."

Her husband claimed her for the next dance. A happy married pair, their obvious joy in each other after five wedded years was the subject of amused comment and mild jokes among their friends. "The everlasting lovers," they were dubbed, and the name suited them as perfectly as they suited each other.

"What's wrong, Julie, old girl?" asked Jim after a few minutes' baffled scrutiny. "Tired?"

"Nothing, nothing. I just feel small, so futile in this crush; sort of trapped, you know. Why *do* the Arnolds have so many people to their things?" Quickly regretting her display of irritation, she added: "It's wonderful, though—the people, the music, the color, and these lovely rooms, like a princess's ball in a fairy tale."

"Yes, great," he agreed. "Lots of strangers here, too; most of them distinguished people from town."

"Who's the tall browned man with Myra, who looks like—well,

like an Indian chief?" She laughed a little at her own pleasantry, just to show Jim that there was nothing troubling her.

"Doesn't he, though? Sort of self-sufficient and superior and a bit indifferent, as if he owned us all and despised the whole tribe of us. I guess you can't blame him much. He probably thinks we're a soft, lazy, self-pampering lot. He's Ralph Tyler, an explorer, just back from some godforsaken place on the edge of nowhere. Been head of some expedition lost somewhere in Asia for years, given up for dead. Discovered a buried city or something; great contribution to civilization and all that, you know. They say he brought back some emeralds worth a king's ransom."

"Do you know him, Jim?"

"Yes; knew him years ago in college. Didn't think he'd remember me after such a long time and all those thrilling adventures, but he did. Honestly, you could have knocked me over with a feather when he came over to me and put out his hand and said, 'Hello there, Jim Romley.' Nice, wasn't it?" Jim's handsome face glowed. He was undoubtedly flattered by the great man's remembrance. He went on enthusiastically: "I'm going to have him out to the house, Julie; that is, if I can get him. Small, handpicked dinner party. What say?"

She shivered again.

"Cold?"

"No, not cold. Just someone walking over my grave." She laughed, amused at the double duty of the superstition in one evening, and glad too that Jim had not noticed that his question had passed unanswered.

Dance followed dance. She wasn't being a success tonight. She knew it, but somehow she couldn't make small talk. Her thoughts kept wandering to that tall browned man who had just come back from the world's end. One or two of her partners, after trying in vain to draw her out, looked at her quizzically, wondering if the impossible had happened. Had Julia and old Jim quarreled?

At last she escaped to a small deserted room on an upper floor, where she could be alone to think. She groped about in her mind for some way to avoid that dinner party. It spelled disaster. She must find some way to keep Ralph Tyler from finding out that she was the wife of his old schoolmate. But if he were going to be here for any length of time, and Jim seemed to think that he would, she would have to meet him. Perhaps she could go away? . . . No, she dared not; anything might happen. Better to be on hand to ward off the blow when it fell. She sighed, suddenly weary and beaten. It was hopeless. And she had been so happy! Just a faint shadow of uneasiness, at first, which had gradually faded as the years slipped away.

She sat for a long time in deep thought. Her face settled into determined lines; she made up her mind. She would ask, plead if necessary, for his silence. It was the only way. It would be hard, humiliating even, but it must be done if she were to continue to be happy in Jim's love. She couldn't bear to look ahead to years without him.

She crossed the room and wrote a note to Ralph Tyler, asking him to meet her in the summerhouse in one of the gardens. She hesitated a moment over the signature, finally writing *Julia Hammond*, in order to prepare him a little for the meeting.

After she had given the note into the hand of a servant for delivery "to Mr. Tyler, the man with Mrs. Redmon," she experienced a slight feeling of relief. "At least I can try," she thought as she made her way to the summerhouse to wait. "Surely, if I tell him about myself and Jim, he'll be merciful."

The man looked curiously at the woman sitting so motionless in the summerhouse in the rock garden. Even in the darkness she felt his gaze upon her, though she lacked the courage to raise her eyes to look at him. She waited expectantly for him to speak.

After what seemed hours but was, she knew, only seconds, she understood that he was waiting for her to break the silence. So she began to speak in a low hesitating voice:

"I suppose you think it strange, this request of mine to meet me here alone; but I had to see you, to talk to you. I wanted to tell you about my marriage to Jim Romley. You know him?"

"Yes, I know him."

"Well," she went on, eagerly now, "you see, we're so happy! Jim's so splendid, and I've tried to be such a good wife. And I thought—I thought—you see, I thought—" The eager voice trailed off on a note of entreaty.

"Yes, you thought?" prompted the man in a noncommittal tone.

"Well, you see, I thought that if you knew how happy we were, and how much I love him, and that since you know Jim, that you—you—"

She stopped. She couldn't go on, she simply couldn't. But she must. There he stood like a long, menacing shadow between her and the future. She began again, this time with insinuating flattery:

"You have so much yourself now—honor, fame, and money—and you've done such splendid things! You've suffered too. How you must have suffered! Oh, I'm glad of your success; you deserve it. You're a hero, a great man. A little thing like that can't matter to you now and it means everything to me, everything. Please spare me my little happiness. Please be kind!"

"But I don't understand." The man's voice was puzzled. "How 'kind'? What is it you're asking?"

Reading masked denial in the question, Julia began to sob softly.

"Don't tell Jim! Please, don't tell Jim! I'll do anything to keep him from knowing, anything."

"But aren't you making a mistake? I—"

"Mistake?" She laughed bitterly. "I see; you think I should have told him. You think that even now I should tell him that I was your mistress once. You don't know Jim. He'd never forgive that. He wouldn't understand that, when a girl has been sick and starving on the streets, anything can happen to her; that she's grateful for food and shelter at any price. You won't tell him, will you?"

"But I'm sure," stammered the tall figure, fumbling for cigarettes, "I'm sure you've made a mistake. I'm sorry. I've been trying to—"

Julia cut him off. She couldn't bear to hear him speak the refusing words, his voice seemed so grimly final. She knew it was useless, but she made a last desperate effort:

"I was so young, so foolish, and so hungry; but Jim wouldn't understand." She choked over the last words.

He shook his head—impatiently, it seemed to the agonized woman.

"Mrs. Romley, I've been trying to tell you that you've made a mistake. I'm sorry. However, I can assure you that your secret is safe with me. It will never be from my lips that Jim Romley hears you have been—er—what you say you have been."

Only the woman's sharply drawn quivering breath indicated that she had heard. A match blazed for a moment as he lighted his cigarette with shaking hands. Julia's frightened eyes picked out his face in the flickering light. She uttered a faint dismayed cry.

She had told the wrong man.

# Freedom

He wondered, as he walked deftly through the impassioned traffic on the Avenue, how she would adjust her life if he were to withdraw from it. . . . How peaceful it would be to have no woman in one's life! These months away took on the appearance of a liberation, a temporary recess from a hateful existence in which he lived in intimacy with someone he did not know and would not now have chosen. . . . He began, again, to speculate on the pattern her life would take without him. Abruptly, it flashed upon him that the vague irritation of many weeks was a feeling of smoldering resentment against her.

The displeasure that this realization caused him increased his ill humor and distaste. He began to dissect her with an acrimomy that astonished himself. Her unanimated beauty seemed now only a thin disguise for an inert mind, and not for the serene beauty of soul which he had attributed to her. He suspected, too, a touch of depravity, perhaps only physical, but more likely mental as well. Reflection convinced him that her appeal for him was bounded by the senses, for witness his disgust and clarity of vision, now that they were separated. How could he have been so blinded? Why, for him she had been the universe; a universe personal and unheedful of outside persons or things. He had adored her in a slavish fashion. He groaned inwardly at his own mental caricature of himself, sitting dumb, staring at her in fatuous worship. What an ass he had been!

His work here was done, but what was there to prevent him from staying away for six months—a year—forever? . . . Never to see her again! . . . He stopped, irresolute. What would she do? He tried to construct a representation of her future without him. In his present new hatred, she became a creature irresistibly given to pleasure at no matter what cost. A sybarite! A parasite too!

He was prayerfully thankful that appreciation of his danger had come before she had sapped from him all physical and spiritual vitality. But her future troubled him even while he assured himself that he knew its road, and laughed ruefully at the picture of her flitting from mate to mate.

A feverish impatience gripped him. Somehow, he must contrive to get himself out of the slough into which his amorous folly had precipitated him. . . . Three years. Good God! At the moment, those three years seemed the most precious of his life. And he had foolishly thrown them away. He had drifted pleasantly, peacefully, without landmarks; would be drifting yet but for the death of a friend whose final affairs had brought him away. . . .

He started. Death! Perhaps she would die. How that would simplify matters for him. But no; she would not die. He laughed without amusement. She would not die; she would outlast him, damn her! . . . An angry resentment, sharp and painful as a whiplash, struck him. Its passing left him calm and determined. . . .

He braced himself and continued to walk. He had decided; he would stay. With this decision, he seemed to be reborn. He felt cool, refreshed, as if he had stepped out from a warm, scented place into a cold, brisk breeze. He was happy. The world had turned to silver and gold, and life again became a magical adventure. Even the placards in the shops shone with the light of paradise upon them. One caught and held his eye. Travel . . . Yes, he would travel; lose himself in India, China, the South Seas . . . Radiance from the most battered vehicle and the meanest pedestrian. Gladness flooded him. He was free.

A year, thick with various adventures, had slid by since that spring day on which he had wrenched himself free. He had lived, been happy, and with no woman in his life. The break had been simple: a telegram hinting at prolonged business and indefinite return. There had been no reply. This had annoyed him, but he told himself it was what he had expected. He would not admit that, perhaps, he had missed her letter in his wanderings. He had persuaded himself to believe what he wanted to believe—that she had not cared. Actually, there had been confusion in his mind, a complex of thoughts which made it difficult to know what he really had thought. He had imagined that he shuddered at the idea that she had accepted the most generous offer. He pitied her. There was, too, a touch of sadness, a sense of something lost, which he irritably explained on the score of her beauty. Beauty of any kind always stirred him. . . . Too bad a woman like that couldn't be decent. He was well rid of her.

But what had she done? How had he taken it? His contemptuous mood visualized her at times, laughing merrily at some jest made by his successor, or again sitting silent, staring into the fire. He would be conscious of every detail of her appearance: her hair simply arranged, her soft dark eyes, her delicate chin propped on hands rivaling the perfection of La Gioconda's. Sometimes there would be a reversion to the emotions which had ensnared him, when he ached with yearning, when he longed for her again. Such moments were rare.

. . .

Another year passed, during which his life had widened, risen, and then crashed. . . .

Dead? How could she be dead? Dead in childbirth, they had told him, both his mistress and the child she had borne him. She had been dead on that spring day when, resentful and angry at her influence in his life, he had reached out toward freedom—to find only a mirage; for he saw quite plainly that now he would never be free. It was she who had escaped him. Each time he had cursed and wondered, it had been a dead woman whom he had cursed and about whom he had wondered. . . . He shivered; he seemed always to be cold now. . . .

Well rid of her! How well he had not known, nor how easily. She was dead. And he had cursed her. But one didn't curse the dead. . . . Didn't one? Damn her! Why couldn't she have lived, or why hadn't she died sooner? For long months he had wondered how she had arranged her life, and all the while she had done nothing but to complete it by dying.

The futility of all his speculations exasperated him. His old resentment returned. She *had* spoiled his life; first by living and then by dying. He hated the fact that she had finished with him, rather than he with her. He could not forgive her. . . . Forgive her? She was dead. He felt somehow that, after all, the dead did not care if you forgave them or not.

Gradually, his mind became puppet to a disturbing tension which drove it back and forth between two thoughts: he had left her; she was dead. These two facts became lodged in his mind like burrs pricking at his breaking faculties. As he recalled the manner of his leaving her, it seemed increasingly brutal. She had died loving him, bearing him a child, and he had left her. He tried to shake off the heavy mental dejection which weighed him down, but his former will and determination deserted him. The vitality of the past, forever dragging him down into black depression, frightened him. The mental fog, thick as soot, into which the news of her death had trapped him, appalled him. He must get himself out. A wild anger seized him. He began to think of his own death, self-inflicted, with feeling that defied analysis. His zest for life became swallowed up in the rising tide of sorrow and mental chaos which was engulfing him.

As autumn approached, with faint notice on his part, his anger and resentment retreated, leaving in their wake a gentle stir of regret and remorse. Imperceptibly, he grew physically weary; a strange sensation of loneliness and isolation enveloped him. A species of timidity came upon him; he felt an unhappy remoteness from people, and began to edge away from life.

His deepening sense of isolation drove him more and more back upon his memories. Sunk in his armchair before the fire, he passed the days and sometimes the nights, for he had lost count of these, merged as they were into one another.

His increasing mental haziness had rejected the fact of her death; often she was there with him, just beyond the firelight or the candlelight. She talked and laughed with him. Sometimes, at night, he woke to see her standing over him or sitting in his chair before the dying fire. By some mysterious process, the glory of first love flamed again in him. He forgot that they had ever parted. His twisted memories visioned her with him in places where she had never been. He had forgotten all but the past, and that was brightly distorted.

He sat waiting for her. He seemed to remember that she had promised to come. Outside, the street was quiet. She was late. Why didn't she come? Childish tears fell over his cold cheeks. He sat weeping in front of the sinking fire.

A nameless dread seized him; she would not come! In the agony of his disappointment, he did not see that the fire had died and the candles had sputtered out. He sat wrapped in immeasurable sadness. He knew that she would not come.

Something in this thought fired his disintegrating brain. She would not come; then he must go to her.

He rose, shaking with cold, and groped toward the door. Yes, he would go to her.

The gleam of a streetlight through a French window caught his attention. He stumbled toward it. His cold fingers fumbled a moment with the catch, but he tore it open with a spark of his old determination and power, and stepped out—and down to the pavement a hundred feet below.

# Sanctuary

# One

On the Southern coast, between Merton and Shawboro, there is a strip of desolation some half a mile wide and nearly ten miles long between the sea and old fields of ruined plantations. Skirting the edge of this narrow jungle is a partly grown-over road which still shows traces of furrows made by the wheels of wagons that have long since rotted away or been cut into firewood. This road is little used, now that the state has built its new highway a bit to the west and wagons are less numerous than automobiles.

In the forsaken road a man was walking swiftly. But in spite of his hurry, at every step he set down his feet with infinite care, for the night was windless and the heavy silence intensified each sound; even the breaking of a twig could be plainly heard. And the man had need of caution as well as haste.

Before a lonely cottage that shrank timidly back from the road the man hesitated a moment, then struck out across the patch of green in front of it. Stepping behind a clump of bushes close to the house, he looked in through the lighted window at Annie Poole, standing at her kitchen table mixing the supper biscuits.

He was a big, black man with pale brown eyes in which there was an odd mixture of fear and amazement. The light showed streaks of gray soil on his heavy, sweating face and great hands, and on his torn clothes. In his woolly hair clung bits of dried leaves and dead grass.

He made a gesture as if to tap on the window, but turned away to the door instead. Without knocking he opened it and went in.

# Two

The woman's brown gaze was immediately on him, though she did not move. She said, "You ain't in no hurry, is you, Jim Hammer?" It wasn't, however, entirely a question.

"Ah's in trubble, Mis' Poole," the man explained, his voice shaking, his fingers twitching.

"W'at you done done now?"

"Shot a man, Mis' Poole."

"Trufe?" The woman seemed calm. But the word was spat out.

"Yas'm. Shot 'im." In the man's tone was something of wonder, as if he himself could not quite believe that he had really done this thing which he affirmed.

"Daid?"

"Dunno, Mis' Poole. Dunno."

"White man o' niggah?"

"Cain't say, Mis' Poole. White man, Ah reckons."

Annie Poole looked at him with cold contempt. She was a tiny, withered woman—fifty perhaps—with a wrinkled face the color of old copper, framed by a crinkly mass of white hair. But about her small figure was some quality of hardness that belied her appearance of frailty. At last she spoke, boring her sharp little eyes into those of the anxious creature before her.

"An' w'at am you lookin' foh me to do 'bout et?"

"Jes' lemme stop till dey's gone by. Hide me till dey passes. Reckon dey ain't fur off now." His begging voice changed to a frightened whimper. "Foh de Lawd's sake, Mis' Poole, lemme stop."

And why, the woman inquired caustically, should she run the dangerous risk of hiding him?

"Obadiah, he'd lemme stop ef he was to home," the man whined.

Annie Poole sighed. "Yas," she admitted slowly, reluctantly, "Ah spec' he would. Obadiah, he's too good to youall no 'count trash." Her slight shoulders lifted in a hopeless shrug. "Yas, Ah reckon he'd do et. Emspecial' seein' how he allus set such a heap o' store by you. Cain't see w'at foh, mahse'f. Ah shuah don' see nuffin' in you but a heap o' dirt."

But a look of irony, of cunning, of complicity passed over her face. She went on, "Still, 'siderin' all an' all, how Obadiah's right fon' o' you, an' how white folks is white folks, Ah'm a-gwine hide you dis one time."

Crossing the kitchen, she opened a door leading into a small bedroom, saying, "Git yo'se'f in dat dere feather baid an' Ah'm a-gwine put de clo's on de top. Don' reckon dey'll fin' you ef dey does look foh you in mah house. An Ah don' spec' dey'll go foh to do dat. Not lessen you been keerless an' let 'em smell you out gittin' hyah." She turned on him a withering look. "But you allus been triflin'. Cain't do nuffin' propah. An' Ah'm a-tellin' you ef dey warn't white folks an' you a po' niggah, Ah shuah wouldn't be lettin' you mess up mah feather baid dis ebenin', 'cose Ah jes' plain don' want you hyah. Ah done kep' mahse'f outen trubble all mah life. So's Obadiah."

"Ah's powahful 'bliged to you, Mis' Poole. You shuah am one good 'oman. De Lawd'll mos' suttinly—"

Annie Poole cut him off. "Dis ain't no time foh all dat kin' o' fiddle-de-roll. Ah does mah duty as Ah sees et 'thout no thanks from you. Ef de Lawd had gib you a white face 'stead o' dat dere black one, Ah shuah would turn you out. Now hush yo' mouf an' git yo'se'f in. An' don' git movin' and scrunchin' undah dose covahs and git yo'se'f kotched in mah house."

Without further comment the man did as he was told. After he had laid his soiled body and grimy garments between her snowy sheets, Annie Poole carefully rearranged the covering and placed piles of freshly laundered linen on top. Then she gave a pat here and there, eyed the result, and, finding it satisfactory, went back to her cooking.

# Three

Jim Hammer settled down to the racking business of waiting until the approaching danger should have passed him by. Soon savory odors seeped in to him and he realized that he was hungry. He wished that Annie Poole would bring him something to eat. Just one biscuit. But she wouldn't, he knew. Not she. She was a hard one, Obadiah's mother.

By and by he fell into a sleep from which he was dragged back by the rumbling sound of wheels in the road outside. For a second fear clutched so tightly at him that he almost leaped from the suffocating shelter of the bed in order to make some active attempt to escape the horror that his capture meant. There was a spasm at his heart, a pain so sharp, so slashing, that he had to suppress an impulse to cry out. He felt himself falling. Down, down, down . . . Everything grew dim and very distant in his memory. . . . Vanished . . . Came rushing back.

Outside there was silence. He strained his ears. Nothing. No footsteps. No voices. They had gone on then. Gone without even stopping to ask Annie Poole if she had seen him pass that way. A sigh of relief slipped from him. His thick lips curled in an ugly, cunning smile. It had been smart of him to think of coming to Obadiah's mother's to hide. She was an old demon, but he was safe in her house.

He lay a short while longer, listening intently, and, hearing nothing, started to get up. But immediately he stopped, his yellow eyes glowing like pale flames. He had heard the unmistakable sound of men coming toward the house. Swiftly he slid back into the heavy, hot stuffiness of the bed and lay listening fearfully.

The terrifying sounds drew nearer. Slowly. Heavily. Just for a moment he thought they were not coming in—they took so long. But there was a light knock and the noise of a door being opened. His whole body went taut. His feet felt frozen, his hands clammy, his tongue like a weighted, dying thing. His pounding heart made it hard for his straining ears to hear what they were saying out there.

"Ebenin', Mistah Lowndes." Annie Poole's voice sounded as it always did, sharp and dry.

There was no answer. Or had he missed it? With slow care he shifted his position, bringing his head nearer the edge of the bed. Still he heard nothing. What were they waiting for? Why didn't they ask about him?

Annie Poole, it seemed, was of the same mind. "Ah don' reckon youall done traipsed way out hyah jes' foh yo' healf," she hinted.

"There's bad news for you, Annie, I'm 'fraid." The sheriff's voice was low and queer.

Jim Hammer visualized him standing out there—a tall, stooped man, his white tobacco-stained mustache drooping limply at the ends, his nose hooked and sharp, his eyes blue and cold. Bill Lowndes was a hard one too. And white.

"W'atall bad news, Mistah Lowndes?" The woman put the question quietly, directly.

"Obadiah—" the sheriff began—hesitated—began again. "Obadiah—ah—er—he's outside, Annie. I'm 'fraid—"

"Shucks! You done missed. Obadiah, he ain't done nuffin', Mistah Lowndes. Obadiah!" she called stridently, "Obadiah! git hyah an' splain yo'se'f."

But Obadiah didn't answer, didn't come in. Other men came in. Came in with steps that dragged and halted. No one spoke. Not even Annie Poole. Something was laid carefully upon the floor.

"Obadiah, chile," his mother said softly, "Obadiah, chile." Then, with sudden alarm, "He ain't daid, is he? Mistah Lowndes! Obadiah, he ain't daid?"

Jim Hammer didn't catch the answer to that pleading question. A new fear was stealing over him.

"There was a to-do, Annie," Bill Lowndes explained gently, "at the garage back o' the factory. Fellow tryin' to steal tires. Obadiah heerd a noise an' run out with two or three others. Scared the rascal all right. Fired off his gun an' run. We allow et to be Jim Hammer. Picked up his cap back there. Never was no 'count. Thievin' an' sly. But we'll git 'im, Annie. We'll git 'im."

The man huddled in the feather bed prayed silently. "Oh, Lawd! Ah didn't go to do et. Not Obadiah, Lawd. You knows dat. You knows et." And into his frenzied brain came the thought that it would be better for him to get up and go out to them before Annie Poole gave him away. For he was lost now. With all his great strength he tried to get himself out of the bed. But he couldn't.

"Oh, Lawd!" he moaned. "Oh, Lawd!" His thoughts were bitter and they ran through his mind like panic. He knew that it had come to pass as it said somewhere in the Bible about the wicked. The Lord had stretched out his hand and smitten him. He was paralyzed. He couldn't move hand or foot. He moaned again. It was all there was left for him to do. For in the terror of this new calamity that had come upon him he had forgotten the waiting danger which was so near out there in the kitchen.

His hunters, however, didn't hear him. Bill Lowndes was saying, "We been a-lookin' for Jim out along the old road. Figured he'd make tracks for Shawboro. You ain't noticed anybody pass this evenin', Annie?"

The reply came promptly, unwaveringly. "No, Ah ain't sees nobody pass. Not yet."

# Four

Jim Hammer caught his breath.

"Well," the sheriff concluded, "we'll be gittin' along. Obadiah was a mighty fine boy. Ef they was all like him—I'm sorry, Annie. Anything I c'n do, let me know."

"Thank you, Mistah Lowndes."

With the sound of the door closing on the departing men, power to move came back to the man in the bedroom. He pushed his dirt-caked feet out from the covers and rose up, but crouched down again. He wasn't cold now, but hot all over and burning. Almost he wished that Bill Lowndes and his men had taken him with them.

Annie Poole had come into the room.

It seemed a long time before Obadiah's mother spoke. When she did there were no tears, no reproaches; but there was a raging fury in her voice as she lashed out, "Git outer mah feather baid, Jim Hammer, an' outen mah house, an' don' nevah stop thankin' yo' Jesus he done gib you dat black face."

# Quicksand

*For E.S.I.*

*My old man died in a fine big house.*
*My ma died in a shack.*
*I wonder where I'm gonna die,*
*Being neither white nor black?*

—LANGSTON HUGHES

# One

Helga Crane sat alone in her room, which at that hour, eight in the evening, was in soft gloom. Only a single reading lamp, dimmed by a great black and red shade, made a pool of light on the blue Chinese carpet, on the bright covers of the books which she had taken down from their long shelves, on the white pages of the opened one selected, on the shining brass bowl crowded with many-colored nasturtiums beside her on the low table, and on the oriental silk which covered the stool at her slim feet. It was a comfortable room, furnished with rare and intensely personal taste, flooded with Southern sun in the day, but shadowy just then with the drawn curtains and single shaded light. Large, too. So large that the spot where Helga sat was a small oasis in a desert of darkness. And eerily quiet. But that was what she liked after her taxing day's work, after the hard classes, in which she gave willingly and unsparingly of herself with no apparent return. She loved this tranquility, this quiet, following the fret and strain of the long hours spent among fellow members of a carelessly unkind and gossiping faculty, following the strenuous rigidity of conduct required in this huge educational community of which she was an insignificant part. This was her rest, this intentional isolation for a short while in the evening, this little time in her own attractive room with her own books. To the rapping of other teachers, bearing fresh scandals, or seeking information, or other more concrete favors, or merely talk, at that hour Helga Crane never opened her door.

An observer would have thought her well fitted to that framing of light and shade. A slight girl of twenty-two years, with narrow, sloping shoulders and delicate but well-turned arms and legs, she had, none the less, an air of radiant, careless health. In vivid green and gold negligee and glistening brocaded mules, deep sunk in the big high-backed chair, against whose dark tapestry her sharply cut face, with skin like yellow satin, was distinctly outlined, she was—to use a hackneyed word—attractive. Black, very broad brows over soft yet penetrating dark eyes, and a pretty mouth, whose sensitive and sensuous lips had a slight questioning petulance and a tiny dissatisfied droop, were the features on which the observer's attention would fasten; though her nose was good, her ears delicately chiseled, and her curly blue-black hair plentiful and always straying in a little wayward, delightful way. Just then it was tumbled, falling unrestrained about her face and onto her shoulders.

Helga Crane tried not to think of her work and the school as she sat there. Ever since her arrival in Naxos she had striven to keep these ends of the days from the intrusion of irritating thoughts and worries. Usually she was successful. But not this evening. Of the books which she had taken from their places she had decided on Marmaduke Pickthall's *Said the Fisherman*. She wanted forgetfulness, complete mental relaxation, rest from thought of any kind. For the day had been more than usually crowded with distasteful encounters and stupid perversities. The sultry hot Southern spring had left her strangely tired, and a little unnerved. And annoying beyond all other happenings had been that affair of the noon period, now again thrusting itself on her already irritated mind.

She had counted on a few spare minutes in which to indulge in the sweet pleasure of a bath and a fresh, cool change of clothing. And instead her luncheon time had been shortened, as had that of everyone else, and immediately after the hurried gulping down of a heavy hot meal the hundreds of students and teachers had been herded into the sun-baked chapel to listen to the banal, the patronizing, and even the insulting remarks of one of the renowned white preachers of the state.

Helga shuddered a little as she recalled some of the statements made by that holy white man of God to the black folk sitting so respectfully before him.

This was, he had told them with obvious sectional pride, the finest school for Negroes anywhere in the country, north or south; in fact, it was better even than a great many schools for white children. And he had dared any Northerner to come south and after looking upon this great institution to say that the Southerner mistreated the Negro. And he had said that if all Negroes would only take a leaf out of the book of Naxos and conduct themselves in the manner of the Naxos products there would be no race problem, because Naxos Negroes knew what was expected of them. They had good sense and they had good taste. They knew enough to stay in their places, and that, said the preacher, showed good taste. He spoke of his great admiration for the Negro race, no other race in so short a time had made so much progress, but he had urgently besought them to know when and where to stop. He hoped, he sincerely hoped, that they wouldn't become avaricious and grasping, thinking only of adding to their earthly goods, for that would be a sin in the sight of Almighty God. And then he had spoken of contentment, embellishing his words with scriptural quotations and pointing out to them that it was their duty to be satisfied in the estate to which they had been called, hewers of wood and drawers of water. And then he had prayed.

Sitting there in her room, long hours after, Helga again felt a surge

of hot anger and seething resentment. And again it subsided in amazement at the memory of the considerable applause which had greeted
the speaker just before he had asked his God's blessing upon them.

The South. Naxos. Negro education. Suddenly she hated them all.
Strange, too, for this was the thing which she had ardently desired
to share in, to be a part of this monument to one man's genius and
vision. She pinned a scrap of paper about the bulb under the lamp's
shade, for, having discarded her book in the certainty that in such a
mood even *Saïd* and his audacious villainy could not charm her, she
wanted an even more soothing darkness. She wished it were vacation,
so that she might get away for a time.

"No, forever!" she said aloud.

The minutes gathered into hours, but still she sat motionless, a
disdainful smile or an angry frown passing now and then across her
face. Somewhere in the room a little clock ticked time away. Somewhere outside a whippoorwill wailed. Evening died. A sweet smell
of early Southern flowers rushed in on a newly risen breeze which
suddenly parted the thin silk curtains at the opened windows. A
slender, frail glass vase fell from the sill with a tingling crash, but
Helga Crane did not shift her position. And the night grew cooler,
and older.

At last she stirred, uncertainly, but with an overpowering desire
for action of some sort. A second she hesitated, then rose abruptly
and pressed the electric switch with determined firmness, flooding
suddenly the shadowy room with a white glare of light. Next she
made a quick nervous tour to the end of the long room, paused a
moment before the old bowlegged secretary that held with almost
articulate protest her schoolteacher paraphernalia of drab books and
papers. Frantically Helga Crane clutched at the lot and then flung
them violently, scornfully toward the wastebasket. It received a part,
allowing the rest to spill untidily over the floor. The girl smiled
ironically, seeing in the mess a simile of her own earnest endeavor
to inculcate knowledge into her indifferent classes.

Yes, it was like that; a few of the ideas which she tried to put into
the minds behind those baffling ebony, bronze, and gold faces reached

their destination. The others were left scattered about. And, like the gay, indifferent wastebasket, it wasn't their fault. No, it wasn't the fault of those minds back of the diverse colored faces. It was, rather, the fault of the method, the general idea behind the system. Like her own hurried shot at the basket, the aim was bad, the material drab and badly prepared for its purpose.

This great community, she thought, was no longer a school. It had grown into a machine. It was now a showplace in the black belt, exemplification of the white man's magnanimity, refutation of the black man's inefficiency. Life had died out of it. It was, Helga decided, now only a big knife with cruelly sharp edges ruthlessly cutting all to a pattern, the white man's pattern. Teachers as well as students were subjected to the paring process, for it tolerated no innovations, no individualisms. Ideas it rejected, and looked with open hostility on one and all who had the temerity to offer a suggestion or ever so mildly express a disapproval. Enthusiasm, spontaneity, if not actually suppressed, were at least openly regretted as unladylike or ungentlemanly qualities. The place was smug and fat with self-satisfaction.

A peculiar characteristic trait, cold, slowly accumulated unreason in which all values were distorted or else ceased to exist, had with surprising ferociousness shaken the bulwarks of that self-restraint which was also, curiously, a part of her nature. And now that it had waned as quickly as it had risen, she smiled again, and this time the smile held a faint amusement, which wiped away the little hardness which had congealed her lovely face. Nevertheless she was soothed by the impetuous discharge of violence, and a sigh of relief came from her.

She said aloud, quietly, dispassionately: "Well, I'm through with that," and, shutting off the hard, bright blaze of the overhead lights, went back to her chair and settled down with an odd gesture of sudden soft collapse, like a person who had been for months fighting the devil and then unexpectedly had turned around and agreed to do his bidding.

Helga Crane had taught in Naxos for almost two years, at first with the keen joy and zest of those immature people who have dreamed dreams of doing good to their fellow men. But gradually this zest was blotted out, giving place to a deep hatred for the trivial hypocrisies and careless cruelties which were, unintentionally perhaps, a part of the Naxos policy of uplift. Yet she had continued to try not only to teach but to befriend those happy singing children, whose charm and distinctiveness the school was so surely ready to destroy. Instinctively Helga was aware that their smiling submissiveness covered many poignant heartaches and perhaps much secret contempt for their instructors. But she was powerless. In Naxos between teacher and student, between condescending authority and smoldering resentment, the gulf was too great, and too few had tried to cross it. It couldn't be spanned by one sympathetic teacher. It was useless to offer her atom of friendship, which under the existing conditions was neither wanted nor understood.

Nor was the general atmosphere of Naxos, its air of self-rightness and intolerant dislike of difference, the best of mediums for a pretty, solitary girl with no family connections. Helga's essentially likable and charming personality was smudged out. She had felt this for a long time. Now she faced with determination that other truth which she had refused to formulate in her thoughts: the fact that she was utterly unfitted for teaching, even for mere existence, in Naxos. She was a failure here. She had, she conceded now, been silly, obstinate, to persist for so long. A failure. Therefore, no need, no use, to stay longer. Suddenly she longed for immediate departure. How good, she thought, to go now, tonight!—and frowned to remember how impossible that would be. "The dignitaries," she said, "are not in their offices, and there will be yards and yards of red tape to unwind, gigantic, impressive spools of it."

And there was James Vayle to be told, and much-needed money to be got. James, she decided, had better be told at once. She looked at the clock racing indifferently on. No, too late. It would have to be tomorrow.

She hated to admit that money was the most serious difficulty. Knowing full well that it was important, she nevertheless rebelled at the unalterable truth that it could influence her actions, block her desires. A sordid necessity to be grappled with. With Helga it was almost a superstition that to concede to money its importance magnified its power. Still, in spite of her reluctance and distaste, her financial situation would have to be faced, and plans made, if she were to get away from Naxos with anything like the haste which she now so ardently desired.

Most of her earnings had gone into clothes, into books, into the furnishings of the room which held her. All her life Helga Crane had loved and longed for nice things. Indeed, it was this craving, this urge for beauty, which had helped to bring her into disfavor in Naxos—"pride" and "vanity," her detractors called it.

The sum owing to her by the school would just a little more than buy her ticket back to Chicago. It was too near the end of the school term to hope to get teaching work anywhere. If she couldn't find something else, she would have to ask Uncle Peter for a loan. Uncle Peter was, she knew, the one relative who thought kindly, or even calmly, of her. Her stepfather, her stepbrothers and -sisters, and the numerous cousins, aunts, and other uncles could not be even remotely considered. She laughed a little, scornfully, reflecting that the antagonism was mutual, or, perhaps, just a trifle keener on her side than on theirs. They feared and hated her. She pitied and despised them. Uncle Peter was different. In his contemptuous way he was fond of her. Her beautiful, unhappy mother had been his favorite sister. Even so, Helga Crane knew that he would be more likely to help her because her need would strengthen his oft-repeated conviction that because of her Negro blood she would never amount to anything, than from motives of affection or loving memory. This knowledge, in its present aspect of truth, irritated her to an astonishing degree. She regarded Uncle Peter almost vindictively, although always he had been extraordinarily generous with her and she fully intended to ask his assistance. "A beggar," she thought ruefully, "cannot expect to choose."

Returning to James Vayle, her thoughts took on the frigidity of complete determination. Her resolution to end her stay in Naxos would of course inevitably end her engagement to James. She had been engaged to him since her first semester there, when both had been new workers and both were lonely. Together they had discussed their work and problems in adjustment and had drifted into a closer relationship. Bitterly she reflected that James had speedily and with entire ease fitted into his niche. He was now completely "naturalized," as they used laughingly to call it. Helga, on the other hand, had never quite achieved the unmistakable Naxos mold, would never achieve it, in spite of much trying. She could neither conform nor be happy in her unconformity. This she saw clearly now, and with cold anger at all the past futile effort. What a waste! How pathetically she had struggled in those first months and with what small success. A lack somewhere. Always she had considered it a lack of understanding on the part of the community, but in her present new revolt she realized that the fault had been partly hers. A lack of acquiescence. She hadn't really wanted to be made over. This thought bred a sense of shame, a feeling of ironical disillusion. Evidently there were parts of her she couldn't be proud of. The revealing picture of her past striving was too humiliating. It was as if she had deliberately planned to steal an ugly thing, for which she had no desire, and had been found out.

Ironically she visualized the discomfort of James Vayle. How her maladjustment had bothered him! She had a faint notion that it was behind his ready assent to her suggestion anent a longer engagement than, originally, they had planned. He was liked and approved of in Naxos and loathed the idea that the girl he was to marry couldn't manage to win liking and approval also. Instinctively Helga had known that secretly he had placed the blame upon her. How right he had been! Certainly his attitude had gradually changed, though he still gave her his attentions. Naxos pleased him and he had become content with life as it was lived there. No longer lonely, he was now one of the community and so beyond the need or the desire to discuss its affairs and its failings with an outsider. She was, she knew, in a queer indefinite way, a disturbing factor. She knew too that a something held him, a something against which he was powerless. The idea that she was in but one nameless way necessary to him filled her with a sensation amounting almost to shame. And yet his mute helplessness against that ancient appeal by which she held him pleased her and fed her vanity—gave her a feeling of power. At the same time she shrank away from it, subtly aware of possibilities she herself couldn't predict.

Helga's own feelings defeated inquiry, but honestly confronted, all pretense brushed aside, the dominant one, she suspected, was relief. At least she felt no regret that tomorrow would mark the end of any claim she had upon him. The surety that the meeting would be a clash annoyed her, for she had no talent for quarreling—when possible, she preferred to flee. That was all.

The family of James Vayle, in nearby Atlanta, would be glad. They had never liked the engagement, had never liked Helga Crane. Her own lack of family disconcerted them. No family. That was the crux of the whole matter. For Helga, it accounted for everything, her failure here in Naxos, her former loneliness in Nashville. It even accounted for her engagement to James. Negro society, she had learned, was as complicated and as rigid in its ramifications as the highest strata of white society. If you couldn't prove your ancestry and connections, you were tolerated, but you didn't "belong." You could be queer, or even attractive, or bad, or brilliant, or even love beauty and such nonsense if you were a Rankin, or a Leslie, or a Scoville; in other words, if you had a family. But if you were just plain Helga Crane, of whom nobody had ever heard, it was presumptuous of you to be anything but inconspicuous and conformable.

To relinquish James Vayle would most certainly be social suicide, for the Vayles were people of consequence. The fact that they were a "first family" had been one of James's attractions for the obscure Helga. She had wanted social background, but—she had not imagined that it could be so stuffy.

She made a quick movement of impatience and stood up. As she did so, the room whirled about her in an impish, hateful way. Familiar objects seemed suddenly unhappily distant. Faintness closed about her like a vise. She swayed, her small, slender hands gripping the chair arms for support. In a moment the faintness receded, leaving in its wake a sharp resentment at the trick which her strained nerves had played upon her. And after a moment's rest she got hurriedly into bed, leaving her room disorderly for the first time.

Books and papers scattered about the floor, fragile stockings and underthings and the startling green and gold negligee dripping about on chairs and stool, met the encounter of the amazed eyes of the girl who came in the morning to awaken Helga Crane.

# Two

She woke in the morning unrefreshed and with that feeling of half-terrified apprehension peculiar to Christmas and birthday mornings. A long moment she lay puzzling under the sun streaming in a golden flow through the yellow curtains. Then her mind returned to the night before. She had decided to leave Naxos. That was it.

Sharply she began to probe her decision. Reviewing the situation carefully, frankly, she felt no wish to change her resolution. Except —that it would be inconvenient. Much as she wanted to shake the dust of the place from her feet forever, she realized that there would be difficulties. Red tape. James Vayle. Money. Other work. Regretfully she was forced to acknowledge that it would be vastly better to wait until June, the close of the school year. Not so long, really. Half of March, April, May, some of June. Surely she could endure for that much longer conditions which she had borne for nearly two years. By an effort of will, her will, it could be done.

But this reflection, sensible, expedient though it was, did not reconcile her. To remain seemed too hard. Could she do it? Was it possible in the present rebellious state of her feelings? The uneasy sense of being engaged with some formidable antagonist, nameless and un-understood, startled her. It wasn't, she was suddenly aware, merely the school and its ways and its decorous stupid people that oppressed her. There was something else, some other more ruthless force, a quality within herself, which was frustrating her, had always frustrated her, kept her from getting the things she had wanted. Still wanted.

But just what did she want? Barring a desire for material security, gracious ways of living, a profusion of lovely clothes, and a goodly share of envious admiration, Helga Crane didn't know, couldn't tell. But there was, she knew, something else. Happiness, she supposed. Whatever that might be. What, exactly, she wondered, was happiness? Very positively she wanted it. Yet her conception of it had no tangibility. She couldn't define it, isolate it, and contemplate it as she could some other abstract things. Hatred, for instance. Or kindness.

The strident ringing of a bell somewhere in the building brought back the fierce resentment of the night. It crystallized her wavering determination.

From long habit her biscuit-colored feet had slipped mechanically out from under the covers at the bell's first unkind jangle. Leisurely she drew them back and her cold anger vanished as she decided that, now, it didn't at all matter if she failed to appear at the monotonous distasteful breakfast which was provided for her by the school as part of her wages.

In the corridor beyond her door was a medley of noises incident to the rising and preparing for the day at the same hour of many schoolgirls—foolish giggling, indistinguishable snatches of merry conversation, distant gurgle of running water, patter of slippered feet, low-pitched singing, good-natured admonitions to hurry, slamming of doors, clatter of various unnamable articles, and—suddenly— calamitous silence.

Helga ducked her head under the covers in the vain attempt to shut out what she knew would fill the pregnant silence—the sharp sarcastic voice of the dormitory matron. It came.

"Well! Even if every last one of you did come from homes where you weren't taught any manners, you might at least try to pretend that you're capable of learning some here, now that you have the opportunity. Who slammed the shower-baths door?"

Silence.

"Well, you needn't trouble to answer. It's rude, as all of you know. But it's just as well, because none of you can tell the truth. Now hurry up. Don't let me hear of a single one of you being late for breakfast. If I do there'll be extra work for everybody on Saturday.

And *please* at least try to act like ladies and not like savages from the backwoods."

On her side of the door, Helga was wondering if it had ever occurred to the lean and desiccated Miss MacGooden that most of her charges had actually come from the backwoods. Quite recently too. Miss MacGooden, humorless, prim, ugly, with a face like dried leather, prided herself on being a "lady" from one of the best families—an uncle had been a congressman in the period of the Reconstruction. She was therefore, Helga Crane reflected, perhaps unable to perceive that the inducement to act like a lady, her own acrimonious example, was slight, if not altogether negative. And thinking on Miss MacGooden's "ladyness," Helga grinned a little as she remembered that one's expressed reason for never having married, or intending to marry. There were, so she had been given to understand, things in the matrimonial state that were of necessity entirely too repulsive for a lady of delicate and sensitive nature to submit to.

Soon the forcibly shut-off noises began to be heard again, as the evidently vanishing image of Miss MacGooden evaporated from the short memories of the ladies-in-making. Preparations for the intake of the day's quota of learning went on again. Almost naturally.

"So much for that!" said Helga, getting herself out of bed.

She walked to the window and stood looking down into the great quadrangle below, at the multitude of students streaming from the six big dormitories which, two each, flanked three of its sides, and assembling into neat phalanxes preparatory to marching in military order to the sorry breakfast in Jones Hall on the fourth side. Here and there a male member of the faculty, important and resplendent in the regalia of an army officer, would pause in his prancing or strutting, to jerk a negligent or offending student into the proper attitude or place. The massed phalanxes increased in size and number, blotting out pavements, bare earth, and grass. And about it all was a depressing silence, a sullenness almost, until with a horrible abruptness the waiting band blared into "The Star-Spangled Banner." The goose step began. Left, right. Left, right. Forward! March! The automatons moved. The squares disintegrated into fours. Into twos. Disappeared into the gaping doors of Jones Hall. After the last pair of marchers had entered, the huge doors were closed. A few unlucky latecomers, apparently already discouraged, tugged halfheartedly at the knobs, and finding, as they had evidently expected, that they were indeed barred out, turned resignedly away.

Helga Crane turned away from the window, a shadow dimming the pale amber loveliness of her face. Seven o'clock it was now. At twelve those children who by some accident had been a little minute or two late would have their first meal after five hours of work and so-called education. Discipline, it was called.

There came a light knocking on her door.

"Come in," invited Helga unenthusiastically. The door opened to admit Margaret Creighton, another teacher in the English department and to Helga the most congenial member of the whole Naxos faculty. Margaret, she felt, appreciated her.

Seeing Helga still in nightrobe seated on the bedside in a mass of cushions, idly dangling a mule across bare toes like one with all the time in the world before her, she exclaimed in dismay: "Helga Crane, do you know what time it is? Why, it's long after half past seven. The students—"

"Yes, I know," said Helga defiantly, "the students are coming out from breakfast. Well, let them. I, for one, wish that there was some way that they could forever stay out from the poisonous stuff thrown at them, literally thrown at them, Margaret Creighton, for food. Poor things."

Margaret laughed. "That's just ridiculous sentiment, Helga, and you know it. But you haven't had any breakfast yourself. Jim Vayle asked if you were sick. Of course nobody knew. You never tell anybody anything about yourself. I said I'd look in on you."

"Thanks awfully," Helga responded indifferently. She was watching the sunlight dissolve from thick orange into pale yellow. Slowly it crept across the room, wiping out in its path the morning shadows. She wasn't interested in what the other was saying.

"If you don't hurry, you'll be late to your first class. Can I help you?" Margaret offered uncertainly. She was a little afraid of Helga. Nearly everyone was.

"No. Thanks all the same." Then quickly in another, warmer tone: "I do mean it. Thanks, a thousand times, Margaret. I'm really awfully grateful, but—you see, it's like this, I'm not going to be late to my class. I'm not going to be there at all."

The visiting girl, standing in relief, like old walnut against the buff-colored wall, darted a quick glance at Helga. Plainly she was curious. But she only said formally: "Oh, then you *are* sick." For something there was about Helga which discouraged questionings.

No, Helga wasn't sick. Not physically. She was merely disgusted. Fed up with Naxos. If that could be called sickness. The truth was that she had made up her mind to leave. That very day. She could no longer abide being connected with a place of shame, lies, hypocrisy, cruelty, servility, and snobbishness. "It ought," she concluded, "to be shut down by law."

"But, Helga, you can't go now. Not in the middle of the term." The kindly Margaret was distressed.

"But I can. And I am. Today."

"They'll never let you," prophesied Margaret.

"*They* can't stop me. Trains leave here for civilization every day. All that's needed is money," Helga pointed out.

"Yes, of course. Everybody knows that. What I mean is that you'll only hurt yourself in your profession. They won't give you a reference if you jump up and leave like this now. At this time of the year. You'll be put on the blacklist. And you'll find it hard to get another teaching job. Naxos has enormous influence in the South. Better wait till school closes."

"Heaven forbid," answered Helga fervently, "that I should ever again want work anywhere in the South! I hate it." And fell silent, wondering for the hundredth time just what form of vanity it was that had induced an intelligent girl like Margaret Creighton to turn what was probably nice live crinkly hair, perfectly suited to her smooth dark skin and agreeable round features, into a dead straight, greasy, ugly mass.

Looking up from her watch, Margaret said: "Well, I've really got to run, or I'll be late myself. And since I'm staying . . . Better think it over, Helga. There's no place like Naxos, you know. Pretty good salaries, decent rooms, plenty of men, and all that. Ta-ta." The door slid to behind her.

But in another moment it opened. She was back. "I do wish you'd stay. It's nice having you here, Helga. We all think so. Even the dead ones. We need a few decorations to brighten our sad lives." And again she was gone.

Helga was unmoved. She was no longer concerned with what anyone in Naxos might think of her, for she was now in love with the piquancy of leaving. Automatically her fingers adjusted the Chinese-looking pillows on the low couch that served for her bed. Her mind was busy with plans for departure. Packing, money, trains, and—could she get a berth?

# Three

On one side of the long, white, hot sand road that split the flat green, there was a little shade, for it was bordered with trees. Helga Crane walked there so that the sun could not so easily get at her. As she went slowly across the empty campus she was conscious of a vague tenderness for the scene spread out before her. It was so incredibly lovely, so appealing, and so facile. The trees in their spring beauty sent through her restive mind a sharp thrill of pleasure. Seductive, charming, and beckoning as cities were, they had not this easy un-human loveliness. The trees, she thought, on city avenues and boulevards, in city parks and gardens, were tamed, held prisoners in a surrounding maze of human beings. Here they were free. It was human beings who were prisoners. It was too bad. In the midst of all this radiant life. They weren't, she knew, even conscious of its presence. Perhaps there was too much of it, and therefore it was less than nothing.

In response to her insistent demand she had been told that Dr. Anderson could give her twenty minutes at eleven o'clock. Well, she supposed that she could say all that she had to say in twenty minutes, though she resented being limited. Twenty minutes. In Naxos, she was as unimportant as that.

He was a new man, this principal, for whom Helga remembered feeling unaccountably sorry, when last September he had first been appointed to Naxos as its head. For some reason she had liked him, although she had seen little of him; he was so frequently away on publicity and money-raising tours. And as yet he had made but few and slight changes in the running of the school. Now she was a little irritated at finding herself wondering just how she was going to tell him of her decision. What did it matter to him? Why should she mind if it did? But there returned to her that indistinct sense of sympathy for the remote silent man with the tired gray eyes, and she wondered again by what fluke of fate such a man, apparently a humane and understanding person, had chanced into the command of this cruel educational machine. Suddenly, her own resolve loomed as an almost direct unkindness. This increased her annoyance and discomfort. A sense of defeat, of being cheated of justification, closed down on her. Absurd!

She arrived at the administration building in a mild rage, as unreasonable as it was futile, but once inside she had a sudden attack of nerves at the prospect of traversing that great outer room which was the workplace of some twenty-odd people. This was a disease from which Helga had suffered at intervals all her life, and it was a point of honor, almost, with her never to give way to it. So, instead of turning away, as she felt inclined, she walked on, outwardly indifferent. Halfway down the long aisle which divided the room, the principal's secretary, a huge black man, surged toward her.

"Good morning, Miss Crane, Dr. Anderson will see you in a few moments. Sit down right here."

She felt the inquiry in the shuttered eyes. For some reason this dissipated her self-consciousness and restored her poise. Thanking him, she seated herself, really careless now of the glances of the stenographers, bookkeepers, clerks. Their curiosity and slightly veiled hostility no longer touched her. Her coming departure had released her from the need for conciliation which had irked her for so long. It was pleasant to Helga Crane to be able to sit calmly looking out of the window onto the smooth lawn, where a few leaves quite prematurely fallen dotted the grass, for once uncaring whether the frock which she wore roused disapproval or envy.

Turning from the window, her gaze wandered contemptuously over the dull attire of the women workers. Drab colors, mostly navy blue, black, brown, unrelieved, save for a scrap of white or tan about the hands and necks. Fragments of a speech made by the dean of women floated through her thoughts—"Bright colors are vulgar"—"Black, gray, brown, and navy blue are the most becoming colors for colored people"—"Dark-complected people shouldn't wear yellow, or green or red."—The dean was a woman from one of the "first families" —a great "race" woman; she, Helga Crane, a despised mulatto; but something intuitive, some unanalyzed driving spirit of loyalty to the inherent racial need for gorgeousness told her that bright colors *were* fitting and that dark-complexioned people *should* wear yellow, green, and red. Black, brown, and gray were ruinous to them, actually destroyed the luminous tones lurking in their dusky skins. One of the loveliest sights Helga had ever seen had been a sooty black girl decked out in a flaming orange dress, which a horrified matron had next day consigned to the dyer. Why, she wondered, didn't someone write *A Plea for Color*?

These people yapped loudly of race, of race consciousness, of race pride, and yet suppressed its most delightful manifestations, love of color, joy of rhythmic motion, naive, spontaneous laughter. Harmony, radiance, and simplicity, all the essentials of spiritual beauty in the race they had marked for destruction.

She came back to her own problems. Clothes had been one of her difficulties in Naxos. Helga Crane loved clothes, elaborate ones. Nevertheless, she had tried not to offend. But with small success, for, although she had affected the deceptively simple variety, the hawk eyes of dean and matrons had detected the subtle difference from their own irreproachably conventional garments. Too, they felt that the colors were queer; dark purples, royal blues, rich greens, deep reds, in soft, luxurious woolens or heavy, clinging silks. And the trimmings—when Helga used them at all—seemed to them odd. Old laces, strange embroideries, dim brocades. Her faultless, slim shoes made them uncomfortable and her small plain hats seemed to them positively indecent. Helga smiled inwardly at the thought that whenever there was an evening affair for the faculty the dear ladies probably held their breaths until she had made her appearance. They existed in constant fear that she might turn out in an evening dress. The proper evening wear in Naxos was afternoon attire. And one could, if one wished, garnish the hair with flowers.

Quick, muted footfalls sounded. The secretary had returned.

"Dr. Anderson will see you now, Miss Crane."

She rose, followed, and was ushered into the guarded sanctum, without having decided just what she was to say. For a moment she felt behind her the open doorway and then the gentle impact of its closing. Before her at a great desk her eyes picked out the figure of a man, at first blurred slightly in outline in that dimmer light. At his "Miss Crane?" her lips formed for speech, but no sound came. She was aware of inward confusion. For her the situation seemed charged, unaccountably, with strangeness and something very like hysteria. An almost overpowering desire to laugh seized her. Then, miraculously, a complete ease, such as she had never known in Naxos, possessed her. She smiled, nodded in answer to his questioning salutation, and with a gracious "Thank you" dropped into the chair which he indicated. She looked at him frankly now, this man still young, thirty-five perhaps, and found it easy to go on in the vein of a simple statement.

"Dr. Anderson, I'm sorry to have to confess that I've failed in my job here. I've made up my mind to leave. Today."

A short, almost imperceptible silence, then a deep voice of peculiarly pleasing resonance, asking gently: "You don't like Naxos, Miss Crane?"

She evaded. "Naxos, the place? Yes, I like it. Who wouldn't like it? It's so beautiful. But I—well—I don't seem to fit here."

The man smiled, just a little. "The school? You don't like the school?"

The words burst from her. "No, I don't like it. I hate it!"

"Why?" The question was detached, too detached.

In the girl blazed a desire to wound. There he sat, staring dreamily out of the window, blatantly unconcerned with her or her answer. Well, she'd tell him. She pronounced each word with deliberate slowness.

"Well, for one thing, I hate hypocrisy. I hate cruelty to students, and to teachers who can't fight back. I hate backbiting, and sneaking, and petty jealousy. Naxos? It's hardly a place at all. It's more like some loathsome, venomous disease. Ugh! Everybody spending his time in a malicious hunting for the weaknesses of others, spying, grudging, scratching."

"I see. And you don't think it might help to cure us, to have someone who doesn't approve of these things stay with us? Even just one person, Miss Crane?"

She wondered if this last was irony. She suspected it was humor and so ignored the half-pleading note in his voice.

"No, I don't! It doesn't do the disease any good. Only irritates it. And it makes me unhappy, dissatisfied. It isn't pleasant to be always made to appear in the wrong, even when I know I'm right."

His gaze was on her now, searching. "Queer," she thought, "how some brown people have gray eyes. Gives them a strange, unexpected appearance. A little frightening."

The man said kindly: "Ah, you're unhappy. And for the reasons you've stated?"

"Yes, partly. Then, too, the people here don't like me. They don't think I'm in the spirit of the work. And I'm not, not if it means suppression of individuality and beauty."

"And does it?"

"Well, it seems to work out that way."

"How old are you, Miss Crane?"

She resented this, but she told him, speaking with what curtness she could command only the bare figure: "Twenty-three."

"Twenty-three. I see. Someday you'll learn that lies, injustice, and hypocrisy are a part of every ordinary community. Most people achieve a sort of protective immunity, a kind of callousness, toward them. If they didn't, they couldn't endure. I think there's less of these evils here than in most places, but because we're trying to do such a big thing, to aim so high, the ugly things show more, they irk some of us more. Service is like clean white linen, even the tiniest speck shows." He went on, explaining, amplifying, pleading.

Helga Crane was silent, feeling a mystifying yearning which sang and throbbed in her. She felt again that urge for service, not now for her people, but for this man who was talking so earnestly of his work, his plans, his hopes. An insistent need to be a part of them sprang in her. With compunction tweaking at her heart for even having entertained the notion of deserting him, she resolved not only to remain until June but to return next year. She was shamed yet stirred. It was not sacrifice she felt now, but actual desire to stay, and to come back next year.

He came, at last, to the end of the long speech, only part of which she had heard. "You see, you understand?" he urged.

"Yes, oh yes, I do."

"What we need is more people like you, people with a sense of values, and proportion, an appreciation of the rarer things of life. You have something to give which we badly need here in Naxos. You mustn't desert us, Miss Crane."

She nodded, silent. He had won her. She knew that she would stay. "It's an elusive something," he went on. "Perhaps I can best explain it by the use of that trite phrase, 'You're a lady.' You have dignity and breeding."

At these words turmoil rose again in Helga Crane. The intricate pattern of the rug which she had been studying escaped her. The shamed feeling which had been her penance evaporated. Only a lacerated pride remained. She took firm hold of the chair arms to still the trembling of her fingers.

"If you're speaking of family, Dr. Anderson, why, I haven't any. I was born in a Chicago slum."

The man chose his words—carefully, he thought. "That doesn't at all matter, Miss Crane. Financial, economic circumstances can't destroy tendencies inherited from good stock. You yourself prove that!"

Concerned with her own angry thoughts, which scurried here and there like trapped rats, Helga missed the import of his words. Her own words, her answer, fell like drops of hail.

"The joke is on you, Dr. Anderson. My father was a gambler who deserted my mother, a white immigrant. It is even uncertain that they were married. As I said at first, I don't belong here. I shall be leaving at once. This afternoon. Good morning."

# Four

Long, soft white clouds, clouds like shreds of incredibly fine cotton, streaked the blue of the early evening sky. Over the flying landscape hung a very faint mist, disturbed now and then by a languid breeze. But no coolness invaded the heat of the train rushing north. The open windows of the stuffy day coach, where Helga Crane sat with others of her race, seemed only to intensify her discomfort. Her head ached with a steady pounding pain. This, added to her wounds of the spirit, made traveling something little short of a medieval torture. Desperately she was trying to right the confusion in her mind. The temper of the morning's interview rose before her like an ugly mutilated creature crawling horribly over the flying landscape of her thoughts. It was no use. The ugly thing pressed down on her, held her. Leaning back, she tried to doze as others were doing. The futility of her effort exasperated her.

Just what had happened to her there in that cool dim room under the quizzical gaze of those piercing gray eyes? Whatever it was had been so powerful, so compelling, that but for a few chance words she would still be in Naxos. And why had she permitted herself to be jolted into a rage so fierce, so illogical, so disastrous, that now after it was spent she sat despondent, sunk in shameful contrition?

As she reviewed the manner of her departure from his presence, it seemed increasingly rude.

She didn't, she told herself, after all, like this Dr. Anderson. He was too controlled, too sure of himself and others. She detested cool, perfectly controlled people. Well, it didn't matter. He didn't matter. But she could not put him from her mind. She set it down to annoyance because of the cold discourtesy of her abrupt action. She disliked rudeness in anyone.

She had outraged her own pride, and she had terribly wronged her mother by her insidious implication. Why? Her thoughts lingered with her mother, long dead. A fair Scandinavian girl in love with life, with love, with passion, dreaming, and risking all in one blind surrender. A cruel sacrifice. In forgetting all but love she had forgotten, or had perhaps never known, that some things the world never forgives. But as Helga knew, she had remembered, or had learned in suffering and longing all the rest of her life. Her daughter hoped she had been happy, happy beyond most human creatures, in the little time it had lasted, the little time before that gay suave scoundrel, Helga's father, had left her. But Helga Crane doubted it. How could she have been? A girl gently bred, fresh from an older, more polished civilization, flung into poverty, sordidness, and dissipation. She visualized her now, sad, cold, and—yes, remote. The tragic cruelties of the years had left her a little pathetic, a little hard, and a little unapproachable.

That second marriage, to a man of her own race, but not of her own kind—so passionately, so instinctively resented by Helga even at the trivial age of six—she now understood as a grievous necessity. Even foolish, despised women must have food and clothing; even unloved little Negro girls must be somehow provided for. Memory, flown back to those years following the marriage, dealt her torturing stabs. Before her rose the pictures of her mother's careful management to avoid those ugly scarifying quarrels which even at this far-off time caused an uncontrollable shudder, her own childish self-effacement, the savage unkindness of her stepbrothers and -sisters, and the jealous, malicious hatred of her mother's husband. Summers, winters, years, passing in one long, changeless stretch of aching misery of soul. Her mother's death, when Helga was fifteen. Her rescue by Uncle Peter, who had sent her to school, a school for Negroes, where for the first time she could breathe freely, where she discovered that because one was dark one was not necessarily loathsome, and could, therefore, consider oneself without repulsion.

Six years. She had been happy there, as happy as a child unused to happiness dared be. There had been always a feeling of strangeness, of outsideness, and one of holding her breath for fear that it wouldn't last. It hadn't. It had dwindled gradually into eclipse of painful isolation. As she grew older, she became gradually aware of a difference between herself and the girls about her. They had mothers, fathers, brothers, and sisters of whom they spoke frequently, and who sometimes visited them. They went home for the vacations which Helga spent in the city where the school was located. They visited each other and knew many of the same people. Discontent for which there was no remedy crept upon her, and she was glad almost when these most peaceful years which she had yet known came to their end. She had been happier, but still horribly lonely.

She had looked forward with pleasant expectancy to working in Naxos when the chance came. And now this! What was it that stood in her way? Helga Crane couldn't explain it, put a name to it. She had tried in the early afternoon in her gentle but staccato talk with James Vayle. Even to herself her explanation had sounded inane and insufficient; no wonder James had been impatient and unbelieving. During their brief and unsatisfactory conversation she had had an odd feeling that he felt somehow cheated. And more than once she had been aware of a suggestion of suspicion in his attitude, a feeling that he was being duped, that he suspected her of some hidden purpose which he was attempting to discover.

Well, that was over. She would never be married to James Vayle now. It flashed upon her that, even had she remained in Naxos, she would never have been married to him. She couldn't have married him. Gradually, too, there stole into her thoughts of him a curious sensation of repugnance, for which she was at a loss to account. It was new, something unfelt before. Certainly she had never loved him overwhelmingly, not, for example, as her mother must have loved her father, but she *had* liked him, and she had expected to love him, after their marriage. People generally did love then, she imagined. No, she had not loved James, but she had wanted to. Acute nausea rose in her as she recalled the slight quivering of his lips sometimes when her hands had unexpectedly touched his; the throbbing vein in his forehead on a gay day when they had wandered off alone across the low hills and she had allowed him frequent kisses under the shelter of some low-hanging willows. Now she shivered a little, even in the hot train, as if she had suddenly come out from a warm scented place into cool, clear air. She must have been mad, she thought; but she couldn't tell why she thought so. This, too, bothered her.

Laughing conversation buzzed about her. Across the aisle a bronze baby, with bright staring eyes, began a fretful whining, which its young mother essayed to silence by a low droning croon. In the seat just beyond, a black and tan young pair were absorbed in the eating of a cold fried chicken, audibly crunching the ends of the crisp, browned bones. A little distance away a tired laborer slept noisily. Near him two children dropped the peelings of oranges and bananas on the already soiled floor. The smell of stale food and ancient tobacco irritated Helga like a physical pain. A man, a white man, strode through the packed car and spat twice, once in the exact center of the dingy door panel, and once into the receptacle which held the drinking water. Instantly Helga became aware of stinging thirst. Her eyes sought the small watch at her wrist. Ten hours to Chicago. Would she be lucky enough to prevail upon the conductor to let her occupy a berth, or would she have to remain here all night, without sleep, without food, without drink, and with that disgusting door panel to which her purposely averted eyes were contantly, involuntarily straying?

Her first effort was unsuccessful. An ill-natured "No, you know you can't," was the answer to her inquiry. But farther on along the road, there was a change of men. Her rebuff had made her reluctant to try again, but the entry of a farmer carrying a basket containing live chickens, which he deposited on the seat (the only vacant one) beside her, strengthened her weakened courage. Timidly, she approached the new conductor, an elderly gray-mustached man of pleasant appearance, who subjected her to a keen, appraising look and then promised to see what could be done. She thanked him, gratefully, and went back to her shared seat, to wait anxiously. After half an hour he returned, saying he could "fix her up," there was a section she could have, adding: "It'll cost you ten dollars." She murmured: "All right. Thank you." It was twice the price, and she needed every penny, but she knew she was fortunate to get it even at that, and so was very thankful, as she followed his tall, loping figure out of that car and through seemingly endless others, and at last into one where she could rest a little.

She undressed and lay down, her thoughts still busy with the morning's encounter. Why hadn't she grasped his meaning? Why, if she had said so much, hadn't she said more about herself and her mother? He would, she was sure, have understood, even sympathized. Why had she lost her temper and given way to angry half-truths? . . . Angry half-truths . . . Angry half- . . .

# Five

Gray Chicago seethed, surged, and scurried about her. Helga shivered a little, drawing her light coat closer. She had forgotten how cold March could be under the pale skies of the North. But she liked it, this blustering wind. She would even have welcomed snow, for it would more clearly have marked the contrast between this freedom and the cage which Naxos had been to her. Not but what it was marked plainly enough by the noise, the dash, the crowds.

Helga Crane, who had been born in this dirty, mad, hurrying city, had no home here. She had not even any friends here. It would have to be, she decided, the Young Women's Christian Association. "Oh dear! The uplift. Poor, poor colored people. Well, no use stewing about it. I'll get a taxi to take me out, bag and baggage, then I'll have a hot bath and a really good meal, peep into the shops—mustn't buy anything—and then for Uncle Peter. Guess I won't phone. More effective if I surprise him."

It was late, very late, almost evening, when finally Helga turned her steps northward, in the direction of Uncle Peter's home. She had put it off as long as she could, for she detested her errand. The fact that that one day had shown her its acute necessity did not decrease her distaste. As she approached the North Side, the distaste grew. Arrived at last at the familiar door of the old stone house, her confidence in Uncle Peter's welcome deserted her. She gave the bell a timid push and then decided to turn away, to go back to her room and phone, or, better yet, to write. But before she could retreat, the door was opened by a strange red-faced maid, dressed primly in black and white. This increased Helga's mistrust. Where, she wondered, was the ancient Rose, who had, ever since she could remember, served her uncle.

The hostile "Well?" of this new servant forcibly recalled the reason for her presence there. She said firmly: "Mr. Nilssen, please."

"Mr. Nilssen's not in," was the pert retort. "Will you see Mrs. Nilssen?"

Helga was startled. "Mrs. Nilssen! I beg your pardon, did you say Mrs. Nilssen?"

"I did," answered the maid shortly, beginning to close the door.

"What is it, Ida?" A woman's soft voice sounded from within.

"Someone for Mr. Nilssen, m'am." The girl looked embarrassed.

In Helga's face the blood rose in a deep red stain. She explained: "Helga Crane, his niece."

"She says she's his niece, m'am."

"Well, have her come in."

There was no escape. She stood in the large reception hall and was annoyed to find herself actually trembling. A woman, tall, exquisitely gowned, with shining gray hair piled high, came forward murmuring in a puzzled voice: "His niece, did you say?"

"Yes, Helga Crane. My mother was his sister, Karen Nilssen. I've been away. I didn't know Uncle Peter had married." Sensitive to atmosphere, Helga had felt at once the latent antagonism in the woman's manner.

"Oh, yes! I remember about you now. I'd forgotten for a moment. *Well*, he isn't exactly your uncle, is he? Your mother wasn't married, was she? I mean, to your father?"

"I—I don't know," stammered the girl, feeling pushed down to the uttermost depths of ignominy.

"Of course she wasn't." The clear, low voice held a positive note. "Mr. Nilssen has been very kind to you, supported you, sent you to school. But you mustn't expect anything else. And you mustn't come here any more. It—well, frankly, it isn't convenient. I'm sure an intelligent girl like yourself can understand that."

"Of course," Helga agreed, coldly, freezingly, but her lips quivered. She wanted to get away as quickly as possible. She reached the door. There was a second of complete silence, then Mrs. Nilssen's voice, a little agitated: "And please remember that my husband is not your uncle. No indeed! Why, that, that would make me your aunt! He's not—"

But at last the knob had turned in Helga's fumbling hand. She gave a little unpremeditated laugh and slipped out. When she was in the street, she ran. Her only impulse was to get as far away from her uncle's house, and this woman, his wife, who so plainly wished to dissociate herself from the outrage of her very existence. She was torn with mad fright, an emotion against which she knew but two weapons: to kick and scream, or to flee.

The day had lengthened. It was evening and much colder, but Helga Crane was unconscious of any change, so shaken she was and burning. The wind cut her like a knife, but she did not feel it. She ceased her frantic running, aware at last of the curious glances of passersby. At one spot, for a moment less frequented than others, she stopped to give heed to her disordered appearance. Here a man, well groomed and pleasant-spoken, accosted her. On such occasions she was wont to reply scathingly, but tonight his pale Caucasian face struck her breaking faculties as too droll. Laughing harshly, she threw at him the words: "You're not my uncle."

He retired in haste, probably thinking her drunk, or possibly a little mad.

Night fell, while Helga Crane in the rushing swiftness of a roaring elevated train sat numb. It was as if all the bogies and goblins that had beset her unloved, unloving, and unhappy childhood had come to life with tenfold power to hurt and frighten. For the wound was deeper in that her long freedom from their presence had rendered her the more vulnerable. Worst of all was the fact that under the stinging hurt she understood and sympathized with Mrs. Nilssen's point of view, as always she had been able to understand her mother's, her stepfather's, and his children's points of view. She saw herself for an obscene sore in all their lives, at all costs to be hidden. She understood, even while she resented. It would have been easier if she had not.

Later in the bare silence of her tiny room she remembered the unaccomplished object of her visit. Money. Characteristically, while admitting its necessity, and even its undeniable desirability, she dismissed its importance. Its elusive quality she had as yet never known. She would find work of some kind. Perhaps the library. The idea clung. Yes, certainly the library. She knew books and loved them.

She stood intently looking down into the glimmering street, far below, swarming with people, merging into little eddies and disengaging themselves to pursue their own individual ways. A few minutes later she stood in the doorway, drawn by an uncontrollable desire to mingle with the crowd. The purple sky showed tremulous clouds piled up, drifting here and there with a sort of endless lack of purpose. Very like the myriad human beings pressing hurriedly on. Looking at these, Helga caught herself wondering who they were, what they did, and of what they thought. What was passing behind those dark molds of flesh? Did they really think at all? Yet, as she stepped out into the moving multicolored crowd, there came to her a queer feeling of enthusiasm, as if she were tasting some agreeable, exotic food— sweetbreads, smothered with truffles and mushrooms, perhaps. And,

oddly enough, she felt, too, that she had come home. She, Helga
Crane, who had no home.

# Six

Helga woke to the sound of rain. The day was leaden gray, and misty
black, and dullish white. She was not surprised, the night had promised it. She made a little frown, remembering that it was today that
she was to search for work.

She dressed herself carefully, in the plainest garments she possessed, a suit of fine blue twill faultlessly tailored, from whose left
pocket peeped a gay kerchief, an unadorned, heavy silk blouse,
a small, smart, fawn-colored hat, and slim brown oxfords, and
chose a brown umbrella. In a nearby street she sought out an appealing little restaurant, which she had noted in her last night's
ramble through the neighborhood, for the thick cups and the queer
dark silver of the Young Women's Christian Association distressed
her.

After a slight breakfast she made her way to the library, that ugly
gray building, where was housed much knowledge and a little wisdom,
on interminable shelves. The friendly person at the desk in the hall
bestowed on her a kindly smile when Helga stated her business and
asked for directions.

"The corridor to your left, then the second door to your right,"
she was told.

Outside the indicated door, for half a second she hesitated,
then braced herself and went in. In less than a quarter of an hour
she came out, in surprised disappointment. "Library training"—
"civil service"—"library school"—"classification"—"cataloguing"
—"training class"—"examination"—"probation period"—flitted
through her mind.

"How erudite they must be!" she remarked sarcastically to herself,
and ignored the smiling curiosity of the desk person as she went

through the hall to the street. For a long moment she stood on the high stone steps above the avenue, then shrugged her shoulders and stepped down. It *was* a disappointment, but of course there were other things. She would find something else. But what? Teaching, even substitute teaching, was hopeless now, in March. She had no business training, and the shops didn't employ colored clerks or salespeople, not even the smaller ones. She couldn't sew, she couldn't cook. Well, she *could* do housework, or wait on table, for a short time at least. Until she got a little money together. With this thought she remembered that the Young Women's Christian Association maintained an employment agency.

"Of course, the very thing!" She exclaimed aloud. "I'll go straight back."

But, though the day was still drear, rain had ceased to fall, and Helga, instead of returning, spent hours in aimless strolling about the hustling streets of the Loop district. When at last she did retrace her steps, the business day had ended and the employment office was closed. This frightened her a little, this and the fact that she had spent money, too much money, for a book and a tapestry purse, things which she wanted but did not need and certainly could not afford. Regretful and dismayed, she resolved to go without her dinner, as a self-inflicted penance, as well as an economy—and she would be at the employment office the first thing tomorrow morning.

But it was not until three days more had passed that Helga Crane sought the Association or any other employment office. And then it was sheer necessity that drove her there, for her money had dwindled to a ridiculous sum. She had put off the hated moment, had assured herself that she was tired, needed a bit of vacation, was due one. It had been pleasant, the leisure, the walks, the lake, the shops and streets with their gay colors, their movement, after the great quiet of Naxos. Now she was panicky.

In the office a few nondescript women sat scattered about on the long row of chairs. Some were plainly uninterested, others wore an air of acute expectancy, which disturbed Helga. Behind a desk two alert young women, both wearing a superior air, were busy writing upon and filing countless white cards. Now and then one stopped to answer the telephone.

"Y.W.C.A. employment. . . . Yes. . . . Spell it, please. . . . Sleep in or out? Thirty dollars? . . . Thank you, I'll send one right over."

Or, "I'm awfully sorry, we haven't anybody right now, but I'll send you the first one that comes in."

Their manners were obtrusively businesslike, but they ignored the already embarrassed Helga. Diffidently she approached the desk. The darker of the two looked up and turned on a little smile.

"Yes?" she inquired.

"I wonder if you can help me? I want work," Helga stated simply.

"Maybe. What kind? Have you references?"

Helga explained. She was a teacher. A graduate of Devon. Had been teaching in Naxos.

The girl was not interested. "Our kind of work wouldn't do for you," she kept repeating at the end of each of Helga's statements. "Domestic mostly."

When Helga said that she was willing to accept work of any kind, a slight, almost imperceptible change crept into her manner and her perfunctory smile disappeared. She repeated her question about the reference. On learning that Helga had none, she said sharply, finally: "I'm sorry, but we never send out help without references."

With a feeling that she had been slapped, Helga Crane hurried out. After some lunch she sought out an employment agency on State Street. An hour passed in patient sitting. Then came her turn to be interviewed. She said, simply, that she wanted work, work of any kind. A competent young woman, whose eyes stared froglike from great tortoise-shell-rimmed glasses, regarded her with an appraising look and asked for her history, past and present, not forgetting the "references." Helga told her that she was a graduate of Devon, had taught in Naxos. But even before she arrived at the explanation of the lack of references, the other's interest in her had faded.

"I'm sorry, but we have nothing that you would be interested in," she said and motioned to the next seeker, who immediately came forward, proffering several much-worn papers.

"References," thought Helga resentfully, bitterly, as she went out the door into the crowded garish street in search of another agency, where her visit was equally vain.

Days of this sort of thing. Weeks of it. And of the futile scanning and answering of newspaper advertisements. She traversed acres of streets, but it seemed that in that whole energetic place nobody wanted her services. At least not the kind that she offered. A few men, both white and black, offered her money, but the price of the money was too dear. Helga Crane did not feel inclined to pay it.

She began to feel terrified and lost. And she was a little hungry too, for her small money was dwindling and she felt the need to economize somehow. Food was the easiest.

In the midst of her search for work she felt horribly lonely too. This sense of loneliness increased, it grew to appalling proportions, encompassing her, shutting her off from all of life around her. Devastated she was, and always on the verge of weeping. It made her feel small and insignificant that in all the climbing massed city no one cared one whit about her.

Helga Crane was not religious. She took nothing on trust. Nevertheless on Sundays she attended the very fashionable, very high services in the Negro Episcopal church on Michigan Avenue. She hoped that some good Christian would speak to her, invite her to return, or inquire kindly if she was a stranger in the city. None did, and she became bitter, distrusting religion more than ever. She was herself unconscious of that faint hint of offishness which hung about her and repelled advances, an arrogance that stirred in people a peculiar irritation. They noticed her, admired her clothes, but that was all, for the self-sufficient uninterested manner adopted instinctively as a protective measure for her acute sensitiveness, in her child days, still clung to her.

An agitated feeling of disaster closed in on her, tightened. Then, one afternoon, coming in from the discouraging round of agencies and the vain answering of newspaper wants to the stark neatness of her room, she found between door and sill a small folded note. Spreading it open, she read:

*Miss Crane:*

*Please come into the employment office as soon as you return.*

*Ida Ross*

Helga spent some time in the contemplation of this note. She was afraid to hope. Its possibilities made her feel a little hysterical. Finally, after removing the dirt of the dusty streets, she went down, down to that room where she had first felt the smallness of her commercial value. Subsequent failures had augmented her feeling of incompetence, but she resented the fact that these clerks were evidently aware of her unsuccess. It required all the pride and indifferent hauteur she could summon to support her in their presence. Her additional arrogance passed unnoticed by those for whom it was assumed. They were interested only in the business for which they had summoned her, that of procuring a traveling companion for a lecturing female on her way to a convention.

"She wants," Miss Ross told Helga, "someone intelligent, someone who can help her get her speeches in order on the train. We thought of you right away. Of course, it isn't permanent. She'll pay your expenses and there'll be twenty-five dollars besides. She leaves tomorrow. Here's her address. You're to go to see her at five o'clock. It's after four now. I'll phone that you're on your way."

The presumptuousness of their certainty that she would snatch at the opportunity galled Helga. She became aware of a desire to be disagreeable. The inclination to fling the address of the lecturing female in their face stirred in her, but she remembered the lone five-dollar bill in the rare old tapestry purse swinging from her arm. She couldn't afford anger. So she thanked them very politely and set out for the home of Mrs. Hayes-Rore on Grand Boulevard, knowing full well that she intended to take the job, if the lecturing one would take her. Twenty-five dollars was not to be looked at with nose in air when one was the owner of but five. And meals—meals for four days at least.

Mrs. Hayes-Rore proved to be a plump lemon-colored woman with badly straightened hair and dirty fingernails. Her direct, penetrating gaze was somewhat formidable. Notebook in hand, she gave Helga the impression of having risen early for consultation with other harassed authorities on the race problem, and having been in conference on the subject all day. Evidently she had had little time or thought for the careful donning of the five-years-behind-the-mode garments which covered her, and which even in their youth could hardly have fitted or suited her. She had a tart personality, and prying. She approved of Helga, after asking her endless questions about her education and her opinions on the race problem, none of which she was permitted to answer, for Mrs. Hayes-Rore either went on to the next or answered the question herself by remarking: "Not that it matters, if you can only do what I want done, and the girls at the Y said that you could. I'm on the Board of Managers, and I know they wouldn't send me anybody who wasn't all right." After this had been repeated twice in a booming, oratorical voice, Helga felt that the Association secretaries had taken an awful chance in sending a person about whom they knew as little as they did about her.

"Yes, I'm sure you'll do. I don't really need ideas, I've plenty of my own. It's just a matter of getting someone to help me get my speeches in order, correct and condense them, you know. I leave at eleven in the morning. Can you be ready by then? . . . That's good. Better be here at nine. Now don't disappoint me. I'm depending on you."

As she stepped into the street and made her way skillfully through the impassioned human traffic, Helga reviewed the plan which she had formed, while in the lecturing one's presence, to remain in New York. There would be twenty-five dollars, and perhaps the amount of her return ticket. Enough for a start. Surely she could get work there. Everybody did. Anyway, she would have a reference.

With her decision she felt reborn. She began happily to paint the future in vivid colors. The world had changed to silver, and life ceased to be a struggle and became a gay adventure. Even the advertisements in the shopwindows seemed to shine with radiance.

Curious about Mrs. Hayes-Rore, on her return to the Y she went into the employment office, ostensibly to thank the girls and to report that the important woman would take her. Was there, she inquired, anything that she needed to know? Mrs. Hayes-Rore had appeared to put such faith in their recommendation of her that she felt almost obliged to give satisfaction. And she added: "I didn't get much chance to ask questions. She seemed so—er—busy."

Both the girls laughed. Helga laughed with them, surprised that she hadn't perceived before how really likable they were.

"We'll be through here in ten minutes. If you're not busy, come in and have your supper with us and we'll tell you about her," promised Miss Ross.


# Seven

Having finally turned her attention to Helga Crane, Fortune now seemed determined to smile, to make amends for her shameful neglect. One had, Helga decided, only to touch the right button, to press the right spring, in order to attract the jade's notice.

For Helga that spring had been Mrs. Hayes-Rore. Ever afterwards, on recalling that day on which with well-nigh empty purse and apprehensive heart she had made her way from the Young Women's Christian Association to the Grand Boulevard home of Mrs. Hayes-Rore, always she wondered at her own lack of astuteness in not seeing in the woman someone who by a few words was to have a part in the shaping of her life.

The husband of Mrs. Hayes-Rore had at one time been a dark thread in the soiled fabric of Chicago's South Side politics, who, departing this life hurriedly and unexpectedly and a little mysteriously, and somewhat before the whole of his suddenly acquired wealth had had time to vanish, had left his widow comfortably established with money and some of that prestige which in Negro circles had been his. All this Helga had learned from the secretaries at the Y.

And from numerous remarks dropped by Mrs. Hayes-Rore herself she was able to fill in the details more or less adequately.

On the train that carried them to New York, Helga had made short work of correcting and condensing the speeches, which Mrs. Hayes-Rore as a prominent "race" woman and an authority on the problem was to deliver before several meetings of the annual convention of the Negro Women's League of Clubs, convening the next week in New York. These speeches proved to be merely patchworks of others' speeches and opinions. Helga had heard other lecturers say the same things in Devon and again in Naxos. Ideas, phrases, and even whole sentences and paragraphs were lifted bodily from previous orations and published works of Wendell Phillips, Frederick Douglass, Booker T. Washington, and other doctors of the race's ills. For variety Mrs. Hayes-Rore had seasoned hers with a peppery dash of Du Bois and a few vinegary statements of her own. Aside from these it was, Helga reflected, the same old thing.

But Mrs. Hayes-Rore was to her, after the first short, awkward period, interesting. Her dark eyes, bright and investigating, had, Helga noted, a humorous gleam, and something in the way she held her untidy head gave the impression of a cat watching its prey so that when she struck, if she so decided, the blow would be unerringly effective. Helga, looking up from a last reading of the speeches, was aware that she was being studied. Her employer sat leaning back, the tips of her fingers pressed together, her head a bit on one side, her small inquisitive eyes boring into the girl before her. And as the train hurled itself frantically toward smoke-infested Newark, she decided to strike.

"Now tell me," she commanded, "how is it that a nice girl like you can rush off on a wild goose chase like this at a moment's notice. I should think your people'd object, or'd make inquiries, or something."

At that command Helga Crane could not help sliding down her eyes to hide the anger that had risen in them. Was she to be forever explaining her people—or lack of them? But she said courteously enough, even managing a hard little smile: "Well, you see, Mrs.

Hayes-Rore, I haven't any people. There's only me, so I can do as I please."

"Ha!" said Mrs. Hayes-Rore.

Terrific, thought Helga Crane, the power of that sound from the lips of this woman. How, she wondered, had she succeeded in investing it with so much incredulity?

"If you didn't have people, you wouldn't be living. Everybody has people, Miss Crane. Everybody."

"*I* haven't, Mrs. Hayes-Rore."

Mrs. Hayes-Rore screwed up her eyes. "Well, that's mighty mysterious, and I detest mysteries." She shrugged, and into those eyes there now came with alarming quickness an accusing criticism.

"It isn't," Helga said defensively, "a mystery. It's a fact and a mighty unpleasant one. Inconvenient too," and she laughed a little, not wishing to cry.

Her tormentor, in sudden embarrassment, turned her sharp eyes to the window. She seemed intent on the miles of red clay sliding past. After a moment, however, she asked gently: "You wouldn't like to tell me about it, would you? It seems to bother you. And I'm interested in girls."

Annoyed, but still hanging, for the sake of the twenty-five dollars, to her self-control, Helga gave her head a little toss and flung out her hands in a helpless, beaten way. Then she shrugged. What did it matter? "Oh, well, if you really want to know. I assure you, it's nothing interesting. Or nasty," she added maliciously. "It's just plain horrid. For me." And she began mockingly to relate her story.

But as she went on, again she had that sore sensation of revolt, and again the torment which she had gone through loomed before her as something brutal and undeserved. Passionately, tearfully, incoherently, the final words tumbled from her quivering petulant lips.

The other woman still looked out of the window, apparently so interested in the outer aspect of the drab sections of the Jersey manufacturing city through which they were passing that, the better to see, she had now so turned her head that only an ear and a small portion of cheek were visible.

During the little pause that followed Helga's recital, the faces of the two women, which had been bare, seemed to harden. It was almost as if they had slipped on masks. The girl wished to hide her turbulent feeling and to appear indifferent to Mrs. Hayes-Rore's opinion of her story. The woman felt that the story, dealing as it did with race intermingling and possibly adultery, was beyond definite discussion. For among black people, as among white people, it is tacitly understood that these things are not mentioned—and therefore they do not exist.

Sliding adroitly out from under the precarious subject to a safer, more decent one, Mrs. Hayes-Rore asked Helga what she was thinking of doing when she got back to Chicago. Had she anything in mind?

Helga, it appeared, hadn't. The truth was she had been thinking of staying in New York. Maybe she could find something there. Everybody seemed to. At least she could make the attempt.

Mrs. Hayes-Rore sighed, for no obvious reason. "Um, maybe I can help you. I know people in New York. Do you?"

"No."

"New York's the lonesomest place in the world if you don't know anybody."

"It couldn't possibly be worse than Chicago," said Helga savagely, giving the table support a violent kick.

They were running into the shadow of the tunnel. Mrs. Hayes-Rore murmured thoughtfully: "You'd better come uptown and stay with me a few days. I may need you. Something may turn up."

It was one of those vicious mornings, windy and bright. There seemed to Helga, as they emerged from the depths of the vast station, to be a whirling malice in the sharp air of this shining city. Mrs. Hayes-Rore's words about its terrible loneliness shot through her mind. She felt its aggressive unfriendliness. Even the great buildings, the flying cabs, and the swirling crowds seemed manifestations of purposed malevolence. And for that first short minute she was awed and frightened and inclined to turn back to that other city, which, though not kind, was yet not strange. This New York seemed somehow more appalling, more scornful, in some inexplicable way even more terrible and uncaring than Chicago. Threatening almost. Ugly. Yes, perhaps she'd better turn back.

The feeling passed, escaped in the surprise of what Mrs. Hayes-Rore was saying. Her oratorical voice boomed above the city's roar. "I suppose I ought really to have phoned Anne from the station. About you, I mean. Well, it doesn't matter. She's got plenty of room. Lives alone in a big house, which is something Negroes in New York don't do. They fill 'em up with lodgers usually. But Anne's funny. Nice, though. You'll like her, and it will be good for you to know her if you're going to stay in New York. She's a widow, my husband's sister's son's wife. The war, you know."

"Oh," protested Helga Crane, with a feeling of acute misgiving, "but won't she be annoyed and inconvenienced by having me brought in on her like this? I supposed we were going to the Y or a hotel or something like that. Oughtn't we really to stop and phone?"

The woman at her side in the swaying cab smiled, a peculiar invincible, self-reliant smile, but gave Helga Crane's suggestion no other attention. Plainly she was a person accustomed to having things her way. She merely went on talking of other plans. "I think maybe I can get you some work. With a new Negro insurance company. They're after me to put quite a tidy sum into it. Well, I'll just tell them that they may as well take you with the money," and she laughed.

"Thanks awfully," Helga said, "but will they like it? I mean being made to take me because of the money."

"They're not being made," contradicted Mrs. Hayes-Rore. "I intended to let them have the money anyway, and I'll tell Mr. Darling so—after he takes you. They ought to be glad to get you. Colored organizations always need more brains as well as more money. Don't worry. And don't thank me again. You haven't got the job yet, you know."

There was a little silence, during which Helga gave herself up to the distraction of watching the strange city and the strange crowds, trying hard to put out of her mind the vision of an easier future which her companion's words had conjured up; for, as had been pointed out, it was, as yet, only a possibility.

Turning out of the park into the broad thoroughfare of Lenox Avenue, Mrs. Hayes-Rore said in a too carefully casual manner: "And, by the way, I wouldn't mention that my people are white, if I were you. Colored people won't understand it, and after all it's your own business. When you've lived as long as I have, you'll know that what others don't know can't hurt you. I'll just tell Anne that you're a friend of mine whose mother's dead. That'll place you well enough and it's all true. I never tell lies. She can fill in the gaps to suit herself and anyone else curious enough to ask."

"Thanks," Helga said again. And so great was her gratitude that she reached out and took her new friend's slightly soiled hand in one of her own fastidious ones, and retained it until their cab turned into a pleasant tree-lined street and came to a halt before one of the dignified houses in the center of the block. Here they got out.

In after years Helga Crane had only to close her eyes to see herself standing apprehensively in the small cream-colored hall, the floor of which was covered with deep silver-hued carpet; to see Mrs. Hayes-Rore pecking the cheek of the tall slim creature beautifully dressed in a cool green tailored frock; to hear herself being introduced to "my niece, Mrs. Grey" as "Miss Crane, a little friend of mine whose mother's died, and I think perhaps a while in New York will be good for her"; to feel her hand grasped in quick sympathy, and to hear Anne Grey's pleasant voice, with its faint note of wistfulness, saying: "I'm so sorry, and I'm glad Aunt Jeanette brought you here. Did you have a good trip? I'm sure you must be worn out. I'll have Lillie take you right up." And to feel like a criminal.

# Eight

A year thick with various adventures had sped by since that spring day on which Helga Crane had set out away from Chicago's indifferent unkindness for New York in the company of Mrs. Hayes-Rore. New York she had found not so unkind, not so unfriendly, not so indifferent. There she had been happy, and secured work, had made acquaintances and another friend. Again she had had that strange transforming experience, this time not so fleetingly, that magic sense of having come home. Harlem, teeming black Harlem, had welcomed her and lulled her into something that was, she was certain, peace and contentment.

The request and recommendation of Mrs. Hayes-Rore had been sufficient for her to obtain work with the insurance company in which that energetic woman was interested. And through Anne it had been possible for her to meet and to know people with tastes and ideas similar to her own. Their sophisticated cynical talk, their elaborate parties, the unobtrusive correctness of their clothes and homes, all appealed to her craving for smartness, for enjoyment. Soon she was able to reflect with a flicker of amusement on that constant feeling of humiliation and inferiority which had encompassed her in Naxos. Her New York friends looked with contempt and scorn on Naxos and all its works. This gave Helga a pleasant sense of avengement. Any shreds of self-consciousness or apprehension which at first she may have felt vanished quickly, escaped in the keenness of her joy at seeming at last to belong somewhere. For she considered that she had, as she put it, "found herself."

Between Anne Grey and Helga Crane there had sprung one of those immediate and peculiarly sympathetic friendships. Uneasy at first, Helga had been relieved that Anne had never returned to the uncomfortable subject of her mother's death so intentionally mentioned on their first meeting by Mrs. Hayes-Rore, beyond a tremulous brief: "You won't talk to me about it, will you? I can't bear the thought of death. Nobody ever talks to me about it. My husband, you know." This Helga discovered to be true. Later, when she knew Anne better, she suspected that it was a bit of a pose assumed for the purpose of doing away with the necessity of speaking regretfully of a husband who had been perhaps not too greatly loved.

After the first pleasant weeks, feeling that her obligation to Anne was already too great, Helga began to look about for a permanent place to live. It was, she found, difficult. She eschewed the Y as too bare, impersonal, and restrictive. Nor did furnished rooms or the idea of a solitary or a shared apartment appeal to her. So she rejoiced when one day Anne, looking up from her book, said lightly: "Helga, since you're going to be in New York, why don't you stay here with me? I don't usually take people. It's too disrupting. Still, it *is* sort of pleasant having somebody in the house and I don't seem to mind you. You don't bore me, or bother me. If you'd like to stay— Think it over."

Helga didn't, of course, require to think it over, because lodgment in Anne's home was in complete accord with what she designated as her "aesthetic sense." Even Helga Crane approved of Anne's house and the furnishings which so admirably graced the big cream-colored rooms. Beds with long, tapering posts to which tremendous age lent dignity and interest, bonneted old highboys, tables that might be by Duncan Phyfe, rare spindle-legged chairs, and others whose ladder backs gracefully climbed the delicate wall panels. These historic things mingled harmoniously and comfortably with brass-bound Chinese tea chests, luxurious deep chairs and davenports, tiny tables of gay color, a lacquered jade-green settee with gleaming black satin cushions, lustrous Eastern rugs, ancient copper, Japanese prints, some fine etchings, a profusion of precious bric-a-brac, and endless shelves filled with books.

Anne Grey herself was, as Helga expressed it, "almost too good to be true." Thirty, maybe, brownly beautiful, she had the face of a golden Madonna, grave and calm and sweet, with shining black hair and eyes. She carried herself as queens are reputed to bear themselves, and probably do not. Her manners were as agreeably gentle as her own soft name. She possessed an impeccably fastidious taste in clothes, knowing what suited her and wearing it with an air of unconscious assurance. The unusual thing, a native New Yorker, she was also a person of distinction, financially independent, well connected and much sought after. And she was interesting, an odd confusion of wit and intense earnestness; a vivid and remarkable person. Yes, undoubtedly, Anne was almost too good to be true. She was almost perfect.

Thus established, secure, comfortable, Helga soon became thoroughly absorbed in the distracting interests of life in New York. Her secretarial work with the Negro insurance company filled her day. Books, the theater, parties, used up the nights. Gradually in the charm of this new and delightful pattern of her life she lost that tantalizing oppression of loneliness and isolation which always, it seemed, had been a part of her existence.

But, while the continuously gorgeous panorama of Harlem fascinated her, thrilled her, the sober mad rush of white New York failed entirely to stir her. Like thousands of other Harlem dwellers, she patronized its shops, its theaters, its art galleries, and its restaurants, and read its papers, without considering herself a part of the monster. And she was satisfied, unenvious. For her this Harlem was enough. Of that white world, so distant, so near, she asked only indifference. No, not at all did she crave, from those pale and powerful people, awareness. Sinister folk, she considered them, who had stolen her birthright. Their past contribution to her life, which had been but shame and grief, she had hidden away from brown folk in a locked closet, "never," she told herself, "to be reopened."

Someday she intended to marry one of those alluring brown or yellow men who danced attendance on her. Already financially successful, any one of them could give to her the things which she had now come to desire, a home like Anne's, cars of expensive makes such as lined the avenue, clothes and furs from Bendel's and Revillon Frères, servants, and leisure.

Always her forehead wrinkled in distaste whenever, involuntarily, which was somehow frequently, her mind turned on the speculative gray eyes and visionary uplifting plans of Dr. Anderson. That other, James Vayle, had slipped absolutely from her consciousness. Of him she never thought. Helga Crane meant, now, to have a home and perhaps laughing, appealing dark-eyed children in Harlem. Her existence was bounded by Central Park, Fifth Avenue, St. Nicholas Park, and 145th Street. Not at all a narrow life, as Negroes live it, as Helga Crane knew it. Everything was there, vice and goodness, sadness and gaiety, ignorance and wisdom, ugliness and beauty, poverty and richness. And it seemed to her that somehow of goodness, gaiety, wisdom, and beauty always there was a little more than of vice, sadness, ignorance, and ugliness. It was only riches that did not quite transcend poverty.

"But," said Helga Crane, "what of that? Money isn't everything. It isn't even the half of everything. And here we have so much else —and by ourselves. It's only outside of Harlem among those others that money really counts for everything."

In the actuality of the pleasant present and the delightful vision of an agreeable future she was contented and happy. She did not analyze this contentment, this happiness, but vaguely, without putting it into words or even so tangible a thing as a thought, she knew it sprang from a sense of freedom, a release from the feeling of smallness which had hedged her in, first during her sorry, unchildlike childhood among hostile white folk in Chicago, and later during her uncomfortable sojourn among snobbish black folk in Naxos.

# Nine

But it didn't last, this happiness of Helga Crane's.

Little by little the signs of spring appeared, but strangely the enchantment of the season, so enthusiastically, so lavishly greeted by the gay dwellers of Harlem, filled her only with restlessness. Somewhere, within her, in a deep recess, crouched discontent. She began to lose confidence in the fullness of her life, the glow began to fade from her conception of it. As the days multiplied, her need of something, something vaguely familiar, but which she could not put a name to and hold for definite examination, became almost intolerable. She went through moments of overwhelming anguish. She felt shut in, trapped. "Perhaps I'm tired, need a tonic or something," she reflected. So she consulted a physician, who, after a long, solemn examination, said that there was nothing wrong, nothing at all. "A change of scene, perhaps for a week or so, or a few days away from work," would put her straight most likely. Helga tried this, tried them both, but it was no good. All interest had gone out of living. Nothing seemed any good. She became a little frightened, and then shocked to discover that, for some unknown reason, it was of herself she was afraid.

Spring grew into summer, languidly at first, then flauntingly. Without awareness on her part, Helga Crane began to draw away from those contacts which had so delighted her. More and more she made lonely excursions to places outside of Harlem. A sensation of estrangement and isolation encompassed her. As the days became hotter and the streets more swarming, a kind of repulsion came upon her. She recoiled in aversion from the sight of the grinning faces and from the sound of the easy laughter of all these people who strolled, aimlessly now, it seemed, up and down the avenues. Not only did the crowds of nameless folk on the street annoy her, she began also actually to dislike her friends.

Even the gentle Anne distressed her. Perhaps because Anne was obsessed by the race problem and fed her obsession. She frequented all the meetings of protest, subscribed to all the complaining magazines, and read all the lurid newspapers spewed out by the Negro yellow press. She talked, wept, and ground her teeth dramatically about the wrongs and shames of her race. At times she lashed her fury to surprising heights for one by nature so placid and gentle. And, though she would not, even to herself, have admitted it, she reveled in this orgy of protest.

"Social equality," "Equal opportunity for all," were her slogans, often and emphatically repeated. Anne preached these things and honestly thought that she believed them, but she considered it an affront to the race, and to all the varicolored peoples that made Lenox and Seventh avenues the rich spectacles which they were, for any Negro to receive on terms of equality any white person.

"To me," asserted Anne Grey, "the most wretched Negro prostitute that walks 135th Street is more than any President of these United States, not excepting Abraham Lincoln." But she turned up her finely carved nose at their lusty churches, their picturesque parades, their naïve clowning on the streets. She would not have desired or even have been willing to live in any section outside the black belt, and she would have refused scornfully, had they been tendered, any invitation from white folk. She hated white people with a deep and burning hatred, with the kind of hatred which, finding itself held in sufficiently numerous groups, was capable someday, on some great provocation, of bursting into dangerously malignant flames.

But she aped their clothes, their manners, and their gracious ways of living. While proclaiming loudly the undiluted good of all things Negro, she yet disliked the songs, the dances, and the softly blurred speech of the race. Toward these things she showed only a disdainful contempt, tinged sometimes with a faint amusement. Like the despised people of the white race, she preferred Pavlova to Florence Mills, John McCormack to Taylor Gordon, Walter Hampden to Paul Robeson. Theoretically, however, she stood for the immediate advancement of all things Negroid, and was in revolt against social inequality.

Helga had been entertained by this racial ardor in one so little affected by racial prejudice as Anne, and by her inconsistencies. But suddenly these things irked her with a great irksomeness and she wanted to be free of this constant prattling of the incongruities, the injustices, the stupidities, the viciousness of white people. It stirred memories, probed hidden wounds, whose poignant ache bred in her surprising oppression and corroded the fabric of her quietism. Sometimes it took all her self-control to keep from tossing sarcastically at Anne Ibsen's remark about there being assuredly something very wrong with the drains, but after all there were other parts of the edifice.

It was at this period of restiveness that Helga met Dr. Anderson again. She had gone, unwillingly, to a meeting, a health meeting, held in a large church—as were most of Harlem's uplift activities—as a substitute for her employer, Mr. Darling. Making her tardy arrival during a tedious discourse by a pompous saffron-hued physician, she was led by the irritated usher, whom she had roused from a nap in which he had been pleasantly freed from the intricacies of Negro health statistics, to a very front seat. Complete silence ensued while she subsided into her chair. The offended doctor looked at the ceiling, at the floor, and accusingly at Helga, and finally continued his lengthy discourse. When at last he had ended and Helga had dared to remove her eyes from his sweating face and look about, she saw with a sudden thrill that Robert Anderson was among her nearest neighbors. A peculiar, not wholly disagreeable quiver ran down her spine. She felt an odd little faintness. The blood rushed to her face. She tried to jeer at herself for being so moved by the encounter.

He, meanwhile, she observed, watched her gravely. And having caught her attention, he smiled a little and nodded.

When all who so desired had spouted to their hearts' content—if to little purpose—and the meeting was finally over, Anderson detached himself from the circle of admiring friends and acquaintances that had gathered around him and caught up with Helga halfway down the long aisle leading out to fresher air.

"I wondered if you were really going to cut me. I see you were," he began, with that half-quizzical smile which she remembered so well.

She laughed. "Oh, I didn't think you'd remember me." Then she added: "Pleasantly, I mean."

The man laughed too. But they couldn't talk yet. People kept breaking in on them. At last, however, they were at the door, and then he suggested that they share a taxi "for the sake of a little breeze." Helga assented.

Constraint fell upon them when they emerged into the hot street, made seemingly hotter by a low-hanging golden moon and the hundreds of blazing electric lights. For a moment, before hailing a taxi, they stood together looking at the slow-moving mass of perspiring human beings. Neither spoke, but Helga was conscious of the man's steady gaze. The prominent gray eyes were fixed upon her, studying her, appraising her. Many times since turning her back on Naxos she had in fancy rehearsed this scene, this re-encounter. Now she found that rehearsal helped not at all. It was so absolutely different from anything that she had imagined.

In the open taxi they talked of impersonal things: books, places, the fascination of New York, of Harlem. But underneath the exchange of small talk lay another conversation of which Helga Crane was sharply aware. She was aware, too, of a strange ill-defined emotion, a vague yearning rising within her. And she experienced a sensation of consternation and keen regret when with a lurching jerk the cab pulled up before the house in 139th Street. So soon, she thought.

But she held out her hand calmly, coolly. Cordially she asked him to call sometime. "It is," she said, "a pleasure to renew our acquaintance." Was it, she was wondering, merely an acquaintance?

He responded seriously that he too thought it a pleasure, and added: "You haven't changed. You're still seeking for something, I think."

At his speech there dropped from her that vague feeling of yearning, that longing for sympathy and understanding which his presence evoked. She felt a sharp stinging sensation and a recurrence of that anger and defiant desire to hurt which had so seared her on that past morning in Naxos. She searched for a biting remark but, finding none venomous enough, she merely laughed a little rude and scornful laugh and, throwing up her small head, bade him an impatient good night and ran quickly up the steps.

Afterward she lay for long hours without undressing, thinking angry self-accusing thoughts, recalling and reconstructing that other explosive contact. That memory filled her with a sort of aching delirium. A thousand indefinite longings beset her. Eagerly she desired to see him again to right herself in his thoughts. Far into the night she lay planning speeches for their next meeting, so that it was long before drowsiness advanced upon her.

When he did call, Sunday, three days later, she put him off on Anne and went out, pleading an engagement, which until then she had not meant to keep. Until the very moment of his entrance she had had no intention of running away, but something, some imp of contumacy, drove her from his presence, though she longed to stay.

Again abruptly had come the uncontrollable wish to wound. Later, with a sense of helplessness and inevitability, she realized that the weapon which she had chosen had been a boomerang, for she herself had felt the keen disappointment of the denial. Better to have stayed and hurled polite sarcasms at him. She might then at least have had the joy of seeing him wince.

In this spirit she made her way to the corner and turned into Seventh Avenue. The warmth of the sun, though gentle on that afternoon, had nevertheless kissed the street into marvelous light and color. Now and then, greeting an acquaintance, or stopping to chat with a friend, Helga was all the time seeing its soft shining brightness on the buildings along its sides or on the gleaming bronze, gold, and copper faces of its promenaders. And another vision, too, came haunting Helga Crane: level gray eyes set down in a brown face which stared out at her, coolly, quizzically, disturbingly. And she was not happy.

The tea to which she had so suddenly made up her mind to go she found boring beyond endurance—insipid drinks, dull conversation, stupid men. The aimless talk glanced from John Wellinger's lawsuit for discrimination because of race against a downtown restaurant and the advantages of living in Europe, especially in France, to the significance, if any, of the Garvey movement. Then it sped to a favorite Negro dancer who had just then secured a foothold on the stage of a current white musical comedy, to other shows, to a new book touching on Negroes. Thence to costumes for a coming masquerade dance, to a new jazz song, to Yvette Dawson's engagement to a Boston lawyer who had seen her one night at a party and proposed to her the next day at noon. Then back again to racial discrimination.

Why, Helga wondered, with unreasoning exasperation, didn' they find something else to talk of? Why must the race problem always creep in? She refused to go on to another gathering. It would, she thought, be simply the same old thing.

On her arrival home she was more disappointed than she cared to admit to find the house in darkness and even Anne gone off some-

where. She would have liked that night to have talked with Anne.
Get her opinion of Dr. Anderson.

Anne it was who the next day told her that he had given up his
work in Naxos; or rather that Naxos had given him up. He had been
too liberal, too lenient, for education as it was inflicted in Naxos.
Now he was permanently in New York, employed as welfare worker
by some big manufacturing concern, which gave employment to
hundreds of Negro men.

"Uplift," sniffed Helga contemptuously, and fled before the on-
slaught of Anne's harangue on the needs and ills of the race.

# Ten

With the waning summer the acute sensitiveness of Helga Crane's
frayed nerves grew keener. There were days when the mere sight of
the serene tan and brown faces about her stung her like a personal
insult. The carefree quality of their laughter roused in her the desire
to scream at them: "Fools, fools! Stupid fools!" This passionate and
unreasoning protest gained in intensity, swallowing up all else like
some dense fog. Life became for her only a hateful place where one
lived in intimacy with people one would not have chosen had one
been given choice. It was, too, an excruciating agony. She was con-
tinually out of temper. Anne, thank the gods! was away, but her
nearing return filled Helga with dismay.

Arriving at work one sultry day, hot and dispirited, she found
waiting a letter, a letter from Uncle Peter. It had originally been sent
to Naxos, and from there it had made the journey back to Chicago
to the Young Women's Christian Association, and then to Mrs.
Hayes-Rore. That busy woman had at last found time between con-
ventions and lectures to readdress it and had sent it on to New York.
Four months, at least, it had been on its travels. Helga felt no curiosity
as to its contents, only annoyance at the long delay, as she ripped
open the thin edge of the envelope and for a space sat staring at the
peculiar foreign script of her uncle.

*715 Sheridan Road*
*Chicago, Ill.*

*Dear Helga:*

*It is now over a year since you made your unfortunate call
here. It was unfortunate for us all, you, Mrs. Nilssen, and
myself. But of course you couldn't know. I blame myself.
I should have written you of my marriage.*

*I have looked for a letter, or some word from you;
evidently, with your usual penetration, you understood
thoroughly that I must terminate my outward relation
with you. You were always a keen one.*

*Of course I am sorry, but it can't be helped. My wife
must be considered, and she feels very strongly about this.*

*You know, of course, that I wish you the best of luck.
But take an old man's advice and don't do as your mother
did. Why don't you run over and visit your Aunt
Katrina? She always wanted you. Maria Kirkeplads, No. 2,
will find her.*

*I enclose what I intended to leave you at my death. It
is better and more convenient that you get it now. I wish
it were more, but even this little may come in handy for a
rainy day.*

*Best wishes for your luck.*

*Peter Nilssen*

Beside the brief, friendly, but none the less final letter there was a
check for five thousand dollars. Helga Crane's first feeling was one
of unreality. This changed almost immediately into one of relief, of
liberation. It was stronger than the mere security from present financial worry which the check promised. Money as money was still
not very important to Helga. But later, while on an errand in the big
general office of the society, her puzzled bewilderment fled. Here the
inscrutability of the dozen or more brown faces, all cast from the
same indefinite mold, and so like her own, seemed pressing forward

against her. Abruptly it flashed upon her that the harrowing irritation of the past weeks was a smoldering hatred. Then she was overcome by another, so actual, so sharp, so horribly painful, that forever afterwards she preferred to forget it. It was as if she were shut up, boxed up, with hundreds of her race, closed up with that something in the racial character which had always been, to her, inexplicable, alien. Why, she demanded in fierce rebellion, should she be yoked to these despised black folk?

Back in the privacy of her own cubicle, self-loathing came upon her. "They're my own people, my own people," she kept repeating over and over to herself. It was no good. The feeling would not be routed. "I can't go on like this," she said to herself. "I simply can't."

There were footsteps. Panic seized her. She'd have to get out. She terribly needed to. Snatching hat and purse, she hurried to the narrow door, saying in a forced, steady voice, as it opened to reveal her employer: "Mr. Darling, I'm sorry, but I've got to go out. Please, may I be excused?"

At his courteous "Certainly, certainly. And don't hurry. It's much too hot," Helga Crane had the grace to feel ashamed, but there was no softening of her determination. The necessity for being alone was too urgent. She hated him and all the others too much.

Outside, rain had begun to fall. She walked bareheaded, bitter with self-reproach. But she rejoiced too. She didn't, in spite of her racial markings, belong to these dark segregated people. She was different. She felt it. It wasn't merely a matter of color. It was something broader, deeper, that made folk kin.

And now she was free. She would take Uncle Peter's money and advice and revisit her aunt in Copenhagen. Fleeting pleasant memories of her childhood visit there flew through her excited mind. She had been only eight, yet she had enjoyed the interest and the admiration which her unfamiliar color and dark curly hair, strange to those pink, white, and gold people, had evoked. Quite clearly now she recalled that her Aunt Katrina had begged for her to be allowed to remain. Why, she wondered, hadn't her mother consented? To

Helga it seemed that it would have been the solution to all their problems, her mother's, her stepfather's, her own.

At home in the cool dimness of the big chintz-hung living room, clad only in a fluttering thing of green chiffon, she gave herself up to daydreams of a happy future in Copenhagen, where there were no Negroes, no problems, no prejudice, until she remembered with perturbation that this was the day of Anne's return from her vacation at the seashore. Worse. There was a dinner party in her honor that very night. Helga sighed. She'd have to go. She couldn't possibly get out of a dinner party for Anne, even though she felt that such an event on a hot night was little short of an outrage. Nothing but a sense of obligation to Anne kept her from pleading a splitting head-ache as an excuse for remaining quietly at home.

Her mind trailed off to the highly important matter of clothes. What should she wear? White? No, everybody would, because it was hot. Green? She shook her head. Anne would be sure to. The blue thing. Reluctantly she decided against it; she loved it, but she had worn it too often. There was that cobwebby black net touched with orange, which she had bought last spring in a fit of extravagance and never worn, because on getting it home both she and Anne had considered it too décolleté, and too outré. Anne's words: "There's not enough of it, and what there is gives you the air of something about to fly," came back to her, and she smiled as she decided that she would certainly wear the black net. For her it would be a symbol. She was about to fly.

She busied herself with some absurdly expensive roses which she had ordered sent in, spending an interminable time in their arrange-ment. At last she was satisfied with their appropriateness in some blue Chinese jars of great age. Anne *did* have such lovely things, she thought as she began conscientiously to prepare for her return, al-though there was really little to do; Lillie seemed to have done every-thing. But Helga dusted the tops of the books, placed the magazines in ordered carelessness, redressed Anne's bed in fresh-smelling sheets of cool linen, and laid out her best pale yellow pajamas of crepe de chine. Finally she set out two tall green glasses and made a great pitcher of lemonade, leaving only the ginger ale and claret to be added on Anne's arrival. She was a little conscience-stricken, so she wanted to be particularly nice to Anne, who had been so kind to her when first she came to New York, a forlorn friendless creature. Yes, she was grateful to Anne; but, just the same, she meant to go. At once.

Her preparations over, she went back to the carved chair from which the thought of Anne's homecoming had drawn her. Characteristically she writhed at the idea of telling Anne of her impending departure and shirked the problem of evolving a plausible and inoffensive excuse for its suddenness. "That," she decided lazily, "will have to look out for itself; I can't be bothered just now. It's too hot."

She began to make plans and to dream delightful dreams of change, of life somewhere else. Someplace where at last she would be permanently satisfied. Her anticipatory thoughts waltzed and eddied about to the sweet silent music of change. With rapture almost, she let herself drop into the blissful sensation of visualizing herself in different, strange places, among approving and admiring people, where she would be appreciated and understood.

# Eleven

It was night. The dinner party was over, but no one wanted to go home. Half past eleven was, it seemed, much too early to tumble into bed on a Saturday night. It was a sulky, humid night, a thick furry night, through which the electric torches shone like silver fuzz—an atrocious night for cabareting, Helga insisted, but the others wanted to go, so she went with them, though half unwillingly. After much consultation and chatter they decided upon a place and climbed into two patiently waiting taxis, rattling things which jerked, wiggled, and groaned, and threatened every minute to collide with others of their kind, or with inattentive pedestrians. Soon they pulled up before a tawdry doorway in a narrow crosstown street and stepped out. The night was far from quiet, the streets far from empty. Clanging trolley bells, quarreling cats, cackling phonographs, raucous laughter, complaining motor horns, low singing, mingled in the familiar medley that is Harlem. Black figures, white figures, little forms, big forms, small groups, large groups, sauntered, or hurried by. It was gay, grotesque, and a little weird. Helga Crane felt singularly apart from it all. Entering the waiting doorway, they descended through a furtive, narrow passage, into a vast subterranean room. Helga smiled, thinking that this was one of those places characterized by the righteous as a hell.

A glare of light struck her eyes, a blare of jazz split her ears. For a moment everything seemed to be spinning round; even she felt that she was circling aimlessly, as she followed with the others the black giant who led them to a small table, where, when they were seated, their knees and elbows touched. Helga wondered that the waiter, indefinitely carved out of ebony, did not smile as he wrote their order: "Four bottles of White Rock, four bottles of ginger ale." Bah! Anne giggled, the others smiled and openly exchanged knowing glances, and under the tables flat glass bottles were extracted from the women's evening scarfs and small silver flasks drawn from the men's hip pockets. In a little moment she grew accustomed to the smoke and din.

They danced, ambling lazily to a crooning melody, or violently twisting their bodies, like whirling leaves, to a sudden streaming rhythm, or shaking themselves ecstatically to a thumping of unseen tomtoms. For the while Helga was oblivious of the reek of flesh, smoke, and alcohol, oblivious of the oblivion of other gyrating pairs, oblivious of the color, the noise, and the grand distorted childishness of it all. She was drugged, lifted, sustained, by the extraordinary music, blown out, ripped out, beaten out, by the joyous, wild, murky orchestra. The essence of life seemed bodily motion. And when suddenly the music died, she dragged herself back to the present with a conscious effort; and a shameful certainty that not only had she been in the jungle, but that she had enjoyed it, began to taunt her. She hardened her determination to get away. She wasn't, she told herself, a jungle creature. She cloaked herself in a faint disgust as she watched the entertainers throw themselves about to the bursts of syncopated jangle, and when the time came again for the patrons to dance, she declined. Her rejected partner excused himself and sought an acquaintance a few tables removed. Helga sat looking curiously about her as the buzz of conversation ceased, strangled by the savage strains of music, and the crowd became a swirling mass. For the hundredth time she marveled at the gradations within this oppressed race of hers. A dozen shades slid by. There was sooty black, shiny black, taupe, mahogany, bronze, copper, gold, orange, yellow, peach, ivory, pinky white, pastry white. There was yellow hair, brown hair, black hair; straight hair, straightened hair, curly hair, crinkly hair, woolly hair. She saw black eyes in white faces, brown eyes in yellow faces, gray eyes in brown faces, blue eyes in tan faces. Africa, Europe, perhaps with a pinch of Asia, in a fantastic motley of ugliness and beauty, semibarbaric, sophisticated, exotic, were here. But she was blind to its charm, purposely aloof and a little contemptuous, and soon her interest in the moving mosaic waned.

She had discovered Dr. Anderson sitting at a table on the far side of the room, with a girl in a shivering apricot frock. Seriously he returned her tiny bow. She met his eyes, gravely smiling, then blushed, furiously, and averted her own. But they went back immediately to the girl beside him, who sat indifferently sipping a colorless liquid from a high glass, or puffing a precariously hanging cigarette. Across dozens of tables, littered with corks, with ashes, with shriveled sandwiches, through slits in the swaying mob, Helga Crane studied her.

She was pale, with a peculiar, almost deathlike pallor. The brilliantly red, softly curving mouth was somehow sorrowful. Her pitch-black eyes, a little aslant, were veiled by long, drooping lashes and surmounted by broad brows, which seemed like black smears. The short dark hair was brushed severely back from the wide forehead. The extreme décolletage of her simple apricot dress showed a skin of unusual color, a delicate, creamy hue, with golden tones. "Almost like an alabaster," thought Helga.

Bang! Again the music died. The moving mass broke, separated.

The others returned. Anne had rage in her eyes. Her voice trembled as she took Helga aside to whisper: "There's your Dr. Anderson over there, with Audrey Denney."

"Yes, I saw him. She's lovely. Who is she?"

"She's Audrey Denney, as I said, and she lives downtown. West Twenty-second Street. Hasn't much use for Harlem any more. It's a wonder she hasn't some white man hanging about. The disgusting creature! I wonder how she inveigled Anderson? But that's Audrey! If there is any desirable man about, trust her to attach him. She ought to be ostracized."

"Why?" asked Helga curiously, noting at the same time that three of the men in their own party had deserted and were now congregated about the offending Miss Denney.

"Because she goes about with white people," came Anne's indignant answer, "and they know she's colored."

"I'm afraid I don't quite see, Anne. Would it be all right if they didn't know she was colored?"

"Now don't be nasty, Helga. You know very well what I mean." Anne's voice was shaking. Helga didn't see, and she was greatly interested, but she decided to let it go. She didn't want to quarrel with Anne, not now, when she had that guilty feeling about leaving her. But Anne was off on her favorite subject, race. And it seemed, too, that Audrey Denney was to her particularly obnoxious.

"Why, she gives parties for white and colored people together. And she goes to white people's parties. It's worse than disgusting, it's positively obscene."

"Oh, come, Anne, you haven't been to any of the parties, I know, so how can you be so positive about the matter?"

"No, but I've heard about them. I know people who've been."

"Friends of yours, Anne?"

Anne admitted that they were, some of them.

"Well, then, they can't be so bad. I mean, if your friends sometimes go, can they? Just what goes on that's so terrible?"

"Why, they drink, for one thing. Quantities, they say."

"So do we, at the parties here in Harlem," Helga responded. An idiotic impulse seized her to leave the place, Anne's presence, then, forever. But of course she couldn't. It would be foolish, and so ugly.

"And the white men dance with the colored women. Now you know, Helga Crane, that can mean only one thing." Anne's voice was trembling with cold hatred. As she ended, she made a little clicking noise with her tongue, indicating an abhorrence too great for words.

"Don't the colored men dance with the white women, or do they sit about, impolitely, while the other men dance with their women?" inquired Helga very softly, and with a slowness approaching almost to insolence. Anne's insinuations were too revolting. She had a slightly sickish feeling, and a flash of anger touched her. She mastered it and ignored Anne's inadequate answer.

"It's the principle of the thing that I object to. You can't get round the fact that her behavior is outrageous, treacherous, in fact. That's what's the matter with the Negro race. They won't stick together. She certainly ought to be ostracized. I've nothing but contempt for her, as has every other self-respecting Negro."

The other women and the lone man left to them—Helga's own escort—all seemingly agreed with Anne. At any rate, they didn't protest. Helga gave it up. She felt that it would be useless to tell them that what she felt for the beautiful, calm, cool girl who had the assurance, the courage, so placidly to ignore racial barriers and give her attention to people was not contempt but envious admiration. So she remained silent, watching the girl.

At the next first sound of music Dr. Anderson rose. Languidly the girl followed his movement, a faint smile parting her sorrowful lips at some remark he made. Her long, slender body swayed with an eager pulsing motion. She danced with grace and abandon, gravely, yet with obvious pleasure, her legs, her hips, her back, all swaying gently, swung by that wild music from the heart of the jungle. Helga turned her glance to Dr. Anderson. Her disinterested curiosity passed. While she still felt for the girl envious admiration, that feeling was now augmented by another, a more primitive emotion. She forgot the garish crowded room. She forgot her friends. She saw only two figures, closely clinging. She felt her heart throbbing. She felt the room receding. She went out the door. She climbed endless stairs. At last, panting, confused, but thankful to have escaped, she found herself again out in the dark night alone, a small crumpled thing in a fragile, flying black and gold dress. A taxi drifted toward her, stopped. She stepped into it, feeling cold, unhappy, misunderstood, and forlorn.

# Twelve

Helga Crane felt no regret as the clifflike towers faded. The sight thrilled her as beauty, grandeur, of any kind always did, but that was all.

The liner drew out from churning slate-colored waters of the river into the open sea. The small seething ripples on the water's surface became little waves. It was evening. In the western sky was a pink and mauve light, which faded gradually into a soft gray-blue obscurity. Leaning against the railing, Helga stared into the approaching night, glad to be at last alone, free of that great superfluity of human beings, yellow, brown, and black, which, as the torrid summer burned to its close, had so oppressed her. No, she hadn't belonged there. Of her attempt to emerge from that inherent aloneness which was part of her very being only dullness had come, dullness and a great aversion.

Almost at once it was time for dinner. Somewhere a bell sounded. She turned and with buoyant steps went down. Already she had begun to feel happier. Just for a moment, outside the dining salon, she hesitated, assailed with a tiny uneasiness which passed as quickly as it had come. She entered softly, unobtrusively. And, after all, she had had her little fear for nothing. The purser, a man grown old in the service of the Scandinavian-American Line, remembered her as the little dark girl who had crossed with her mother years ago, and so she must sit at his table. Helga liked that. It put her at her ease and made her feel important.

Everyone was kind in the delightful days which followed, and her first shyness under the politely curious glances of turquoise eyes of her fellow travelers soon slid from her. The old forgotten Danish of her childhood began to come, awkwardly at first, from her lips, under their agreeable tutelage. Evidently they were interested, curious, and perhaps a little amused about this Negro girl on her way to Denmark alone.

Helga was a good sailor, and mostly the weather was lovely with the serene calm of the lingering September summer, under whose sky the sea was smooth, like a length of watered silk, unruffled by the stir of any wind. But even the two rough days found her on deck, reveling like a released bird in her returned feeling of happiness and freedom, that blessed sense of belonging to herself alone and not to a race. Again, she had put the past behind her with an ease which astonished even herself. Only the figure of Dr. Anderson obtruded itself with surprising vividness to irk her because she could get no meaning from that keen sensation of covetous exasperation that had so surprisingly risen within her on the night of the cabaret party. This question Helga Crane recognized as not entirely new; it was but a revival of the puzzlement experienced when she had fled so abruptly from Naxos more than a year before. With the recollection of that previous flight and subsequent half questioning a dim disturbing notion came to her. She wasn't, she couldn't be, in love with the man. It was a thought too humiliating, and so quickly dismissed. Nonsense! Sheer nonsense! When one is in love, one strives to please. Never, she decided, had she made an effort to be pleasing to Dr. Anderson. On the contrary, she had always tried, deliberately, to irritate him. She was, she told herself, a sentimental fool.

Nevertheless, the thought of love stayed with her, not prominent, definite, but shadowy, incoherent. And in a remote corner of her consciousness lurked the memory of Dr. Anderson's serious smile and gravely musical voice.

On the last morning Helga rose at dawn, a dawn outside old Copenhagen. She lay lazily in her long chair watching the feeble sun creeping over the ship's great green funnels with sickly light; watching the purply gray sky change to opal, to gold, to pale blue. A few other passengers, also early risen, excited by the prospect of renewing old attachments, of glad homecomings after long years, paced nervously back and forth. Now, at the last moment, they were impatient, but apprehensive fear, too, had its place in their rushing emotions. Impatient Helga Crane was not. But she *was* apprehensive. Gradually, as the ship drew into the lazier waters of the dock, she became prey to sinister fears and memories. A deep pang of misgiving nauseated her at the thought of her aunt's husband, acquired since Helga's childhood visit. Painfully, vividly, she remembered the frightened anger of Uncle Peter's new wife, and looking back at her precipitate departure from America, she was amazed at her own stupidity. She had not even considered the remote possibility that her aunt's husband might be like Mrs. Nilssen. For the first time in nine days she wished herself back in New York, in America.

The little gulf of water between the ship and the wharf lessened. The engines had long ago ceased their whirring, and now the buzz of conversation, too, died down. There was a sort of silence. Soon the welcoming crowd on the wharf stood under the shadow of the great sea monster, their faces turned up to the anxious ones of the passengers who hung over the railing. Hats were taken off, handkerchiefs were shaken out and frantically waved. Chatter. Deafening shouts. A little quiet weeping. Sailors and laborers were yelling and rushing about. Cables were thrown. The gangplank was laid.

Silent, unmoving, Helga Crane stood looking intently down into the gesticulating crowd. Was anyone waving to her? She couldn't tell. She didn't in the least remember her aunt, save as a hazy pretty lady. She smiled a little at the thought that her aunt, or anyone waiting there in the crowd below, would have no difficulty in singling her out. But—had she been met? When she descended the gangplank she was still uncertain and was trying to decide on a plan of procedure in the event that she had not. A telegram before she went through customs? Telephone? A taxi?

But, again, she had all her fears and questionings for nothing. A smart woman in olive green came toward her at once. And, even in the fervent gladness of her relief, Helga took in the carelessly trailing purple scarf and correct black hat that completed the perfection of her aunt's costume, and had time to feel herself a little shabbily dressed. For it was her aunt; Helga saw that at once. The resemblance to her own mother was unmistakable. There was the same long nose, the same beaming blue eyes, the same straying pale brown hair so like sparkling beer. And the tall man with the fierce mustache who followed carrying hat and stick must be Herr Dahl, Aunt Katrina's husband. How gracious he was in his welcome, and how anxious to air his faulty English, now that her aunt had finished kissing her and exclaimed in Danish: "Little Helga! Little Helga! Goodness! But how you have grown!"

Laughter from all three.

"Welcome to Denmark, to Copenhagen, to our home," said the new uncle in queer, proud, oratorical English. And to Helga's smiling, grateful "Thank you," he returned: "Your trunks? Your checks?" also in English, and then lapsed into Danish.

"Where in the world are the Fischers? We must hurry the customs."

Almost immediately they were joined by a breathless couple, a young gray-haired man and a fair, tiny, doll-like woman. It developed that they had lived in England for some years and so spoke English, real English, well. They were both breathless, all apologies and explanations.

"So early!" sputtered the man, Herr Fischer. "We inquired last night and they said nine. It was only by accident that we called again this morning to be sure. Well, you can imagine the rush we were in when they said eight! And of course we had trouble in finding a cab. One always does if one is late." All this in Danish. Then to Helga in English: "You see, I was especially asked to come because Fru Dahl didn't know if you remembered your Danish, and your uncle's English—well—"

More laughter.

At last, the customs having been hurried and a cab secured, they were off, with much chatter, through the toylike streets, weaving perilously in and out among the swarms of bicycles.

It had begun, a new life for Helga Crane.

# Thirteen

She liked it, this new life. For a time it blotted from her mind all else. She took to luxury as the proverbial duck to water. And she took to admiration and attention even more eagerly.

It was pleasant to wake on that first afternoon, after the insisted-upon nap, with that sensation of lavish contentment and well-being enjoyed only by impecunious sybarites waking in the houses of the rich. But there was something more than mere contentment and well-being. To Helga Crane it was the realization of a dream that she had dreamed persistently ever since she was old enough to remember such vague things as daydreams and longings. Always she had wanted, not money, but the things which money could give, leisure, attention, beautiful surroundings. Things. Things. Things.

So it was more than pleasant, it was important, this awakening in the great high room which held the great high bed on which she lay, small but exalted. It was important because to Helga Crane it was the day, so she decided, to which all the sad forlorn past had led, and from which the whole future was to depend. This, then, was where she belonged. This was her proper setting. She felt consoled at last for the spiritual wounds of the past.

A discreet knocking on the tall paneled door sounded. In response to Helga's "Come in" a respectful rosy-faced maid entered and Helga lay for a long minute watching her adjust the shutters. She was conscious, too, of the girl's sly curious glances at her, although her general attitude was quite correct, willing and disinterested. In New York, America, Helga would have resented this sly watching. Now, here, she was only amused. Marie, she reflected, had probably never seen a Negro outside the pictured pages of her geography book.

Another knocking. Aunt Katrina entered, smiling at Helga's quick, lithe spring from the bed. They were going out to tea, she informed Helga. What, the girl inquired, did one wear to tea in Copenhagen, meanwhile glancing at her aunt's dark purple dress and bringing forth a severely plain blue crepe frock. But no! It seemed that that wouldn't at all do.

"Too sober," pronounced Fru Dahl. "Haven't you something lively, something bright?" And, noting Helga's puzzled glance at her own subdued costume, she explained laughingly: "Oh, I'm an old married lady, and a Dane. But you, you're young. And you're a foreigner, and different. You must have bright things to set off the color of your lovely brown skin. Striking things, exotic things. You must make an impression."

"I've only these," said Helga Crane, timidly displaying her wardrobe on couch and chairs. "Of course I intend to buy here. I didn't want to bring over too much that might be useless."

"And you were quite right too. Umm. Let's see. That black there, the one with the cerise and purple trimmings. Wear that."

Helga was shocked. "But for tea, Aunt! Isn't it too gay? Too— too—*outré*?"

"Oh dear, no. Not at all, not for you. Just right." Then after a little pause she added: "And we're having people in to dinner tonight, quite a lot. Perhaps we'd better decide on our frocks now." For she was, in spite of all her gentle kindness, a woman who left nothing to chance. In her own mind she had determined the role that Helga was to play in advancing the social fortunes of the Dahls of Copenhagen, and she meant to begin at once.

At last, after much trying on and scrutinizing, it was decided that Marie should cut a favorite emerald-green velvet dress a little lower in the back and add some gold and mauve flowers, "to liven it up a bit," as Fru Dahl put it.

"Now that," she said, pointing to the Chinese-red dressing gown in which Helga had wrapped herself when at last the fitting was over, "suits you. Tomorrow we'll shop. Maybe we can get something that color. That black and orange thing there is good too, but too high. What a prim American maiden you are, Helga, to hide such a fine back and shoulders. Your feet are nice too, but you ought to have higher heels—and buckles."

Left alone, Helga began to wonder. She was dubious, too, and not a little resentful. Certainly she loved color with a passion that perhaps only Negroes and Gypsies know. But she had a deep faith in the perfection of her own taste, and no mind to be bedecked in flaunting flashy things. Still—she had to admit that Fru Dahl was right about the dressing gown. It did suit her. Perhaps an evening dress. And she knew that she had lovely shoulders, and her feet *were* nice.

When she was dressed in the shining black taffeta with its bizarre trimmings of purple and cerise, Fru Dahl approved her and so did Herr Dahl. Everything in her responded to his "She's beautiful; beautiful!" Helga Crane knew she wasn't that, but it pleased her that he could think so, and say so. Aunt Katrina smiled in her quiet, assured way, taking to herself her husband's compliment to her niece. But a little frown appeared over the fierce mustache, as he said in his precise, faintly feminine voice: "She ought to have earrings, long ones. Is it too late for Garborg's? We could call up."

And call up they did. And Garborg, the jeweler, in Fredericks-gaarde waited for them. Not only were earrings bought, long ones brightly enameled, but glittering shoe buckles and two great bracelets. Helga's sleeves being long, she escaped the bracelets for the moment. They were wrapped to be worn that night. The earrings, however, and the buckles came into immediate use and Helga felt like a ver-itable savage as they made their leisurely way across the pavement from the shop to the waiting motor. This feeling was intensified by the many pedestrians who stopped to stare at the queer dark creature, strange to their city. Her cheeks reddened, but both Herr and Fru Dahl seemed oblivious of the stares or the audible whispers in which Helga made out the one frequently recurring word "*sorte*," which she recognized as the Danish word for "black."

Her Aunt Katrina merely remarked: "A high color becomes you, Helga. Perhaps tonight a little rouge—" To which her husband nod-ded in agreement and stroked his mustache meditatively. Helga Crane said nothing.

They were pleased with the success she was at the tea, or rather the coffee—for no tea was served—and later at dinner. Helga herself felt like nothing so much as some new and strange species of pet dog being proudly exhibited. Everyone was very polite and very friendly, but she felt the massed curiosity and interest, so discreetly hidden under the polite greetings. The very atmosphere was tense with it. "As if I had horns, or three legs," she thought. She was really nervous and a little terrified, but managed to present an outward smiling composure. This was assisted by the fact that it was taken for granted that she knew nothing or very little of the language. So she had only to bow and look pleasant. Herr and Fru Dahl did the talking, answered the questions. She came away from the coffee feeling that she had acquitted herself well in the first skirmish. And, in spite of the mental strain, she had enjoyed her prominence.

If the afternoon had been a strain, the evening was something more. It was more exciting too. Marie had indeed "cut down" the prized green velvet, until, as Helga put it, it was "practically nothing but a skirt." She was thankful for the barbaric bracelets, for the dangling earrings, for the beads about her neck. She was even thankful for the rouge on her burning cheeks and for the very powder on her back. No other woman in the stately pale blue room was so greatly exposed. But she liked the small murmur of wonder and admiration which rose when Uncle Poul brought her in. She liked the compliments in the men's eyes as they bent over her hand. She liked the subtle half-understood flattery of her dinner partners. The women too were kind, feeling no need for jealousy. To them this girl, this Helga Crane, this mysterious niece of the Dahls, was not to be reckoned seriously in their scheme of things. True, she was attractive, unusual, in an exotic, almost savage way, but she wasn't one of them. She didn't at all count.

Near the end of the evening, as Helga sat effectively posed on a red satin sofa, the center of an admiring group, replying to questions about America and her trip over, in halting, inadequate Danish, there came a shifting of the curious interest away from herself. Following the others' eyes, she saw that there had entered the room a tallish man with a flying mane of reddish-blond hair. He was wearing a great black cape, which swung gracefully from his huge shoulders, and in his long, nervous hand he held a wide soft hat. An artist, Helga decided at once, taking in the broad streaming tie. But how affected! How theatrical!

With Fru Dahl he came forward and was presented. "Herr Olsen, Herr Axel Olsen." To Helga Crane that meant nothing. The man, however, interested her. For an imperceptible second he bent over her hand. After that he looked intently at her for what seemed to her an incredibly rude length of time from under his heavy drooping lids. At last, removing his stare of startled satisfaction, he wagged his leonine head approvingly.

"Yes, you're right. She's amazing. Marvelous," he muttered.

Everyone else in the room was deliberately not staring. About Helga there sputtered a little staccato murmur of manufactured conversation. Meanwhile she could think of no proper word of greeting to the outrageous man before her. She wanted, very badly, to laugh. But the man was as unaware of her omission as of her desire. His words flowed on and on, rising and rising. She tried to follow, but his rapid Danish eluded her. She caught only words, phrases, here and there. "Superb eyes . . . color . . . neck column . . . yellow . . . hair . . . alive . . . wonderful . . ." His speech was for Fru Dahl. For a bit longer he lingered before the silent girl, whose smile had become a fixed aching mask, still gazing appraisingly, but saying no word to her, and then moved away with Fru Dahl, talking rapidly and excitedly to her and her husband, who joined them for a moment at the far side of the room. Then he was gone as suddenly as he had come.

"Who is he?" Helga put the question timidly to a hovering young army officer, a very smart captain just back from Sweden. Plainly he was surprised.

"Herr Olsen, Herr Axel Olsen, the painter. Portraits, you know."

"Oh," said Helga, still mystified.

"I guess he's going to paint you. You're lucky. He's queer. Won't do everybody."

"Oh, no. I mean, I'm sure you're mistaken. He didn't ask, didn't say anything about it."

The young man laughed. "Ha-ha! That's good! He'll arrange that with Herr Dahl. He evidently came just to see you, and it was plain that he was pleased." He smiled approvingly.

"Oh," said Helga again. Then at last she laughed. It was so funny. The great man hadn't addressed a word to her. Here she was, a curiosity, a stunt, at which people came and gazed. And was she to be treated like a secluded young miss, a Danish *frøkken*, not to be consulted personally even on matters affecting her personally? She, Helga Crane, who almost all her life had looked after herself, was she now to be looked after by Aunt Katrina and her husband? It didn't seem real.

It was late, very late, when finally she climbed into the great bed after having received an auntly kiss. She lay long awake reviewing the events of the crowded day. She was happy again. Happiness covered her like the lovely quilts under which she rested. She was mystified too. Her aunt's words came back to her. "You're young and a foreigner and—and different." Just what did that mean, she wondered. Did it mean that the difference was to be stressed, accented? Helga wasn't so sure that she liked that. Hitherto all her efforts had been toward similarity to those about her.

"How odd," she thought sleepily, "and how different from America!"

# Fourteen

The young officer had been right in his surmise. Axel Olsen was going to paint Helga Crane. Not only was he going to paint her, but he was to accompany her and her aunt on their shopping expedition. Aunt Katrina was frankly elated. Uncle Poul was also visibly pleased. Evidently they were not above kowtowing to a lion. Helga's own feelings were mixed; she was amused, grateful, and vexed. It had all been decided and arranged without her, and, also, she was a little afraid of Olsen. His stupendous arrogance awed her.

The day was an exciting, not easily to be forgotten one. Definitely, too, it conveyed to Helga her exact status in her new environment. A decoration. A curio. A peacock. Their progress through the shops was an event; an event for Copenhagen as well as for Helga Crane. Her dark, alien appearance was to most people an astonishment. Some stared surreptitiously, some openly, and some stopped dead in front of her in order more fully to profit by their stares. *"Den Sorte"* dropped freely, audibly, from many lips.

The time came when she grew used to the stares of the population. And the time came when the population of Copenhagen grew used to her outlandish presence and ceased to stare. But at the end of that first day it was with thankfulness that she returned to the sheltering walls of the house on Maria Kirkplads.

They were followed by numerous packages, whose contents all had been selected or suggested by Olsen and paid for by Aunt Katrina. Helga had only to wear them. When they were opened and the things spread out upon the sedate furnishings of her chamber, they made a rather startling array. It was almost in a mood of rebellion that Helga faced the fantastic collection of garments incongruously laid out in the quaint, stiff, pale old room. There were batik dresses in which mingled indigo, orange, green, vermilion, and black; dresses of velvet and chiffon in screaming colors, blood red, sulphur yellow, sea green; and one black and white thing in striking combination. There was a black Manila shawl strewn with great scarlet and lemon flowers, a leopard-skin coat, a glittering opera cape. There were turbanlike hats of metallic silks, feathers, and furs, strange jewelry, enameled or set with odd semiprecious stones, a nauseous Eastern perfume, shoes with dangerously high heels. Gradually Helga's perturbation subsided in the unusual pleasure of having so many new and expensive clothes at one time. She began to feel a little excited, incited.

Incited. That was it, the guiding principle of her life in Copenhagen. She was incited to make an impression, a voluptuous impression. She was incited to inflame attention and admiration. She was dressed for it, subtly schooled for it. And after a little while she gave herself up wholly to the fascinating business of being seen, gaped at, desired. Against the solid background of Herr Dahl's wealth and generosity she submitted to her aunt's arrangement of her life to one end, the amusing one of being noticed and flattered. Intentionally she kept to the slow, faltering Danish. It was, she decided, more attractive than a nearer perfection. She grew used to the extravagant things with which Aunt Katrina chose to dress her. She managed, too, to retain that air of remoteness which had been in America so disastrous to her friendships. Here in Copenhagen it was merely a little mysterious and added another clinging wisp of charm.

Helga Crane's new existence was intensely pleasant to her; it gratified her augmented sense of self-importance. And it suited her. She had to admit that the Danes had the right idea. To each his own milieu. Enhance what was already in one's possession. In America Negroes sometimes talked loudly of this, but in their hearts they repudiated it. In their lives too. They didn't want to be like themselves. What they wanted, asked for, begged for, was to be like their white overlords. They were ashamed to be Negroes, but not ashamed to beg to be something else. Something inferior. Not quite genuine. Too bad!

Helga Crane didn't, however, think often of America, except in unfavorable contrast to Denmark. For she had resolved never to return to the existence of ignominy which the New World of opportunity and promise forced upon Negroes. How stupid she had been ever to have thought that she could marry and perhaps have children in a land where every dark child was handicapped at the start by the shroud of color! She saw, suddenly, the giving birth to little, helpless, unprotesting Negro children as a sin, an unforgivable outrage. More black folk to suffer indignities. More dark bodies for mobs to lynch. No, Helga Crane didn't think often of America. It was too humiliating, too disturbing. And she wanted to be left to the peace which had come to her. Her mental difficulties and questionings had become simplified. She now believed sincerely that there was a law of compensation, and that sometimes it worked. For all those early desolate years she now felt recompensed. She recalled a line that had impressed her in her lonely schooldays: "The far-off interest of tears."

To her, Helga Crane, it had come at last, and she meant to cling to it. So she turned her back on painful America, resolutely shutting out the griefs, the humiliations, the frustrations, which she had endured there.

Her mind was occupied with other and nearer things.

The charm of the old city itself, with its odd architectural mixture of medievalism and modernity, and the general air of well-being which pervaded it impressed her. Even in the so-called poor sections there was none of that untidiness and squalor which she remembered as the accompaniment of poverty in Chicago, New York, and the Southern cities of America. Here the doorsteps were always white from constant scrubbings, the women neat, and the children washed and provided with whole clothing. Here were no tatters and rags, no beggars. But, then, begging, she learned, was an offense punishable by law. Indeed, it was unnecessary in a country where everyone considered it a duty somehow to support himself and his family by honest work; or, if misfortune and illness came upon one, everyone else, including the state, felt bound to give assistance, a lift on the road to the regaining of independence.

After the initial shyness and consternation at the sensation caused by her strange presence had worn off, Helga spent hours driving or walking about the city, at first in the protecting company of Uncle Poul or Aunt Katrina or both, or sometimes Axel Olsen. But later, when she had become a little familiar with the city, and its inhabitants a little used to her, and when she had learned to cross the streets in safety, dodging successfully the innumerable bicycles like a true Copenhagener, she went often alone, loitering on the long bridge which spanned the placid lakes, or watching the pageant of the blue-clad, sprucely tailored soldiers in the daily parade at Amalienborg Palace, or in the historic vicinity of the long, low-lying Exchange, a picturesque structure in picturesque surroundings, skirting as it did the great canal, which always was alive with many small boats, flying broad white sails and pressing close on the huge ruined pile of the palace of Christiansborg. There was also the Gammelstrand, the congregating place of the vendors of fish, where daily was enacted a spirited and interesting scene between sellers and buyers, and where Helga's appearance always roused lively and audible, but friendly, interest, long after she became in other parts of the city an accepted curiosity. Here it was that one day an old countrywoman asked her to what manner of mankind she belonged and at Helga's replying: "I'm a Negro," had become indignant, retorting angrily that, just because she was old and a countrywoman she could not be so easily fooled, for she knew as well as everyone else that Negroes were black and had woolly hair.

Against all this walking the Dahls had at first uttered mild protest. "But, Aunt dear, I have to walk, or I'll get fat," Helga asserted. "I've never, never in all my life, eaten so much." For the accepted style of entertainment in Copenhagen seemed to be a round of dinner parties, at which it was customary for the hostess to tax the full capacity not only of her dining room but of her guests as well. Helga enjoyed these dinner parties, as they were usually spirited affairs, the conversation brilliant and witty, often in several languages. And always she came in for a goodly measure of flattering attention and admiration.

There were, too, those popular afternoon gatherings for the express purpose of drinking coffee together, where between much talk, interesting talk, one sipped the strong and steaming beverage from exquisite cups fashioned of Royal Danish porcelain and partook of an infinite variety of rich cakes and *smørrebrød*. This *smørrebrød*, dainty sandwiches of an endless and tempting array, was distinctly a Danish institution. Often Helga wondered just how many of these delicious sandwiches she had consumed since setting foot on Denmark's soil. Always, wherever food was served, appeared the inevitable *smørrebrød*, in the home of the Dahls, in every other home that she visited, in hotels, in restaurants.

At first she had missed, a little, dancing, for, though excellent dancers, the Danes seemed not to care a great deal for that pastime, which so delightfully combines exercise and pleasure. But in the winter there was skating, solitary or in gay groups. Helga liked this sport, though she was not very good at it. There were, however, always plenty of efficient and willing men to instruct and to guide her over the glittering ice. One could, too, wear such attractive skating things.

But mostly it was with Axel Olsen that her thoughts were occupied. Brilliant, bored, elegant, urbane, cynical, worldly, he was a type entirely new to Helga Crane, familiar only, and that but little, with the restricted society of American Negroes. She was aware, too, that this amusing if conceited man was interested in her. They were, because he was painting her, much together. Helga spent long mornings in the eccentric studio opposite the Folkemuseum, and Olsen came often to the Dahl home, where, as Helga and the man himself knew, he was something more than welcome. But in spite of his expressed interest and even delight in her exotic appearance, in spite of his constant attendance upon her, he gave no sign of the more personal kind of concern which—encouraged by Aunt Katrina's mild insinuations and Uncle Poul's subtle questionings—she had tried to secure. Was it, she wondered, race that kept him silent, held him back? Helga Crane frowned on this thought, putting it furiously from her, because it disturbed her sense of security and permanence in her new life, pricked her self-assurance.

Nevertheless she was startled when on a pleasant afternoon while drinking coffee in the Hotel Vivili, Aunt Katrina mentioned, almost casually, the desirability of Helga's making a good marriage.

"Marriage, Aunt dear!"

"Marriage," firmly repeated her aunt, helping herself to another anchovy and olive sandwich. "You are," she pointed out, "twenty-five."

"Oh, Aunt, I couldn't! I mean, there's nobody here for me to marry." In spite of herself and her desire not to be, Helga was shocked.

"Nobody?" There was, Fru Dahl asserted, Captain Frederick Skaargaard—and very handsome he was, too—and he would have money. And there was Herr Hans Tietgen, not so handsome, of course, but clever and a good businessman; he too would be rich, very rich, someday. And there was Herr Karl Pedersen, who had a good berth with the Landmands-bank and considerable shares in a prosperous cement factory at Aalborg. There was, too, Christian Lende, the young owner of the new Odin Theater. Any of these Helga might marry, was Aunt Katrina's opinion. "And," she added, "others." Or maybe Helga herself had some ideas.

Helga had. She didn't, she responded, believe in mixed marriages, "between races, you know." They brought only trouble—to the children—as she herself knew but too well from bitter experience.

Fru Dahl thoughtfully lit a cigarette. Eventually, after a satisfactory glow had manifested itself, she announced: "Because your mother was a fool. Yes, she was! If she'd come home after she married, or after you were born, or even after your father—er—went off like that, it would have been different. If even she'd left you when she was here. But why in the world she should have married again, and a person like that, I can't see. She wanted to keep you, she insisted on it, even over his protest, I think. She loved you so much, she said. . . . And so she made you unhappy. Mothers, I suppose, are like that. Selfish. And Karen was always stupid. If you've got any brains at all they came from your father."

Into this Helga would not enter. Because of its obvious partial truths she felt the need for disguising caution. With a detachment that amazed herself she asked if Aunt Katrina didn't think, really, that miscegenation was wrong, in fact as well as principle.

"Don't," was her aunt's reply, "be a fool too, Helga. We don't think of those things here. Not in connection with individuals, at least." And almost immediately she inquired: "Did you give Herr Olsen my message about dinner tonight?"

"Yes, Aunt." Helga was cross, and trying not to show it.

"He's coming?"

"Yes, Aunt," with precise politeness.

"What about him?"

"I don't know. *What* about him?"

"He likes you?"

"I don't know. How can I tell that?" Helga asked with irritating reserve, her concentrated attention on the selection of a sandwich. She had a feeling of nakedness. Outrage.

Now Fru Dahl was annoyed and showed it. "What nonsense! Of course you know. Any girl does," and her satin-covered foot tapped, a little impatiently, the old tiled floor.

"Really, I don't know, Aunt," Helga responded in a strange voice, a strange manner, coldly formal, levelly courteous. Then suddenly contrite, she added: "Honestly, I don't. I can't tell a thing about him," and fell into a little silence. "Not a thing," she repeated. But the phrase, though audible, was addressed to no one. To herself.

She looked out into the amazing orderliness of the street. Instinctively she wanted to combat this searching into the one thing which, here, surrounded by all other things which for so long she had so positively wanted, made her a little afraid. Started vague premonitions.

Fru Dahl regarded her intently. It would be, she remarked with a return of her outward casualness, by far the best of all possibilities. Particularly desirable. She touched Helga's hand with her fingers in a little affectionate gesture. Very lightly.

Helga Crane didn't immediately reply. There was, she knew, so much reason—from one viewpoint—in her aunt's statement. She could only acknowledge it. "I know that," she told her finally. Inwardly she was admiring the cool, easy way in which Aunt Katrina had brushed aside the momentary acid note of the conversation and resumed her customary pitch. It took, Helga thought, a great deal of security. Balance.

"Yes," she was saying, while leisurely lighting another of those long, thin, brown cigarettes which Helga knew from distressing experience to be incredibly nasty tasting, "it would be the ideal thing for you, Helga." She gazed penetratingly into the masked face of her niece and nodded, as though satisfied with what she saw there. "And you of course realize that you are a very charming and beautiful girl. Intelligent too. If you put your mind to it, there's no reason in the world why you shouldn't—" Abruptly she stopped, leaving her implication at once suspended and clear. Behind her there were footsteps. A small gloved hand appeared on her shoulder. In the short moment before turning to greet Fru Fischer she said quietly, meaningly: "Or else stop wasting your time, Helga."

Helga Crane said: "Ah, Fru Fischer. It's good to see you." She meant it. Her whole body was tense with suppressed indignation. Burning inside like the confined fire of a hot furnace. She was so harassed that she smiled in self-protection. And suddenly she was oddly cold. An intimation of things distant, but nonetheless disturbing, oppressed her with a faintly sick feeling. Like a heavy weight, a stone weight, just where, she knew, was her stomach.

Fru Fischer was late. As usual. She apologized profusely. Also as usual. And, yes, she would have some coffee. And some *smørrebrød.* Though she must say that the coffee here at the Vivili was atrocious. Simply atrocious. "I don't see how you stand it." And the place was getting so common, always so many Bolsheviks and Japs and things. And she didn't—"begging your pardon, Helga"—like that hideous American music they were forever playing, even if it was considered very smart. "Give me," she said, "the good old-fashioned Danish melodies of Gade and Heise. Which reminds me, Herr Olsen says that Nielsen's *Helios* is being performed with great success just now in England. But I suppose you know all about it, Helga. He's already told you. What?" This last was accompanied with an arch and insinuating smile.

A shrug moved Helga Crane's shoulders. Strange she'd never before noticed what a positively disagreeable woman Fru Fischer was. Stupid, too.

# Fifteen

Well into Helga's second year in Denmark came an indefinite discontent. Not clear, but vague, like a storm gathering far on the horizon. It was long before she would admit that she was less happy than she had been during her first year in Copenhagen, but she knew that it was so. And this subconscious knowledge added to her growing restlessness and little mental insecurity. She desired ardently to combat this wearing down of her satisfaction with her life, with herself. But she didn't know how.

Frankly the question came to this: what was the matter with her? Was there, without her knowing it, some peculiar lack in her? Absurd. But she began to have a feeling of discouragement and hopelessness. Why couldn't she be happy, content, somewhere? Other people managed, somehow, to be. To put it plainly, didn't she know how? Was she incapable of it?

And then on a warm spring day came Anne's letter telling of her coming marriage to Anderson, who retained still his shadowy place in Helga Crane's memory. It added, somehow, to her discontent, and to her growing dissatisfaction with her peacock's life. This, too, annoyed her.

What, she asked herself, was there about that man which had the power always to upset her? She began to think back to her first encounter with him. Perhaps if she hadn't come away— She laughed. Derisively. "Yes, if I hadn't come away, I'd be stuck in Harlem. Working every day of my life. Chattering about the race problem."

Anne, it seemed, wanted her to come back for the wedding. This, Helga had no intention of doing. True, she had liked and admired Anne better than anyone she had ever known, but even for her she wouldn't cross the ocean.

Go back to America, where they hated Negroes! To America, where Negroes were not people. To America, where Negroes were allowed to be beggars only, of life, of happiness, of security. To America, where everything had been taken from those dark ones, liberty, respect, even the labor of their hands. To America, where, if one had Negro blood, one mustn't expect money, education, or, sometimes, even work whereby one might earn bread. Perhaps she was wrong to bother about it now that she was so far away. Helga couldn't, however, help it. Never could she recall the shames and often the absolute horrors of the black man's existence in America without the quickening of her heart's beating and a sensation of disturbing nausea. It was too awful. The sense of dread of it was almost a tangible thing in her throat.

And certainly she wouldn't go back for any such idiotic reason as Anne's getting married to that offensive Robert Anderson. Anne was really too amusing. Just why, she wondered, and how had it come about that he was being married to Anne? And why did Anne, who had so much more than so many others—more than enough—want Anderson too? Why couldn't she— "I think," she told herself, "I'd better stop. It's none of my business. I don't care in the least. Besides," she added irrelevantly, "I hate such nonsensical soul searching."

One night not long after the arrival of Anne's letter with its curious news, Helga went with Olsen and some other young folk to the great Circus, a vaudeville house, in search of amusement on a rare off night. After sitting through several numbers they reluctantly arrived at the conclusion that the whole entertainment was dull, unutterably dull, and apparently without alleviation, and so not to be borne. They were reaching for their wraps when out upon the stage pranced two black men, American Negroes undoubtedly, for as they danced and cavorted they sang in the English of America an old ragtime song that Helga remembered hearing as a child, "Everybody Gives Me Good Advice." At its conclusion the audience applauded with delight. Only Helga Crane was silent, motionless.

More songs, old, all of them old, but new and strange to that audience. And how the singers danced, pounding their thighs, slapping their hands together, twisting their legs, waving their abnormally long arms, throwing their bodies about with a loose ease! And how the enchanted spectators clapped and howled and shouted for more!

Helga Crane was not amused. Instead she was filled with a fierce hatred for the cavorting Negroes on the stage. She felt shamed, betrayed, as if these pale pink and white people among whom she lived had suddenly been invited to look upon something in her which she had hidden away and wanted to forget. And she was shocked at the avidity with which Olsen beside her drank it in.

But later, when she was alone, it became quite clear to her that all along they had divined its presence, had known that in her was something, some characteristic, different from any that they themselves possessed. Else why had they decked her out as they had? Why subtly indicated that she was different? And they hadn't despised it. No, they had admired it, rated it as a precious thing, a thing to be enhanced, preserved. Why? She, Helga Crane, didn't admire it. She suspected that no Negroes, no Americans, did. Else why their constant slavish imitation of traits not their own? Why their constant begging to be considered as exact copies of other people? Even the enlightened, the intelligent ones demanded nothing more. They were all beggars like the motley crowd in the old nursery rhyme:

> *Hark! Hark!*
> *The dogs do bark.*
> *The beggars are coming to town.*
> *Some in rags,*
> *Some in tags,*
> *And some in velvet gowns.*

The incident left her profoundly disquieted. Her old unhappy questioning mood came again upon her, insidiously stealing away more of the contentment from her transformed existence.

But she returned again and again to the Circus, always alone, gazing intently and solemnly at the gesticulating black figures, an ironical and silently speculative spectator. For she knew that into her plan for her life had thrust itself a suspensive conflict in which were fused doubts, rebellion, expediency, and urgent longings.

It was at this time that Axel Olsen asked her to marry him. And now Helga Crane was surprised. It was a thing that at one time she had much wanted, had tried to bring about, and had at last relinquished as impossible of achievement. Not so much because of its apparent hopelessness as because of a feeling, intangible almost, that, excited and pleased as he was with her, her origin a little repelled him, and that, prompted by some impulse of racial antagonism, he had retreated into the fastness of a protecting habit of self-ridicule.

A mordantly personal pride and sensitiveness deterred Helga from further efforts at incitation.

True, he had made, one morning, while holding his brush poised for a last, a very last stroke on the portrait, one admirably draped suggestion, speaking seemingly to the pictured face. Had he insinuated marriage, or something less—and easier? Or had he paid her only a rather florid compliment, in somewhat dubious taste? Helga, who had not at the time been quite sure, had remained silent, striving to appear unhearing.

Later, having thought it over, she flayed herself for a fool. It wasn't, she should have known, in the manner of Axel Olsen to pay florid compliments in questionable taste. And had it been marriage that he had meant, he would, of course, have done the proper thing. He wouldn't have stopped—or, rather, have begun—by making his wishes known to her when there was Uncle Poul to be formally consulted. She had been, she told herself, insulted. And a goodly measure of contempt and wariness was added to her interest in the man. She was able, however, to feel a gratifying sense of elation in the remembrance that she had been silent, ostensibly unaware of his utterance, and therefore, as far as he knew, not affronted.

This simplified things. It did away with the quandary in which the confession to the Dahls of such a happening would have involved her, for she couldn't be sure that they, too, might not put it down to the difference of her ancestry. And she could still go attended by him, and envied by others, to openings in Kongens Nytorv, to showings at the Royal Academy or the Charlottenborg. He could still call for her and Aunt Katrina of an afternoon or go with her to Magasin du Nord to select a scarf or a length of silk, of which Uncle Poul could say casually in the presence of interested acquaintances: "Um, pretty scarf"—or "frock"—"you're wearing, Helga. Is that the new one Olsen helped you with?"

Her outward manner toward him changed not at all, save that gradually she became, perhaps, a little more detached and indifferent. But definitely Helga Crane had ceased, even remotely, to consider him other than as someone amusing, desirable, and convenient to have about—if one was careful. She intended, presently, to turn her attention to one of the others. The decorative captain of the Hussars, perhaps. But in the ache of her growing nostalgia, which, try as she might, she could not curb, she no longer thought with any seriousness on either Olsen or Captain Skaargaard. She must, she felt, see America again first. When she returned—

Therefore, where before she would have been pleased and proud at Olsen's proposal, she was now truly surprised. Strangely, she was aware also of a curious feeling of repugnance, as her eyes slid over his face, as smiling, assured, with just the right note of fervor, he made his declaration and request. She was astonished. Was it possible? Was it really this man that she had thought, even wished, she could marry?

He was, it was plain, certain of being accepted, as he was always certain of acceptance, of adulation, in any and every place that he deigned to honor with his presence. Well, Helga was thinking, that wasn't as much his fault as her own, her aunt's, everyone's. He was spoiled, childish almost.

To his words, once she had caught their content and recovered from her surprise, Helga paid not much attention. They would, she knew, be absolutely appropriate ones, and they didn't at all matter. They meant nothing to her—now. She was too amazed to discover suddenly how intensely she disliked him, disliked the shape of his head, the mop of his hair, the line of his nose, the tones of his voice, the nervous grace of his long fingers; disliked even the very look of his irreproachable clothes. And for some inexplicable reason she was a little frightened and embarrassed, so that when he had finished speaking, for a short space there was only stillness in the small room, into which Aunt Katrina had tactfully had him shown. Even Thor, the enormous Persian, curled on the window ledge in the feeble late afternoon sun, had rested for the moment from his incessant purring under Helga's idly stroking fingers.

Helga, her slight agitation vanished, told him that she was surprised. His offer was, she said, unexpected. Quite.

A little sardonically, Olsen interrupted her. He smiled too. "But of course I expected surprise. It is, is it not, the proper thing? And always you are proper, Frøkken Helga, always."

Helga, who had a stripped, naked feeling under his direct glance, drew herself up stiffly. Herr Olsen needn't, she told him, be sarcastic. She *was* surprised. He must understand that she was being quite sincere, quite truthful about that. Really, she hadn't expected him to do her so great an honor.

He made a little impatient gesture. Why, then, had she refused, ignored, his other, earlier suggestion?

At that Helga Crane took a deep indignant breath and was again, this time for an almost imperceptible second, silent. She had, then, been correct in her deduction. Her sensuous, petulant mouth hardened. That he should so frankly—so insolently, it seemed to her—admit his outrageous meaning was too much. She said coldly: "Because, Herr Olsen, in my country the men, of my race, at least, don't make such suggestions to decent girls. And thinking that you were a gentleman, introduced to me by my aunt, I chose to think myself mistaken, to give you the benefit of the doubt."

"Very commendable, my Helga—and wise. Now you have your reward. Now I offer you marriage."

"Thanks," she answered, "thanks, awfully."

"Yes," and he reached for her slim cream hand, now lying quiet on Thor's broad orange and black back. Helga let it lie in his large pink one, noting their contrast. "Yes, because I, poor artist that I am, cannot hold out against the deliberate lure of you. You disturb me. The longing for you does harm to my work. You creep into my brain and madden me," and he kissed the small ivory hand. Quite decorously, Helga thought, for one so maddened that he was driven, against his inclination, to offer her marriage. But immediately, in extenuation, her mind leapt to the admirable casualness of Aunt Katrina's expressed desire for this very thing, and recalled the unruffled calm of Uncle Poul under any and all circumstances. It was, as she had long ago decided, security. Balance.

"But," the man before her was saying, "for me it will be an experience. It may be that with you, Helga, for wife, I will become great. Immortal. Who knows? I didn't want to love you, but I had to. That is the truth. I make of myself a present to you. For love." His voice held a theatrical note. At the same time he moved forward, putting out his arms. His hands touched air. For Helga had moved back. Instantly he dropped his arms and took a step away, repelled by something suddenly wild in her face and manner. Sitting down, he passed a hand over his face with a quick, graceful gesture.

Tameness returned to Helga Crane. Her ironic gaze rested on the face of Axel Olsen, his leonine head, his broad nose—"broader than my own"—his bushy eyebrows, surmounting thick, drooping lids, which hid, she knew, sullen blue eyes. He stirred sharply, shaking off his momentary disconcertion.

In his assured, despotic way he went on: "You know, Helga, you are a contradiction. You have been, I suspect, corrupted by the good Fru Dahl, which is perhaps as well. Who knows? You have the warm impulsive nature of the women of Africa, but, my lovely, you have, I fear, the soul of a prostitute. You sell yourself to the highest buyer. I should of course be happy that it is I. And I am." He stopped, contemplating her, lost apparently, for the second, in pleasant thoughts of the future.

To Helga he seemed to be the most distant, the most unreal figure in the world. She suppressed a ridiculous impulse to laugh. The effort sobered her. Abruptly she was aware that in the end, in some way, she would pay for this hour. A quick brief fear ran through her, leaving in its wake a sense of impending calamity. She wondered if for this she would pay all that she'd had.

And, suddenly, she didn't at all care. She said, lightly but firmly: "But you see, Herr Olsen, I'm not for sale. Not to you. Not to any white man. I don't at all care to be owned. Even by you."

The drooping lids lifted. The look in the blue eyes was, Helga thought, like the surprised stare of a puzzled baby. He hadn't at all grasped her meaning.

She proceeded, deliberately: "I think you don't understand me. What I'm trying to say is this: I don't want you. I wouldn't under any circumstances marry you," and since she was, as she put it, being brutally frank, she added: "*Now.*"

He turned a little away from her, his face white but composed, and looked down into the gathering shadows in the little park before the house. At last he spoke, in a queer frozen voice: "You refuse me?"

"Yes," Helga repeated with intentional carelessness. "I refuse you."

The man's full upper lip trembled. He wiped his forehead, where the gold hair was now lying flat and pale and lusterless. His eyes still avoided the girl in the high-backed chair before him. Helga felt a shiver of compunction. For an instant she regretted that she had not been a little kinder. But wasn't it after all the greatest kindness to be cruel? But more gently, less indifferently, she said: "You see, I couldn't marry a white man. I simply couldn't. It isn't just you, not just personal, you understand. It's deeper, broader than that. It's racial. Someday maybe you'll be glad. We can't tell, you know; if we were married, you might come to be ashamed of me, to hate me, to hate all dark people. My mother did that."

"I have offered you marriage, Helga Crane, and you answer me with some strange talk of race and shame. What nonsense is this?"

Helga let that pass because she couldn't, she felt, explain. It would be too difficult, too mortifying. She had no words which could adequately, and without laceration to her pride, convey to him the pitfalls into which very easily they might step. "I might," she said, "have considered it once—when I first came. But you, hoping for a more informal arrangement, waited too long. You missed the moment. I had time to think. Now I couldn't. Nothing is worth the risk. We might come to hate each other. I've been through it, or something like it. I know. I couldn't do it. And I'm glad."

Rising, she held out her hand, relieved that he was still silent. "Good afternoon," she said formally. "It has been a great honor—"

"A tragedy," he corrected, barely touching her hand with his moist fingertips.

"Why?" Helga countered, and for an instant felt as if something sinister and internecine flew back and forth between them like poison.

"I mean," he said, and quite solemnly, "that though I don't entirely understand you, yet in a way I do too. And—" He hesitated. Went on. "I think that my picture of you is, after all, the true Helga Crane. Therefore—a tragedy. For someone. For me? Perhaps."

"Oh, the picture!" Helga lifted her shoulders in a little impatient motion.

Ceremoniously Axel Olsen bowed himself out, leaving her grateful for the urbanity which permitted them to part without too much awkwardness. No other man, she thought, of her acquaintance could have managed it so well—except, perhaps, Robert Anderson.

"I'm glad," she declared to herself in another moment, "that I refused him. And," she added honestly, "I'm glad that I had the chance. He took it awfully well, though—for a tragedy." And she made a tiny frown.

The picture—she had never quite, in spite of her deep interest in him, and her desire for his admiration and approval, forgiven Olsen for that portrait. It wasn't, she contended, herself at all, but some disgusting sensual creature with her features. Herr and Fru Dahl had not exactly liked it either, although collectors, artists, and critics had been unanimous in their praise and it had been hung on the line at an annual exhibition, where it had attracted much flattering attention and many tempting offers.

Now Helga went in and stood for a long time before it, with its creator's parting words in mind: ". . . a tragedy . . . my picture is, after all, the true Helga Crane." Vehemently she shook her head. "It isn't, it isn't at all," she said aloud. Bosh! Pure artistic bosh and conceit. Nothing else. Anyone with half an eye could see that it wasn't at all like her.

"Marie," she called to the maid passing in the hall, "do you think this is a good picture of me?"

Marie blushed. Hesitated. "Of course, Frøkken, I know Herr Olsen is a great artist, but no, I don't like that picture. It looks bad, wicked. Begging your pardon, Frøkken."

"Thanks, Marie, I don't like it either."

Yes, anyone with half an eye could see that it wasn't she.

# Sixteen

Glad though the Dahls may have been that their niece had had the chance of refusing the hand of Axel Olsen, they were anything but glad that she had taken that chance. Very plainly they said so, and quite firmly they pointed out to her the advisability of retrieving the opportunity, if, indeed, such a thing were possible. But it wasn't, even had Helga been so inclined, for, they were to learn from the columns of *Politikken*, Axel Olsen had gone off suddenly to some queer place in the Balkans. To rest, the newspapers said. To get Frøkken Crane out of his mind, the gossips said.

Life in the Dahl ménage went on, smoothly as before, but not so pleasantly. The combined disappointment and sense of guilt of the Dahls and Helga colored everything. Though she had resolved not to think that they felt that she had, as it were, "let them down," Helga knew that they did. They had not so much expected as hoped that she would bring down Olsen, and so secure the link between the merely fashionable set to which they belonged and the artistic one after which they hankered. It was of course true that there were others, plenty of them. But there was only one Olsen. And Helga, for some idiotic reason connected with race, had refused him. Certainly there was no use in thinking, even, of the others. If she had refused him, she would refuse any and all for the same reason. It was, it seemed, all-embracing.

"It isn't," Uncle Poul had tried to point out to her, "as if there were hundreds of mulattoes here. That, I can understand, might make it a little different. But there's only you. You're unique here, don't you see? Besides, Olsen has money and enviable position. Nobody'd dare to say or even to think anything odd or unkind of you or him. Come now, Helga, it isn't this foolishness about race. Not here in Denmark. You've never spoken of it before. It can't be just that. You're too sensible. It must be something else. I wish you'd try to explain. You don't perhaps like Olsen?"

Helga had been silent, thinking what a severe wrench to Herr

Dahl's ideas of decency was this conversation. For he had an almost fanatic regard for reticence, and a peculiar shrinking from what he looked upon as indecent exposure of the emotions.

"Just what is it, Helga?" he asked again, because the pause had grown awkward for him.

"I can't explain any better than I have," she had begun tremulously, "it's just something—something deep down inside of me," and had turned away to hide a face convulsed by threatening tears.

But that, Uncle Poul had remarked with a reasonableness that was wasted on the miserable girl before him, was nonsense, pure nonsense.

With a shaking sigh and a frantic dab at her eyes, in which had come a despairing look, she had agreed that perhaps it was foolish, but she couldn't help it. "Can't you, won't you understand, Uncle Poul?" she begged, with a pleading look at the kindly worldly man who at that moment had been thinking that this strange exotic niece of his wife's was indeed charming. He didn't blame Olsen for taking it rather hard.

The thought passed. She was weeping. With no effort at restraint. Charming, yes. But insufficiently civilized. Impulsive. Imprudent. Selfish.

"Try, Helga, to control yourself," he had urged gently. He detested tears. "If it distresses you so, we won't talk of it again. You, of course, must do as you yourself wish. Both your aunt and I want only that you should be happy." He had wanted to make an end of this fruitless wet conversation.

Helga had made another little dab at her face with the scrap of lace and raised shining eyes to his face. She had said, with sincere regret: "You've been marvelous to me, you and Aunt Katrina. Angelic. I don't want to seem ungrateful. I'd do anything for you, anything in the world but this."

Herr Dahl had shrugged. A little sardonically he had smiled. He had refrained from pointing out that this was the only thing she could do for them, the only thing that they had asked of her. He had been too glad to be through with the uncomfortable discussion.

So life went on. Dinners, coffees, theaters, pictures, music, clothes.

More dinners, coffees, theaters, clothes, music. And that nagging aching for America increased. Augmented by the uncomfortableness of Aunt Katrina's and Uncle Poul's disappointment with her, that tormenting nostalgia grew to an unbearable weight. As spring came on with many gracious tokens of following summer, she found her thoughts straying with increasing frequency to Anne's letter and to Harlem, its dirty streets, swollen now, in the warmer weather, with dark, gay humanity.

Until recently she had had no faintest wish ever to see America again. Now she began to welcome the thought of a return. Only a visit, of course. Just to see, to prove to herself that there was nothing there for her. To demonstrate the absurdity of even thinking that there could be. And to relieve the slight tension here. Maybe when she came back—

Her definite decision to go was arrived at with almost bewildering suddenness. It was after a concert at which Dvořák's "New World Symphony" had been wonderfully rendered. Those wailing undertones of "Swing Low, Sweet Chariot" were too poignantly familiar. They struck into her longing heart and cut away her weakening defenses. She knew at least what it was that had lurked formless and undesignated these many weeks in the back of her troubled mind. Incompleteness.

"I'm homesick, not for America, but for Negroes. That's the trouble."

For the first time Helga Crane felt sympathy rather than contempt and hatred for that father, whom so often and so angrily she had blamed for his desertion of her mother. She understood, now, his rejection, his repudiation, of the formal calm her mother had represented. She understood his yearning, his intolerable need for the inexhaustible humor and the incessant hope of his own kind, his need for those things, not material, indigenous to all Negro environments. She understood and could sympathize with his facile surrender to the irresistible ties of race, now that they dragged at her own heart. And as she attended parties, the theater, the opera, and mingled with people on the streets, meeting only pale serious faces when she longed for brown laughing ones, she was able to forgive him. Also, it was as if in this understanding and forgiving she had come upon knowledge of almost sacred importance.

Without demur, opposition, or recrimination Herr and Fru Dahl accepted Helga's decision to go back to America. She had expected that they would be glad and relieved. It was agreeable to discover that she had done them less than justice. They were, in spite of their extreme worldliness, very fond of her, and would, as they declared, miss her greatly. And they did want her to come back to them, as they repeatedly insisted. Secretly they felt as she did, that perhaps when she returned— So it was agreed upon that it was only for a brief visit, "for your friend's wedding," and that she was to return in the early fall.

The last day came. The last good-byes were said. Helga began to regret that she was leaving. Why couldn't she have two lives, or why couldn't she be satisfied in one place? Now that she was actually off, she felt heavy at heart. Already she looked back with infinite regret at the two years in the country which had given her so much of pride, of happiness, of wealth, and of beauty.

Bells rang. The gangplank was hoisted. The dark strip of water widened. The running figures of friends suddenly grown very dear grew smaller, blurred into a whole, and vanished. Tears rose in Helga Crane's eyes, fear in her heart.

Good-bye, Denmark! Good-bye. Good-bye!

# Seventeen

A summer had ripened and fall begun. Anne and Dr. Anderson had returned from their short Canadian wedding journey. Helga Crane, lingering still in America, had tactfully removed herself from the house in 139th Street to a hotel. It was, as she could point out to curious acquaintances, much better for the newly married Andersons not to be bothered with a guest, not even with such a close friend as she, Helga, had been to Anne.

Actually, though she herself had truly wanted to get out of the house when they came back, she had been a little surprised and a great deal hurt that Anne had consented so readily to her going. She might at least, thought Helga indignantly, have acted a little bit as if she had wanted her to stay. After writing for her to come, too.

Pleasantly unaware was Helga that Anne, more silently wise than herself, more determined, more selfish, and less inclined to leave anything to chance, understood perfectly that in a large measure it was the voice of Robert Anderson's inexorable conscience that had been the chief factor in bringing about her second marriage—his ascetic protest against the sensuous, the physical. Anne had perceived that the decorous surface of her new husband's mind regarded Helga Crane with that intellectual and aesthetic appreciation which attractive and intelligent women would always draw from him, but that underneath that well-managed section, in a more lawless place where she herself never hoped or desired to enter, was another, a vagrant primitive groping toward something shocking and frightening to the cold asceticism of his reason. Anne knew also that, though she herself was lovely—more beautiful than Helga—and interesting, with her he had not to struggle against that nameless and to him shameful impulse, that sheer delight, which ran through his nerves at mere proximity to Helga. And Anne intended that her marriage should be a success. She intended that her husband should be happy. She was sure that it could be managed by tact and a little cleverness on her own part. She was truly fond of Helga, but seeing how she had grown more charming, more aware of her power, Anne wasn't so sure that her sincere and urgent request to come over for her wedding hadn't been a mistake. She was, however, certain of herself. She could look out for her husband. She could carry out what she considered her obligation to him, keep him undisturbed, unhumiliated. It was impossible that she could fail. Unthinkable.

Helga, on her part, had been glad to get back to New York. How glad, or why, she did not truly realize. And though she sincerely meant to keep her promise to Aunt Katrina and Uncle Poul and return to Copenhagen, summer, September, October, slid by and she made no move to go. Her uttermost intention had been a six or eight weeks' visit, but the feverish rush of New York, the comic tragedy of Harlem, still held her. As time went on, she became a little bored, a little restless, but she stayed on. Something of that wild surge of gladness that had swept her on the day when with Anne and Anderson she had again found herself surrounded by hundreds, thousands, of dark-eyed brown folk remained with her. *These* were her people. Nothing, she had come to understand now, could ever change that. Strange that she had never truly valued this kinship until distance had shown her its worth. How absurd she had been to think that another country, other people, could liberate her from the ties which bound her forever to these mysterious, these terrible, these fascinating, these lovable, dark hordes. Ties that were of the spirit. Ties not only superficially entangled with mere outline of features or color of skin. Deeper. Much deeper than either of these.

Thankful for the appeasement of that loneliness which had again tormented her like a fury, she gave herself up to the miraculous joyousness of Harlem. The easement which its heedless abandon brought to her was a real, a very definite thing. She liked the sharp contrast to her pretentious stately life in Copenhagen. It was as if she had passed from the heavy solemnity of a church service to a gorgeous carefree revel.

Not that she intended to remain. No. Helga Crane couldn't, she told herself and others, live in America. In spite of its glamour, existence in America, even in Harlem, was for Negroes too cramped, too uncertain, too cruel; something not to be endured for a lifetime if one could escape; something demanding a courage greater than was in her. No. She couldn't stay. Nor, she saw now, could she remain away. Leaving, she would have to come back.

This knowledge, this certainty of the division of her life into two parts in two lands, into physical freedom in Europe and spiritual freedom in America, was unfortunate, inconvenient, expensive. It was, too, as she was uncomfortably aware, even a trifle ridiculous, and mentally she caricatured herself moving shuttlelike from continent to continent. From the prejudiced restrictions of the New World to the easy formality of the Old, from the pale calm of Copenhagen to the colorful lure of Harlem.

Nevertheless she felt a slightly pitying superiority over those Negroes who were apparently so satisfied. And she had a fine contempt for the blatantly patriotic black Americans. Always when she encountered one of those picturesque parades in the Harlem streets, the Stars and Stripes streaming ironically, insolently, at the head of the procession, tempered for her, a little, her amusement at the childish seriousness of the spectacle. It was too pathetic.

But when mental doors were deliberately shut on those skeletons that stalked lively and in full health through the consciousness of every person of Negro ancestry in America—conspicuous black, obvious brown, or indistinguishable white—life was intensely amusing, interesting, absorbing, and enjoyable; singularly lacking in that tone of anxiety which the insecurities of existence seemed to ferment in other peoples.

Yet Helga herself had an acute feeling of insecurity, for which she could not account. Sometimes it amounted to fright almost. "I must," she would say then, "get back to Copenhagen." But the resolution gave her not much pleasure. And for this she now blamed Axel Olsen. It was, she insisted, he who had driven her back, made her unhappy in Denmark. Though she knew well that it wasn't. Misgivings, too, rose in her. Why hadn't she married him? Anne was married—she would not say Anderson— Why not she? It would serve Anne right if she married a white man. But she knew in her soul that she wouldn't. "Because I'm a fool," she said bitterly.

# Eighteen

One November evening, impregnated still with the kindly warmth of the dead Indian summer, Helga Crane was leisurely dressing in pleasant anticipation of the party to which she had been asked for that night. It was always amusing at the Tavenors'. Their house was large and comfortable, the food and music always of the best, and the type of entertainment always unexpected and brilliant. The drinks, too, were sure to be safe.

And Helga, since her return, was more than ever popular at parties. Her courageous clothes attracted attention, and her deliberate lure —as Olsen had called it—held it. Her life in Copenhagen had taught her to expect and accept admiration as her due. This attitude, she found, was as effective in New York as across the sea. It was, in fact, even more so. And it was more amusing too. Perhaps because it was somehow a bit more dangerous.

In the midst of curious speculation as to the possible identity of the other guests, with an indefinite sense of annoyance she wondered if Anne would be there. There was of late something about Anne that was to Helga distinctly disagreeable, a peculiar half-patronizing attitude, mixed faintly with distrust. Helga couldn't define it, couldn't account for it. She had tried. In the end she had decided to dismiss it, to ignore it.

"I suppose," she said aloud, "it's because she's married again. As if anybody couldn't get married. Anybody. That is, if mere marriage is all one wants."

Smoothing away the tiny frown from between the broad black brows, she got herself into a little shining, rose-colored slip of a frock knotted with a silver cord. The gratifying result soothed her ruffled feelings. It didn't really matter, this new manner of Anne's. Nor did the fact that Helga knew that Anne disapproved of her. Without words Anne had managed to make that evident. In her opinion, Helga had lived too long among the enemy, the detestable pale faces. She understood them too well, was too tolerant of their ignorant stupidities. If they had been Latins, Anne might conceivably have forgiven the disloyalty. But Nordics! Lynchers! It was too traitorous. Helga smiled a little, understanding Anne's bitterness and hate, and a little of its cause. It was of a piece with that of those she so virulently hated. Fear. And then she sighed a little, for she regretted the waning of Anne's friendship. But, in view of diverging courses of their lives, she felt that even its complete extinction would leave her undevastated. Not that she wasn't still grateful to Anne for many things. It was only that she had other things now. And there would, forever, be Robert Anderson between them. A nuisance. Shutting them off from their previous confident companionship and understanding. "And anyway," she said again, aloud, "he's nobody much to have married. Anybody could have married him. Anybody. If a person wanted only to be married— If it had been somebody like Olsen— That would be different—something to crow over, perhaps."

The party was even more interesting than Helga had expected. Helen, Mrs. Tavenor, had given vent to a malicious glee and had invited representatives of several opposing Harlem political and social factions, including the West Indian, and abandoned them helplessly to each other. Helga's observing eyes picked out several great and near great sulking or obviously trying hard not to sulk in widely separated places in the big rooms. There were present, also, a few white people, to the open disapproval or discomfort of Anne and several others. There too, poised, serene, certain, surrounded by masculine black and white, was Audrey Denney.

"Do you know, Helen," Helga confided, "I've never met Miss Denney. I wish you'd introduce me. Not this minute. Later, when you can manage it. Not so—er—apparently by request, you know."

Helen Tavenor laughed. "No, you wouldn't have met her, living as you did with Anne Grey. Anderson, I mean. She's Anne's particular pet aversion. The mere sight of Audrey is enough to send her into a frenzy for a week. It's too bad, too, because Audrey's an awfully interesting person and Anne's said some pretty awful things about her. *You'll* like her, Helga."

Helga nodded. "Yes, I expect to. And I know about Anne. One night—" She stopped, for across the room she saw, with a stab of surprise, James Vayle. "Where, Helen did you get him?"

"Oh, that? That's something the cat brought in. Don't ask which one. He came with somebody, I don't remember who. I think he's shocked to death. Isn't he lovely? The dear baby. I was going to introduce him to Audrey and tell her to do a good job of vamping on him as soon as I could remember the darling's name, or when it got noisy enough so he wouldn't hear what I called him. But you'll do just as well. Don't tell me you know him!" Helga made a little nod. "Well! And I suppose you met him at some shockingly wicked place in Europe. That's always the way with those innocent-looking men."

"Not quite. I met him ages ago in Naxos. We were engaged to be married. Nice, isn't he? His name's Vayle. James Vayle."

"Nice," said Helen throwing out her hands in a characteristic dramatic gesture—she had beautiful hands and arms—"is exactly the word. Mind if I run off? I've got somebody here who's going to sing. *Not* spirituals. And I haven't the faintest notion where he's got to. The cellar, I'll bet."

James Vayle hadn't, Helga decided, changed at all. Someone claimed her for a dance and it was some time before she caught his eyes, half questioning, upon her. When she did, she smiled in a friendly way over her partner's shoulder and was rewarded by a dignified little bow. Inwardly she grinned, flattered. He hadn't forgotten. He was still hurt. The dance over, she deserted her partner and deliberately made her way across the room to James Vayle. He was for the moment embarrassed and uncertain. Helga Crane, however, took care of that, thinking meanwhile that Helen was right. Here he did seem frightfully young and delightfully unsophisticated. He must be, though, every bit of thirty-two or more.

"They say," was her bantering greeting, "that if one stands on the corner of 135th Street and Seventh Avenue long enough one will eventually see all the people one has ever known or met. It's pretty true, I guess. Not literally of course." He was, she saw, getting himself together. "It's only another way of saying that everybody, almost, sometime sooner or later comes to Harlem, even you."

He laughed. "Yes, I guess that is true enough. I didn't come to stay, though." And then he was grave, his earnest eyes searchingly upon her.

"Well, anyway, you're here now, so let's find a quiet corner if that's possible, where we can talk. I want to hear all about you."

For a moment he hung back and a glint of mischief shone in Helga's eyes. "I see," she said, "you're just the same. However, you needn't be anxious. This isn't Naxos, you know. Nobody's watching us, or if they are, they don't care a bit what we do."

At that he flushed a little, protested a little, and followed her. And when at last they had found seats in another room, not so crowded, he said: "I didn't expect to see you here. I thought you were still abroad."

"Oh, I've been back some time, ever since Dr. Anderson's marriage. Anne, you know, is a great friend of mine. I used to live with her. I came for the wedding. But, of course, I'm not staying. I didn't think I'd be here this long."

"You don't mean that you're going to live over there? Do you really like it so much better?"

"Yes and no, to both questions. I was awfully glad to get back, but I wouldn't live here always. I couldn't. I don't think that any of us who've lived abroad for any length of time would ever live here altogether again if they could help it."

"Lot of them do, though," James Vayle pointed out.

"Oh, I don't mean tourists who rush over to Europe and rush all over the Continent and rush back to America thinking they know Europe. I mean people who've actually lived there, actually lived among the people."

"I still maintain that they nearly all come back here eventually to live."

"That's because they can't help it," Helga Crane said firmly. "Money, you know."

"Perhaps, I'm not so sure. I was in the war. Of course, that's not really living over there, but I saw the country and the difference in treatment. But, I can tell you, I was pretty darn glad to get back. All the fellows were." He shook his head solemnly. "I don't think anything, money or lack of money, keeps us here. If it was only that, if we really wanted to leave, we'd go all right. No, it's something else, something deeper than that."

"And just what do you think it is?"

"I'm afraid it's hard to explain, but I suppose it's just that we like to be together. I simply can't imagine living forever away from colored people."

A suspicion of a frown drew Helga's brows. She threw out rather tartly: "I'm a Negro too, you know."

"Well, Helga, you were always a little different, a little dissatisfied, though I don't pretend to understand you at all. I never did," he said a little wistfully.

And Helga, who was beginning to feel that the conversation had taken an impersonal and disappointing tone, was reassured and gave him her most sympathetic smile and said almost gently: "And now let's talk about you. You're still at Naxos?"

"Yes, I'm still there. I'm assistant principal now."

Plainly it was a cause for enthusiastic congratulation, but Helga could only manage a tepid "How nice!" Naxos was to her too remote, too unimportant. She did not even hate it now.

How long, she asked, would James be in New York?

He couldn't say. Business, important business for the school, had brought him. It was, he said, another tone creeping into his voice, another look stealing over his face, awfully good to see her. She was looking tremendously well. He hoped he would have the opportunity of seeing her again.

But of course. He must come to see her. Anytime, she was always in, or would be for him. And how did he like New York, Harlem?

He didn't, it seemed, like it. It was nice to visit, but not to live in. Oh, there were so many things he didn't like about it, the rush, the lack of home life, the crowds, the noisy meaninglessness of it all.

On Helga's face there had come that pityingly sneering look peculiar to imported New Yorkers when the city of their adoption is attacked by alien Americans. With polite contempt she inquired: "And is that all you don't like?"

At her tone the man's bronze face went purple. He answered coldly, slowly, with a faint gesture in the direction of Helen Tavenor, who stood conversing gaily with one of her white guests: "And I don't like that sort of thing. In fact I detest it."

"Why?" Helga was striving hard to be casual in her manner.

James Vayle, it was evident, was beginning to be angry. It was also evident that Helga Crane's question had embarrassed him. But he seized the bull by the horns and said: "You know as well as I do, Helga, that it's the colored girls these men come up here to see. They wouldn't think of bringing their wives." And he blushed furiously at his own implication. The blush restored Helga's good temper. James was really too funny.

"That," she said softly, "is Hugh Wentworth, the novelist, you know." And she indicated a tall olive-skinned girl being whirled about to the streaming music in the arms of a towering black man. "And that is his wife. She isn't colored, as you've probably been thinking. And now let's change the subject again."

"All right! And this time let's talk about you. You say you don't intend to live here. Don't you ever intend to marry, Helga?"

"Someday, perhaps. I don't know. Marriage—that means children, to me. And why add more suffering to the world? Why add any more unwanted, tortured Negroes to America? Why *do* Negroes have children? Surely it must be sinful. Think of the awfulness of being responsible for the giving of life to creatures doomed to endure such wounds to the flesh, such wounds to the spirit, as Negroes have to endure."

James was aghast. He forgot to be embarrassed. "But, Helga! Good heavens! Don't you see that if we—I mean people like us—don't have children, the others will still have? That's one of the things that's the matter with us. The race is sterile at the top. Few, very few Negroes of the better class have children, and each generation has to wrestle again with the obstacles of the preceding ones: lack of money, education, and background. I feel very strongly about this. We're the ones who must have the children if the race is to get anywhere."

"Well, I for one don't intend to contribute any to the cause. But how serious we are! And I'm afraid that I've really got to leave you. I've already cut two dances for your sake. Do come to see me."

"Oh, I'll come to see you all right. I've got several things that I want to talk to you about and one thing especially."

"Don't," Helga mocked, "tell me you're going to ask me again to marry you."

"That," he said, "is just what I intend to do."

Helga Crane was suddenly deeply ashamed and very sorry for James Vayle, so she told him laughingly that it was shameful of him to joke with her like that, and before he could answer she had gone tripping off with a handsome coffee-colored youth whom she had beckoned from across the room with a little smile.

Later she had to go upstairs to pin up a place in the hem of her dress which had caught on a sharp chair corner. She finished the temporary repair and stepped out into the hall, and somehow, she never quite knew exactly just how, into the arms of Robert Anderson. She drew back and looked up, smiling, to offer an apology.

And then it happened. He stooped and kissed her, a long kiss, holding her close. She fought against him with all her might. Then, strangely, all power seemed to ebb away, and a long-hidden, half-understood desire welled up in her with the suddenness of a dream. Helga Crane's own arms went up about the man's neck. When she drew away, consciously confused and embarrassed, everything seemed to have changed in a space of time which she knew to have been only seconds. Sudden anger seized her. She pushed him indignantly aside and with a little pat for her hair and dress went slowly down to the others.

# Nineteen

That night riotous and colorful dreams invaded Helga Crane's prim hotel bed. She woke in the morning weary and a bit shocked at the uncontrolled fancies which had visited her. Catching up a filmy scarf, she paced back and forth across the narrow room and tried to think. She recalled her flirtations and her mild engagement with James Vayle. She was used to kisses. But none had been like that of last night. She lived over those brief seconds, thinking not so much of the man whose arms had held her as of the ecstasy which had flooded her. Even recollection brought a little onrush of emotion that made her sway a little. She pulled herself together and began to fasten on the solid fact of Anne and experienced a pleasant sense of shock in the realization that Anne was to her exactly what she had been before the incomprehensible experience of last night. She still liked her in the same degree and in the same manner. She still felt slightly annoyed with her. She still did not envy her marriage with Anderson. By some mysterious process the emotional upheaval which had racked her had left all the rocks of her existence unmoved. Outwardly nothing had changed.

Days, weeks, passed; outwardly serene; inwardly tumultuous. Helga met Dr. Anderson at the social affairs to which often they were both asked. Sometimes she danced with him, always in perfect silence. She couldn't, she absolutely couldn't, speak a word to him when they were thus alone together, for at such times lassitude emcompassed her; the emotion which had gripped her retreated, leaving a strange tranquility, troubled only by a soft stir of desire. And shamed by his silence, his apparent forgetting, always after these dances she tried desperately to persuade herself to believe what she wanted to believe: that it had not happened, that she had never had that irrepressible longing. It was of no use.

As the weeks multiplied, she became aware that she must get herself out of the mental quagmire into which that kiss had thrown her. And she should be getting herself back to Copenhagen, but she had now no desire to go.

Abruptly one Sunday in a crowded room, in the midst of teacups and chatter, she knew that she couldn't go, that she hadn't since that kiss intended to go without exploring to the end that unfamiliar path into which she had strayed. Well, it was of no use lagging behind or pulling back. It was of no use trying to persuade herself that she didn't want to go on. A species of fatalism fastened on her. She felt that, ever since that last day in Naxos long ago, somehow she had known that this thing would happen. With this conviction came an odd sense of elation. While making a pleasant assent to some remark of a fellow guest she put down her cup and walked without haste, smiling and nodding to friends and acquaintances on her way, to that part of the room where he stood looking at some examples of African carving. Helga Crane faced him squarely. As he took the hand which she held out with elaborate casualness, she noted that his trembled slightly. She was secretly congratulating herself on her own calm when it failed her. Physical weariness descended on her. Her knees wobbled. Gratefully she slid into the chair which he hastily placed for her. Timidity came over her. She was silent. He talked. She did not listen. He came at last to the end of his long dissertation on African sculpture, and Helga Crane felt the intentness of his gaze upon her.

"Well?" she questioned.

"I want very much to see you, Helga. Alone."

She held herself tensely on the edge of her chair, and suggested: "Tomorrow?"

He hesitated a second and then said quickly: "Why, yes, that's all right."

"Eight o'clock?"

"Eight o'clock," he agreed.

Eight o'clock tomorrow came. Helga Crane never forgot it. She had carried away from yesterday's meeting a feeling of increasing elation. It had seemed to her that she hadn't been so happy, so exalted, in years, if ever. All night, all day, she had mentally prepared herself for the coming consummation; physically too, spending hours before the mirror.

Eight o'clock had come at last and with it Dr. Anderson. Only then had uneasiness come upon her and a feeling of fear for possible exposure. For Helga Crane wasn't, after all, a rebel from society, Negro society. It did mean something to her. She had no wish to stand alone. But these late fears were overwhelmed by the hardiness of insistent desire; and she had got herself down to the hotel's small reception room.

It was, he had said, awfully good of her to see him. She instantly protested. No, she had wanted to see him. He looked at her surprised. "You know, Helga," he had begun with an air of desperation, "I can't forgive myself for acting such a swine at the Tavenors' party. I don't at all blame you for being angry and not speaking to me except when you had to."

But that, she exclaimed, was simply too ridiculous. "I wasn't angry a bit." And it had seemed to her that things were not exactly going forward as they should. It seemed that he had been very sincere, and very formal. Deliberately. She had looked down at her hands and inspected her bracelets, for she had felt that to look at him would be, under the circumstances, too exposing.

"I was afraid," he went on, "that you might have misunderstood; might have been unhappy about it. I could kick myself. It was, it must have been, Tavenor's rotten cocktails."

Helga Crane's sense of elation had abruptly left her. At the same time she had felt the need to answer carefully. No, she replied, she hadn't thought of it at all. It had meant nothing to her. She had been kissed before. It was really too silly of him to have been at all bothered about it. "For what," she had asked, "is one kiss more or less, these days, between friends?" She had even laughed a little.

Dr. Anderson was relieved. He had been, he told her, no end upset. Rising, he said: "I see you're going out. I won't keep you."

Helga Crane too had risen. Quickly. A sort of madness had swept over her. She felt that he had belittled and ridiculed her. And thinking this, she had suddenly savagely slapped Robert Anderson with all her might, in the face.

For a short moment they had both stood stunned, in the deep silence which had followed that resounding slap. Then, without a word of contrition or apology, Helga Crane had gone out of the room and upstairs.

She had, she told herself, been perfectly justified in slapping Dr. Anderson, but she was not convinced. So she had tried hard to make herself very drunk in order that sleep might come to her, but had managed only to make herself very sick.

Not even the memory of how all living had left his face, which had gone a taupe-gray hue, or the despairing way in which he had lifted his head and let it drop, or the trembling hands which he had pressed into his pockets, brought her any scrap of comfort. She had ruined everything. Ruined it because she had been so silly as to close her eyes to all indications that pointed to the fact that no matter what the intensity of his feelings or desires might be, he was not the sort of man who would for any reason give up one particle of his own good opinion of himself. Not even for her. Not even though he knew that she had wanted so terribly something special from him.

Something special. And now she had forfeited it forever. Forever. Helga had an instantaneous shocking perception of what forever meant. And then, like a flash, it was gone, leaving an endless stretch of dreary years before her appalled vision.

# Twenty

The day was a rainy one. Helga Crane, stretched out on her bed, felt herself so broken physically, mentally, that she had given up thinking. But back and forth in her staggered brain wavering, incoherent thoughts shot shuttlelike. Her pride would have shut out these humiliating thoughts and painful visions of herself. The effort was too great. She felt alone, isolated from all other human beings, separated even from her own anterior existence by the disaster of yesterday. Over and over, she repeated: "There's nothing left but to go now." Her anguish seemed unbearable.

For days, for weeks, voluptuous visions had haunted her. Desire had burned in her flesh with uncontrollable violence. The wish to give herself had been so intense that Dr. Anderson's surprising, trivial apology loomed as a direct refusal of the offering. Whatever outcome she had expected, it had been something else than this, this mortification, this feeling of ridicule and self-loathing, this knowledge that she had deluded herself. It was all, she told herself, as unpleasant as possible.

Almost she wished she could die. Not quite. It wasn't that she was afraid of death, which had, she thought, its picturesque aspects. It was rather that she knew she would not die. And death, after the debacle, would but intensify its absurdity. Also, it would reduce her, Helga Crane, to unimportance, to nothingness. Even in her unhappy present state, that did not appeal to her. Gradually, reluctantly, she began to know that the blow to her self-esteem, the certainty of having proved herself a silly fool, was perhaps the severest hurt which she had suffered. It was her self-assurance that had gone down in the crash. After all, what Dr. Anderson thought didn't matter. She could escape from the discomfort of his knowing gray eyes. But she couldn't escape from sure knowledge that she had made a fool of herself. This angered her further and she struck the wall with her hands and jumped up and began hastily to dress herself. She couldn't go on with the analysis. It was too hard. Why bother, when she could add nothing to the obvious fact that she had been a fool?

"I can't stay in this room any longer. I must get out or I'll choke." Her self-knowledge had increased her anguish. Distracted, agitated, incapable of containing herself, she tore open drawers and closets, trying desperately to take some interest in the selection of her apparel.

It was evening and still raining. In the streets, unusually deserted, the electric lights cast dull glows. Helga Crane, walking rapidly, aimlessly, could decide on no definite destination. She had not thought to take umbrella or even rubbers. Rain and wind whipped cruelly about her, drenching her garments and chilling her body. Soon the foolish little satin shoes which she wore were sopping wet. Unheeding these physical discomforts, she went on, but at the open corner of 138th Street a sudden more ruthless gust of wind ripped the small hat from her head. In the next minute the black clouds opened wider and spilled their water with unusual fury. The streets became swirling rivers. Helga Crane, forgetting her mental torment, looked about anxiously for a sheltering taxi. A few taxis sped by, but inhabited, so she began desperately to struggle through wind and rain toward one of the buildings, where she could take shelter in a store or a doorway. But another whirl of wind lashed her and, scornful of her slight strength, tossed her into the swollen gutter.

Now she knew beyond all doubt that she had no desire to die, and certainly not there nor then. Not in such a messy wet manner. Death had lost all of its picturesque aspects to the girl lying soaked and soiled in the flooded gutter. So, though she was very tired and very weak, she dragged herself up and succeeded finally in making her way to the store whose blurred light she had marked for her destination.

She had opened the door and had entered before she was aware that, inside, people were singing a song which she was conscious of having heard years ago—hundreds of years, it seemed. Repeated over and over, she made out the words:

> ". . . *Showers of blessings,*
> *Showers of blessings . . .*"

She was conscious too of a hundred pairs of eyes upon her as she stood there, drenched and disheveled, at the door of this improvised meeting house.

> ". . . *Showers of blessings . . .*"

The appropriateness of the song, with its constant reference to showers, the ridiculousness of herself in such surroundings, was too much for Helga Crane's frayed nerves. She sat down on the floor, a dripping heap, and laughed and laughed and laughed.

It was into a shocked silence that she laughed. For at the first hysterical peal the words of the song had died in the singers' throats, and the wheezy organ had lapsed into stillness. But in a moment there were hushed solicitous voices; she was assisted to her feet and led haltingly to a chair near the low platform at the far end of the room. On one side of her a tall angular black woman under a queer hat sat down, on the other a fattish yellow man with huge outstanding ears and long, nervous hands.

The singing began again, this time a low wailing thing:

> "*Oh, the bitter shame and sorrow*
> *That a time could ever be,*
> *When I let the Savior's pity*
> *Plead in vain, and proudly answered:*
> "*All of self and none of Thee,*
> *All of self and none of Thee.*"
>
> *Yet He found me, I beheld Him,*
> *Bleeding on the cursed tree;*

*Heard Him pray: "Forgive them, Father."*
*And my wistful heart said faintly,*
*"Some of self and some of Thee,*
*Some of self and some of Thee."*

There were, it appeared, endless moaning verses. Behind Helga a woman had begun to cry audibly, and soon, somewhere else, another. Outside, the wind still bellowed. The wailing singing went on:

*" '. . . Less of self and more of Thee,*
*Less of self and more of Thee.' "*

Helga too began to weep, at first silently, softly; then with great racking sobs. Her nerves were so torn, so aching, her body so wet, so cold! It was a relief to cry unrestrainedly, and she gave herself freely to soothing tears, not noticing that the groaning and sobbing of those about her had increased, unaware that the grotesque ebony figure at her side had begun gently to pat her arm to the rhythm of the singing and to croon softly: "Yes, chile, yes, chile." Nor did she notice the furtive glances that the man on her other side cast at her between his fervent shouts of "Amen!" and "Praise God for a sinner!"

She did notice, though, that the tempo, the atmosphere of the place, had changed, and gradually she ceased to weep and gave her attention to what was happening about her. Now they were singing:

*". . . Jesus knows all about my troubles . . ."*

Men and women were swaying and clapping their hands, shouting and stamping their feet to the frankly irreverent melody of the song. Without warning the woman at her side threw off her hat, leaped to her feet, waved her long arms, and shouted shrilly: "Glory! Hallelujah!" and then in wild, ecstatic fury jumped up and down before Helga, clutching at the girl's soaked coat, and screamed: "Come to Jesus, you pore los' sinner!" Alarmed for the fraction of a second, involuntarily Helga had shrunk from her grasp, wriggling out of the wet coat when she could not loosen the crazed creature's hold. At the sight of the bare arms and neck growing out of the clinging red dress, a shudder shook the swaying man at her right. On the face of the dancing woman before her a disapproving frown gathered. She shrieked: "A scarlet 'oman. Come to Jesus, you pore los' Jezebel!"

At this the short brown man on the platform raised a placating hand and sanctimoniously delivered himself of the words: "Remembah de words of our Mastah: 'Let him that is without sin cast de first stone.' Let us pray for our errin' sistah."

Helga Crane was amused, angry, disdainful, as she sat there, listening to the preacher praying for her soul. But though she was contemptuous, she was being too well entertained to leave. And it was, at least, warm and dry. So she stayed, listening to the fervent exhortation to God to save her and to the zealous shoutings and groanings of the congregation. Particularly she was interested in the writhings and weepings of the feminine portion, which seemed to predominate. Little by little the performance took on an almost Bacchic vehemence. Behind her, before her, beside her, frenzied women gesticulated, screamed, wept, and tottered to the praying of the preacher, which had gradually become a cadenced chant. When at last he ended, another took up the plea in the same moaning chant, and then another. It went on and on without pause with the persistence of some unconquerable faith exalted beyond time and reality.

Fascinated, Helga Crane watched until there crept upon her an indistinct horror of an unknown world. She felt herself in the presence of a nameless people, observing rites of a remote obscure origin. The faces of the men and women took on the aspect of a dim vision. "This," she whispered to herself, "is terrible. I must get out of here." But the horror held her. She remained motionless, watching, as if she lacked the strength to leave the place—foul, vile, and terrible, with its mixture of breaths, its contact of bodies, its concerted convulsions, all in wild appeal for a single soul. Her soul.

And as Helga watched and listened, gradually a curious influence penetrated her; she felt an echo of the weird orgy resound in her own heart; she felt herself possessed by the same madness; she too felt a brutal desire to shout and to sling herself about. Frightened at the strength of the obsession, she gathered herself for one last effort to escape, but vainly. In rising, weakness and nausea from last night's unsuccessful attempt to make herself drunk overcame her. She had eaten nothing since yesterday. She fell forward against the crude railing which enclosed the little platform. For a single moment she remained there in silent stillness, because she was afraid she was going to be sick. And in that moment she was lost—or saved. The yelling figures about her pressed forward, closing her in on all sides. Maddened, she grasped at the railing, and with no previous intention began to yell like one insane, drowning every other clamor, while torrents of tears streamed down her face. She was unconscious of the words she uttered, or their meaning: "Oh, God, mercy, mercy. Have mercy on me!" but she repeated them over and over.

From those about her came a thunderclap of joy. Arms were stretched toward her with savage frenzy. The women dragged themselves upon their knees or crawled over the floor like reptiles, sobbing and pulling their hair and tearing off their clothing. Those who succeeded in getting near to her leaned forward to encourage the unfortunate sister, dropping hot tears and beads of sweat upon her bare arms and neck.

The thing became real. A miraculous calm came upon her. Life seemed to expand and to become very easy. Helga Crane felt within her a supreme aspiration toward the regaining of simple happiness, a happiness unburdened by the complexities of the lives she had known. About her the tumult and the shouting continued, but in a lesser degree. Some of the more exuberant worshipers had fainted into inert masses, the voices of others were almost spent. Gradually the room grew quiet and almost solemn, and to the kneeling girl time seemed to sink back into the mysterious grandeur and holiness of far-off simpler centuries.

# Twenty-One

On leaving the mission Helga Crane had started straight back to her room at the hotel. With her had gone the fattish yellow man who had sat beside her. He had introduced himself as the Reverend Mr. Pleasant Green in proffering his escort, for which Helga had been grateful because she had still felt a little dizzy and much exhausted. So great had been this physical weariness that as she had walked beside him, without attention to his verbose information about his own "field," as he called it, she had been seized with a hateful feeling of vertigo and obliged to lay firm hold on his arm to keep herself from falling. The weakness had passed as suddenly as it had come. Silently they had walked on. And gradually Helga had recalled that the man beside her had himself swayed slightly at their close encounter, and that frantically for a fleeting moment he had gripped at a protruding fence railing. That man! Was it possible? As easy as that?

Instantly across her still half-hypnotized consciousness little burning darts of fancy had shot themselves. No. She couldn't. It would be too awful. Just the same, what or who was there to hold her back? Nothing. Simply nothing. Nobody. Nobody at all.

Her searching mind had become in a moment quite clear. She cast at the man a speculative glance, aware that for a tiny space she had looked into his mind, a mind striving to be calm. A mind that was certain that it was secure because it was concerned only with things of the soul, spiritual things, which to him meant religious things. But actually a mind by habit at home amongst the mere material aspect of things, and at that moment consumed by some longing for the ecstasy that might lurk behind the gleam of her cheek, the flying wave of her hair, the pressure of her slim fingers on his heavy arm. An instant's flashing vision it had been and it was gone at once. Escaped in the aching of her own senses and the sudden disturbing fear that she herself had perhaps missed the supreme secret of life.

After all, there was nothing to hold her back. Nobody to care. She stopped sharply, shocked at what she was on the verge of considering. Appalled at where it might lead her.

The man—what was his name?—thinking that she was almost about to fall again, had reached out his arms to her. Helga Crane had deliberately stopped thinking. She had only smiled, a faint provocative smile, and pressed her fingers deep into his arms until a wild look had come into his slightly bloodshot eyes.

The next morning she lay for a long while, scarcely breathing, while she reviewed the happenings of the night before. Curious. She couldn't be sure that it wasn't religion that had made her feel so utterly different from dreadful yesterday. And gradually she became a little sad, because she realized that with every hour she would get a little further away from this soothing haziness, this rest from her long trouble of body and of spirit; back into the clear bareness of her own small life and being, from which happiness and serenity always faded just as they had shaped themselves. And slowly bitterness crept into her soul. Because, she thought, all I've ever had in life has been things—except just this one time. At that she closed her eyes, for even remembrance caused her to shiver a little.

Things, she realized, hadn't been, weren't, enough for her. She'd have to have something else besides. It all came back to that old question of happiness. Surely this was it. Just for a fleeting moment Helga Crane, her eyes watching the wind scattering the gray-white clouds and so clearing a speck of blue sky, questioned her ability to retain, to bear, this happiness at such cost as she must pay for it. There was, she knew, no getting round that. The man's agitation and sincere conviction of sin had been too evident, too illuminating. The question returned in a slightly new form. Was it worth the risk? Could she take it? Was she able? Though what did it matter—now?

And all the while she knew in one small corner of her mind that such thinking was useless. She had made her decision. Her resolution. It was a chance at stability, at permanent happiness, that she meant to take. She had let so many other things, other chances, escape her. And anyway there was God; He would perhaps make it come out all right. Still confused and not so sure that it wasn't the fact that she was "saved" that had contributed to this after feeling of well-being, she clutched the hope, the desire to believe that now at last she had found some One, some Power, who was interested in her. Would help her.

She meant, however, for once in her life to be practical. So she would make sure of both things, God and man.

Her glance caught the calendar over the little white desk. The tenth of November. The steamer *Oscar II* sailed today. Yesterday she had half thought of sailing with it. Yesterday. How far away!

With the thought of yesterday came the thought of Robert Anderson and a feeling of elation, revenge. She had put herself beyond the need of help from him. She had made it impossible for herself ever again to appeal to him. Instinctively she had the knowledge that he would be shocked. Grieved. Horribly hurt even. Well, let him!

The need to hurry suddenly obsessed her. She must. The morning was almost gone. And she meant, if she could manage it, to be married today. Rising, she was seized with a fear so acute that she had to lie down again. For the thought came to her that she might fail. Might not be able to confront the situation. That would be too dreadful. But she became calm again. How could he, a naïve creature like that, hold out against her? If she pretended to distress? To fear? To remorse? He couldn't. It would be useless for him even to try. She screwed up her face into a little grin, remembering that even if protestations were to fail there were other ways.

And, too, there was God.

# Twenty-Two

And so in the confusion of seductive repentance Helga Crane was married to the grandiloquent Reverend Mr. Pleasant Green, that rattish yellow man who had so kindly, so unctuously, proffered his escort to her hotel on the memorable night of her conversion. With him she willingly, even eagerly, left the sins and temptations of New

York behind her to, as he put it, "labor in the vineyard of the Lord" in the tiny Alabama town where he was pastor to a scattered and primitive flock. And where, as the wife of the preacher, she was a person of relative importance. Only relative.

Helga did not hate him, the town, or the people. No. Not for a long time.

As always, at first the novelty of the thing, the change, fascinated her. There was a recurrence of the feeling that now, at last, she had found a place for herself, that she was really living. And she had her religion, which in her new status as a preacher's wife had of necessity become real to her. She believed in it. Because in its coming it had brought this other thing, this anesthetic satisfaction for her senses. Hers was, she declared to herself, a truly spiritual union. This one time in her life, she was convinced, she had not clutched a shadow and missed the actuality. She felt compensated for all previous humiliations and disappointments and was glad. If she remembered that she had had something like this feeling before, she put the unwelcome memory from her with the thought: "This time I know I'm right. This time it will last."

Eagerly she accepted everything, even that bleak air of poverty which, in some curious way, regards itself as virtuous, for no other reason than that it is poor. And in her first hectic enthusiasm she intended and planned to do much good to her husband's parishioners. Her young joy and zest for the uplifting of her fellow men came back to her. She meant to subdue the cleanly scrubbed ugliness of her own surroundings to soft inoffensive beauty, and to help the other women to do likewise. Too, she would help them with their clothes, tactfully point out that sunbonnets, no matter how gay, and aprons, no matter how frilly, were not quite the proper things for Sunday church wear. There would be a sewing circle. She visualized herself instructing the children, who seemed most of the time to run wild, in ways of gentler deportment. She was anxious to be a true helpmate, for in her heart was a feeling of obligation, of humble gratitude.

In her ardor and sincerity Helga even made some small beginnings. True, she was not very successful in this matter of innovations. When she went about to try to interest the women in what she considered more appropriate clothing and in inexpensive ways of improving their homes according to her ideas of beauty, she was met, always, with smiling agreement and good-natured promises. "Yuh all is right, Mis' Green," and "Ah suttinly will, Mis' Green," fell courteously on her ear at each visit.

She was unaware that afterward they would shake their heads sullenly over their washtubs and ironing boards. And that among themselves they talked with amusement, or with anger, of "dat uppity, meddlin' No'the'nah," and "pore Reve'end," who in their opinion "would 'a done bettah to 'a ma'ied Clementine Richards." Knowing, as she did, nothing of this, Helga was unperturbed. But even had she known, she would not have been disheartened. The fact that it was difficult but increased her eagerness and made the doing of it seem only the more worth while. Sometimes she would smile to think how changed she was.

And she was humble too. Even with Clementine Richards, a strapping black beauty of magnificent Amazon proportions and bold shining eyes of jetlike hardness. A person of awesome appearance. All chains, strings of beads, jingling bracelets, flying ribbons, feathery neckpieces, and flowery hats. Clementine was inclined to treat Helga with an only partially concealed contemptuousness, considering her a poor thing without style, and without proper understanding of the worth and greatness of the man, Clementine's own adored pastor, whom Helga had somehow had the astounding good luck to marry. Clementine's admiration of the Reverend Mr. Pleasant Green was open. Helga was at first astonished. Until she learned that there was really no reason why it should be concealed. Everybody was aware of it. Besides, open adoration was the prerogative, the almost religious duty, of the female portion of the flock. If this unhidden and exaggerated approval contributed to his already oversized pomposity, so much the better. It was what they expected, liked, wanted. The greater his own sense of superiority became, the more flattered they were by his notice and small attentions, the more they cast at him killing glances, the more they hung enraptured on his words.

In the days before her conversion, with its subsequent blurring of her sense of humor, Helga might have amused herself by tracing the relation of this constant ogling and flattering to the proverbially large families of preachers; the often disastrous effect on their wives of this constant stirring of the senses by extraneous women. Now, however, she did not even think of it.

She was too busy. Every minute of the day was full. Necessarily. And to Helga this was a new experience. She was charmed by it. To be mistress in one's own house, to have a garden, and chickens, and a pig; to have a husband—and to be "right with God"—what pleasure did that other world which she had left contain that could surpass these? Here, she had found, she was sure, the intangible thing for which, indefinitely, always she had craved. It had received embodiment.

Everything contributed to her gladness in living. And so for a time she loved everything and everyone. Or thought she did. Even the weather. And it was truly lovely. By day a glittering gold sun was set in an unbelievably bright sky. In the evening silver buds sprouted in a Chinese blue sky, and the warm day was softly soothed by a slight, cool breeze. And night! Night, when a languid moon peeped through the wide-opened windows of her little house, a little mockingly, it may be. Always at night's approach Helga was bewildered by a disturbing medley of feelings. Challenge. Anticipation. And a small fear.

In the morning she was serene again. Peace had returned. And she could go happily, inexpertly, about the humble tasks of her household, cooking, dishwashing, sweeping, dusting, mending, and darning. And there was the garden. When she worked there, she felt that life was utterly filled with the glory and the marvel of God.

Helga did not reason about this feeling, as she did not at that time reason about anything. It was enough that it was there, coloring all her thoughts and acts. It endowed the four rooms of her ugly brown house with a kindly radiance, obliterating the stark bareness of its white plaster walls and the nakedness of its uncovered painted floors. It even softened the choppy lines of the shiny oak furniture and subdued the awesome horribleness of the religious pictures.

And all the other houses and cabins shared in this illumination.

And the people. The dark undecorated women unceasingly concerned with the actual business of life, its rounds of births and christenings, of loves and marriages, of deaths and funerals, were to Helga miraculously beautiful. The smallest, dirtiest, brown child, barefooted in the fields or muddy roads, was to her an emblem of the wonder of life, of love, and of God's goodness.

For the preacher, her husband, she had a feeling of gratitude amounting almost to sin. Beyond that, she thought of him not at all. But she was not conscious that she had shut him out from her mind. Besides, what need to think of him? He was there. She was at peace, and secure. Surely their two lives were one, and the companionship in the Lord's grace so perfect that to think about it would be tempting providence. She had done with soul searching.

What did it matter that he consumed his food, even the softest varieties, audibly? What did it matter that, though he did not work with his hands, not even in the garden, his fingernails were always rimmed with black? What did it matter that he failed to wash his fat body, or to shift his clothing, as often as Helga herself did? There were things that more than outweighed these. In the certainty of his goodness, his righteousness, his holiness, Helga somehow overcame her first disgust at the odor of sweat and stale garments. She was even able to be unaware of it. Herself, Helga had come to look upon as a finicky, showy thing of unnecessary prejudices and fripperies. And when she sat in the dreary structure, which had once been a stable belonging to the estate of a wealthy horse-racing man and about which the odor of manure still clung, now the church and social center of the Negroes of the town, and heard him expound with verbal extravagance the gospel of blood and love, of hell and heaven, of fire and gold streets, pounding with clenched fists the frail table before him or shaking those fists in the faces of the congregation like direct personal threats, or pacing wildly back and forth and even sometimes shedding great tears as he besought them to repent, she was, she told herself, proud and gratified that he belonged to her. In some strange way she was able to ignore the atmosphere of self-satisfaction which poured from him like gas from a leaking pipe.

And night came at the end of every day. Emotional, palpitating, amorous, all that was living in her sprang like rank weeds at the tingling thought of night, with a vitality so strong that it devoured all shoots of reason.

# Twenty-Three

After the first exciting months Helga was too driven, too occupied, and too sick to carry out any of the things for which she had made such enthusiastic plans, or even to care that she had made only slight progress toward their accomplishment. For she, who had never thought of her body save as something on which to hang lovely fabrics, had now constantly to think of it. It had persistently to be pampered to secure from it even a little service. Always she felt extraordinarily and annoyingly ill, having forever to be sinking into chairs. Or, if she was out, to be pausing by the roadside, clinging desperately to some convenient fence or tree, waiting for the horrible nausea and hateful faintness to pass. The light, carefree days of the past, when she had not felt heavy and reluctant or weak and spent, receded more and more with increasing vagueness, like a dream passing from a faulty memory.

The children used her up. There were already three of them, all born within the short space of twenty months. Two great healthy twin boys, whose lovely bodies were to Helga like rare figures carved out of amber, and in whose sleepy and mysterious black eyes all that was puzzling, evasive, and aloof in life seemed to find expression. No matter how often or how long she looked at these two small sons of hers, never did she lose a certain delicious feeling in which were mingled pride, tenderness, and exaltation. And there was a girl, sweet, delicate, and flowerlike. Not so healthy or so loved as the boys, but still miraculously her own proud and cherished possession.

So there was no time for the pursuit of beauty, or for the uplifting of other harassed and teeming women, or for the instruction of their neglected children.

Her husband was still, as he had always been, deferentially kind and incredulously proud of her—and verbally encouraging. Helga tried not to see that he had rather lost any personal interest in her, except for the short spaces between the times when she was preparing for or recovering from childbirth. She shut her eyes to the fact that his encouragement had become a little platitudinous, limited mostly to "The Lord will look out for you," "We must accept what God sends," or "My mother had nine children and was thankful for every one." If she was inclined to wonder a little just how they were to manage with another child on the way, he would point out to her that her doubt and uncertainty were a stupendous ingratitude. Had not the good God saved her soul from hellfire and eternal damnation? Had He not in His great kindness given her three small lives to raise up for His glory? Had He not showered her with numerous other mercies (evidently too numerous to be named separately)?

"You must," the Reverend Mr. Pleasant Green would say unctuously, "trust the Lord more fully, Helga."

This pabulum did not irritate her. Perhaps it was the fact that the preacher was, now, not so much at home that even lent to it a measure of real comfort. For the adoring women of his flock, noting how with increasing frequency their pastor's house went unswept and undusted, his children unwashed, and his wife untidy, took pleasant pity on him and invited him often to tasty orderly meals, specially prepared for him, in their own clean houses.

Helga, looking about in helpless dismay and sick disgust at the disorder around her, the permanent assembly of partly emptied medicine bottles on the clock shelf, the perpetual array of drying baby clothes on the chair backs, the constant debris of broken toys on the floor, the unceasing litter of half-dead flowers on the table, dragged in by the toddling twins from the forlorn garden, failed to blame him for the thoughtless selfishness of these absences. And she was thankful, whenever possible, to be relieved from the ordeal of cooking. There were times when, having had to retreat from the kitchen in lumbering haste with her sensitive nose gripped between tightly squeezing fingers, she had been sure that the greatest kindness that

God could ever show to her would be to free her forever from the sight and smell of food.

How, she wondered, did other women, other mothers, manage? Could it be possible that, while presenting such smiling and contented faces, they were all always on the edge of health? All always worn out and apprehensive? Or was it only she, a poor weak city-bred thing, who felt that the strain of what the Reverend Mr. Pleasant Green had so often gently and patiently reminded her was a natural thing, an act of God, was almost unendurable?

One day on her round of visiting—a church duty, to be done no matter how miserable one was—she summoned up sufficient boldness to ask several women how they felt, how they managed. The answers were a resigned shrug, or an amused snort, or an upward rolling of eyeballs with a mention of "de Lawd" looking after us all.

" 'Tain't nothin', nothin' at all, chile," said one, Sary Jones, who, as Helga knew, had had six children in about as many years. "Yuh all takes it too ha'd. Jes' remembah et's natu'al fo' a 'oman to hab chilluns an' don' fret so."

"But," protested Helga, "I'm always so tired and half sick. That can't be natural."

"Laws, chile, we's all ti'ed. An' Ah reckons we's all gwine a be ti'ed till kingdom come. Jes' make de bes' of et, honey. Jes' make de bes' yuh can."

Helga sighed, turning her nose away from the steaming coffee which her hostess had placed for her and against which her squeamish stomach was about to revolt. At the moment the compensations of immortality seemed very shadowy and very far away.

"Jes' remembah," Sary went on, staring sternly into Helga's thin face, "we all gits ouah res' by an' by. In de nex' worl' we's all recompense'. Jes' put yo' trus' in de Sabioah."

Looking at the confident face of the little bronze figure on the opposite side of the immaculately spread table, Helga had a sensation of shame that she should be less than content. Why couldn't she be as trusting and as certain that her troubles would not overwhelm her as Sary Jones was? Sary, who in all likelihood had toiled every day of her life since early childhood except on those days, totaling perhaps sixty, following the birth of her six children. And who by dint of superhuman saving had somehow succeeded in feeding and clothing them and sending them all to school. Before her Helga felt humbled and oppressed by the sense of her own unworthiness and lack of sufficient faith.

"Thanks, Sary," she said, rising in retreat from the coffee, "you've done me a world of good. I'm really going to try to be more patient."

So, though with growing yearning she longed for the great ordinary things of life, hunger, sleep, freedom from pain, she resigned herself to doing without them. The possibility of alleviating her burdens by a greater faith became lodged in her mind. She gave herself up to it. It *did* help. And the beauty of leaning on the wisdom of God, of trusting, gave her a queer sort of satisfaction. Faith was really quite easy. One had only to yield. To ask no questions. The more weary, the more weak, she became, the easier it was. Her religion was to her a kind of protective coloring, shielding her from the cruel light of an unbearable reality.

This utter yielding in faith to what had been sent her found her favor, too, in the eyes of her neighbors. Her husband's flock began to approve and commend this submission and humility to a superior wisdom. The womenfolk spoke more kindly and more affectionately of the preacher's Northern wife. "Pore Mis' Green, wid all dem small chilluns at once. She suah do hab it ha'd. An' she don' nebah complains an' frets no mo'e. Jes' trus' in de Lawd lak de Good Book say. Mighty sweet lil' 'oman too."

Helga didn't bother much about the preparations for the coming child. Actually and metaphorically she bowed her head before God, trusting in Him to see her through. Secretly she was glad that she had not to worry about herself or anything. It was a relief to be able to put the entire responsibility on someone else.

# Twenty-Four

It began, this next childbearing, during the morning services of a breathless hot Sunday while the fervent choir soloist was singing: "Ah am freed of mah sorrow," and lasted far into the small hours of Tuesday morning. It seemed, for some reason, not to go off just right. And when, after that long frightfulness, the fourth little dab of amber humanity which Helga had contributed to a despised race was held before her for maternal approval, she failed entirely to respond properly to this sop of consolation for the suffering and horror through which she had passed. There was from her no pleased, proud smile, no loving, possessive gesture, no manifestation of interest in the important matters of sex and weight. Instead she deliberately closed her eyes, mutely shutting out the sickly infant, its smiling father, the soiled midwife, the curious neighbors, and the tousled room.

A week she lay so. Silent and listless. Ignoring food, the clamoring children, the comings and goings of solicitous, kindhearted women, her hovering husband, and all of life about her. The neighbors were puzzled. The Reverend Mr. Pleasant Green was worried. The midwife was frightened.

On the floor, in and out among the furniture and under her bed, the twins played. Eager to help, the churchwomen crowded in and, meeting there others on the same laudable errand, stayed to gossip and to wonder. Anxiously the preacher sat, Bible in hand, beside his wife's bed, or in a nervous half-guilty manner invited the congregated parishioners to join him in prayer for the healing of their sister. Then, kneeling, they would beseech God to stretch out His all-powerful hand on behalf of the afflicted one, softly at first, but with rising vehemence, accompanied by moans and tears, until it seemed that the God to whom they prayed must in mercy to the sufferer grant relief. If only so that she might rise up and escape from the tumult, the heat, and the smell.

Helga, however, was unconcerned, undisturbed by the commotion about her. It was all part of the general unreality. Nothing reached her. Nothing penetrated the kind darkness into which her bruised spirit had retreated. Even that red-letter event, the coming to see her of the old white physician from downtown, who had for a long time stayed talking gravely to her husband, drew from her no interest. Nor for days was she aware that a stranger, a nurse from Mobile, had been added to her household, a brusquely efficient woman who produced order out of chaos and quiet out of bedlam. Neither did the absence of the children, removed by good neighbors at Miss Hartley's insistence, impress her. While she had gone down into that appalling blackness of pain, the ballast of her brain had got loose and she hovered for a long time somewhere in that delightful borderland on the edge of unconsciousness, an enchanted and blissful place where peace and incredible quiet encompassed her.

After weeks she grew better, returned to earth, set her reluctant feet to the hard path of life again.

"Well, here you are!" announced Miss Hartley in her slightly harsh voice one afternoon just before the fall of evening. She had for some time been standing at the bedside gazing down at Helga with an intent speculative look.

"Yes," Helga agreed in a thin little voice, "I'm back." The truth was that she had been back for some hours. Purposely she had lain silent and still, wanting to linger forever in that serene haven, that effortless calm where nothing was expected of her. There she could watch the figures of the past drift by. There was her mother, whom she had loved from a distance and finally so scornfully blamed, who appeared as she had always remembered her, unbelievably beautiful, young, and remote. Robert Anderson, questioning, purposely detached, affecting, as she realized now, her life in a remarkably cruel degree; for at last she understood clearly how deeply, how passionately, she must have loved him. Anne, lovely, secure, wise, selfish. Axel Olsen, conceited, worldly, spoiled. Audrey Denney, placid, taking quietly and without fuss the things which she wanted. James Vayle, snobbish, smug, servile. Mrs. Hayes-Rore, important, kind, determined. The Dahls, rich, correct, climbing. Flashingly, fragmentarily, other long-forgotten figures, women in gay fashionable frocks and men in formal black and white, glided by in bright rooms to distant, vaguely familiar music.

It was refreshingly delicious, this immersion in the past. But it was finished now. It was over. The words of her husband, the Reverend Mr. Pleasant Green, who had been standing at the window looking mournfully out at the scorched melon patch, ruined because Helga had been ill so long and unable to tend it, were confirmation of that.

"The Lord be praised," he said, and came forward. It was distinctly disagreeable. It was even more disagreeable to feel his moist hand on hers. A cold shiver brushed over her. She closed her eyes. Obstinately and with all her small strength she drew her hand away from him. Hid it far down under the bedcovering, and turned her face away to hide a grimace of unconquerable aversion. She cared nothing, at that moment, for his hurt surprise. She knew only that, in the hideous agony that for interminable hours—no, centuries—she had borne, the luster of religion had vanished; that revulsion had come upon her; that she hated this man. Between them the vastness of the universe had come.

Miss Hartley, all-seeing and instantly aware of a situation, as she had been quite aware that her patient had been conscious for some time before she herself had announced the fact, intervened, saying firmly: "I think it might be better if you didn't try to talk to her now. She's terribly sick and weak yet. She's still got some fever and we mustn't excite her or she's liable to slip back. And we don't want that, do we?"

No, the man, her husband, responded, they didn't want that. Reluctantly he went from the room with a last look at Helga, who was lying on her back with one frail, pale hand under her small head, her curly black hair scattered loose on the pillow. She regarded him from behind dropped lids. The day was hot, her breasts were covered only by a nightgown of filmy crepe, a relic of prematrimonial days, which had slipped from one carved shoulder. He flinched. Helga's petulant lip curled, for she well knew that this fresh reminder of her desirability was like the flick of a whip.

Miss Hartley carefully closed the door after the retreating husband.

"It's time," she said, "for your evening treatment, and then you've got to try to sleep for a while. No more visitors tonight."

Helga nodded and tried unsuccessfully to make a little smile. She was glad of Miss Hartley's presence. It would, she felt, protect her from so much. She mustn't, she thought to herself, get well too fast. Since it seemed she was going to get well. In bed she could think, could have a certain amount of quiet. Of aloneness.

In that period of racking pain and calamitous fright Helga had learned what passion and credulity could do to one. In her was born angry bitterness and an enormous disgust. The cruel, unrelieved suffering had beaten down her protective wall of artificial faith in the infinite wisdom, in the mercy, of God. For had she not called in her agony on Him? And He had not heard. Why? Because, she knew now, He wasn't there. Didn't exist. Into that yawning gap of unspeakable brutality had gone, too, her belief in the miracle and wonder of life. Only scorn, resentment, and hate remained—and ridicule. Life wasn't a miracle, a wonder. It was, for Negroes at least, only a great disappointment. Something to be got through with as best one could. No one was interested in them or helped them. God! Bah! And they were only a nuisance to other people.

Everything in her mind was hot and cold, beating and swirling about. Within her emaciated body raged disillusion. Chaotic turmoil. With the obscuring curtain of religion rent, she was able to look about her and see with shocked eyes this thing that she had done to herself. She couldn't, she thought ironically, even blame God for it, now that she knew that He didn't exist. No. No more than she could pray to Him for the death of her husband, the Reverend Mr. Pleasant Green. The white man's God. And His great love for all people regardless of race! What idiotic nonsense she had allowed herself to believe. How could she, how could anyone, have been so deluded? How could ten million black folk credit it when daily before their eyes was enacted its contradiction? Not that she at all cared about the ten million. But herself. Her sons. Her daughter. These would grow to manhood, to womanhood, in this vicious, this hypocritical land. The dark eyes filled with tears.

"I wouldn't," the nurse advised, "do that. You've been dreadfully sick, you know. I can't have you worrying. Time enough for that when you're well. Now you must sleep all you possibly can."

Helga did sleep. She found it surprisingly easy to sleep. Aided by Miss Hartley's rather masterful discernment, she took advantage of the ease with which this blessed enchantment stole over her. From her husband's praisings, prayers, and caresses she sought refuge in sleep, and from the neighbors' gifts, advice, and sympathy.

There was that day on which they told her that the last sickly infant, born of such futile torture and lingering torment, had died after a short week of slight living. Just closed his eyes and died. No vitality. On hearing it Helga too had just closed her eyes. Not to die. She was convinced that before her there were years of living. Perhaps of happiness even. For a new idea had come to her. She had closed her eyes to shut in any telltale gleam of the relief which she felt. One less. And she had gone off into sleep.

And there was that Sunday morning on which the Reverend Mr. Pleasant Green had informed her that they were that day to hold a special thanksgiving service for her recovery. There would, he said, be prayers, special testimonies, and songs. Was there anything particular she would like to have said, to have prayed for, to have sung? Helga had smiled from sheer amusement as she replied that there was nothing. Nothing at all. She only hoped that they would enjoy themselves. And, closing her eyes that he might be discouraged from longer tarrying, she had gone off into sleep.

Waking later to the sound of joyous religious abandon floating in through the opened windows, she had asked a little diffidently that she be allowed to read. Miss Hartley's sketchy brows contracted into a dubious frown. After a judicious pause she had answered: "No, I don't think so." Then, seeing the rebellious tears which had sprung into her patient's eyes, she added kindly: "But I'll read to you a little if you like."

That, Helga replied, would be nice. In the next room on a high-up shelf was a book. She'd forgotten the name, but its author was Anatole France. There was a story, "The Procurator of Judea." Would Miss Hartley read that? "Thanks. Thanks awfully."

" 'Laelius Lamia, born in Italy of illustrious parents,' " began the nurse in her slightly harsh voice.

Helga drank it in.

" '. . . For to this day the women bring down doves to the altar as their victims. . . .' "

Helga closed her eyes.

" '. . . Africa and Asia have already enriched us with a considerable number of gods. . . .' "

Miss Hartley looked up. Helga had slipped into slumber while the superbly ironic ending which she had so desired to hear was yet a long way off. A dull tale, was Miss Hartley's opinion, as she curiously turned the pages to see how it turned out.

" 'Jesus? . . . Jesus—of Nazareth? I cannot call him to mind.' "

"Huh! she muttered, puzzled. "Silly." And closed the book.

# Twenty-Five

During the long process of getting well, between the dreamy intervals when she was beset by the insistent craving for sleep, Helga had had too much time to think. At first she had felt only an astonished anger at the quagmire in which she had engulfed herself. She had ruined her life. Made it impossible ever again to do the things that she wanted, have the things that she loved, mingle with the people she liked. She had, to put it as brutally as anyone could, been a fool. The damnedest kind of a fool. And she had paid for it. Enough. More than enough.

Her mind, swaying back to the protection that religion had afforded her, almost she wished that it had not failed her. An illusion. Yes. But better, far better, than this terrible reality. Religion had, after all, its uses. It blunted the perceptions. Robbed life of its crudest truths. Especially it had its uses for the poor—and the blacks.

For the blacks. The Negroes.

And this, Helga decided, was what ailed the whole Negro race in America, this fatuous belief in the white man's God, this childlike trust in full compensation for all woes and privations in "kingdom come." Sary Jones's absolute conviction, "In de nex' worl' we's all recompense'," came back to her. And ten million souls were as sure of it as was Sary. How the white man's God must laugh at the great joke he had played on them! Bound them to slavery, then to poverty and insult, and made them bear it unresistingly, uncomplainingly almost, by sweet promises of mansions in the sky by and by.

"Pie in the sky," Helga said aloud derisively, forgetting for the moment Miss Hartley's brisk presence, and so was a little startled at hearing her voice from the adjoining room saying severely: "My goodness! No! I should say you can't have pie. It's too indigestible. Maybe when you're better—"

"That," assented Helga, "is what I said. Pie—by and by. That's the trouble."

The nurse looked concerned. Was this an approaching relapse? Coming to the bedside, she felt at her patient's pulse while giving her a searching look. No. "You'd better," she admonished, a slight edge to her tone, "try to get a little nap. You haven't had any sleep today, and you can't get too much of it. You've got to get strong, you know."

With this Helga was in full agreement. It seemed hundreds of years since she had been strong. And she would need strength. For in some way she was determined to get herself out of this bog into which she had strayed. Or—she would have to die. She couldn't endure it. Her suffocation and shrinking loathing were too great. Not to be borne. Again. For she had to admit that it wasn't new, this feeling of dissatisfaction, of asphyxiation. Something like it she had experienced before. In Naxos. In New York. In Copenhagen. This differed only in degree. And it was of the present and therefore seemingly more reasonable. The other revulsions were of the past, and now less explainable.

The thought of her husband roused in her a deep and contemptuous hatred. At his every approach she had forcibly to subdue a furious inclination to scream out in protest. Shame, too, swept over her at every thought of her marriage. Marriage. This sacred thing of which parsons and other Christian folk ranted so sanctimoniously, how immoral—according to their own standards—it could be! But Helga felt also a modicum of pity for him, as for one already abandoned. She meant to leave him. And it was, she had to concede, all of her own doing, this marriage. Nevertheless, she hated him.

The neighbors and church folk came in for their share of her all-embracing hatred. She hated their raucous laughter, their stupid acceptance of all things, and their unfailing trust in "de Lawd." And more than all the rest she hated the jangling Clementine Richards, with her provocative smirkings, because she had not succeeded in marrying the preacher and thus saving her, Helga, from that crowning idiocy.

Of the children Helga tried not to think. She wanted not to leave them—if that were possible. The recollection of her own childhood, lonely, unloved, rose too poignantly before her for her to consider calmy such a solution. Though she forced herself to believe that this was different. There was not the element of race, of white and black. They were all black together. And they would have their father. But to leave them would be a tearing agony, a rending of deepest fibers. She felt that through all the rest of her lifetime she would be hearing their cry of "Mummy, Mummy, Mummy," through sleepless nights. No. She couldn't desert them.

How, then, was she to escape from the oppression, the degradation, that her life had become? It was so difficult. It was terribly difficult. It was almost hopeless. So for a while—for the immediate present, she told herself—she put aside the making of any plan for her going. "I'm still," she reasoned, "too weak, too sick. By and by, when I'm really strong—"

It was so easy and so pleasant to think about freedom and cities, about clothes and books, about the sweet mingled smell of Houbigant and cigarettes in softly lighted rooms filled with inconsequential chatter and laughter and sophisticated tuneless music. It was so hard to think out a feasible way of retrieving all these agreeable, desired things. Just then. Later. When she got up. By and by. She must rest. Get strong. Sleep. Then, afterwards, she could work out some arrangement. So she dozed and dreamed in snatches of sleeping and waking, letting time run on. Away.

And hardly had she left her bed and become able to walk again without pain, hardly had the children returned from the homes of the neighbors, when she began to have her fifth child.

# Passing

*For Carl Van Vechten and*
*Fania Marinoff*

*One three centuries removed*
*From the scenes his fathers loved,*
*Spicy grove, cinnamon tree,*
*What is Africa to me?*

—COUNTEE CULLEN

Part One

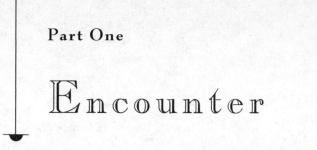

Encounter

# One

It was the last letter in Irene Redfield's little pile of morning mail. After her other ordinary and clearly directed letters the long envelope of thin Italian paper with its almost illegible scrawl seemed out of place and alien. And there was, too, something mysterious and slightly furtive about it. A thin sly thing which bore no return address to betray the sender. Not that she hadn't immediately known who its sender was. Some two years ago she had one very like it in outward appearance. Furtive, but yet in some peculiar, determined way a little flaunting. Purple ink. Foreign paper of extraordinary size.

It had been, Irene noted, postmarked in New York the day

before. Her brows came together in a tiny frown. The frown, however, was more from perplexity than from annoyance; though there was in her thoughts an element of both. She was wholly unable to comprehend such an attitude towards danger as she was sure the letter's contents would reveal; and she disliked the idea of opening and reading it.

This, she reflected, was of a piece with all that she knew of Clare Kendry. Stepping always on the edge of danger. Always aware, but not drawing back or turning aside. Certainly not because of any alarms or feeling of outrage on the part of others.

And for a swift moment Irene Redfield seemed to see a pale small girl sitting on a ragged blue sofa, sewing pieces of bright red cloth together, while her drunken father, a tall, powerfully built man, raged threateningly up and down the shabby room, bellowing curses and making spasmodic lunges at her which were not the less frightening because they were, for the most part, ineffectual. Sometimes he did manage to reach her. But only the fact that the child had edged herself and her poor sewing over to the farthermost corner of the sofa suggested that she was in any way perturbed by this menace to herself and her work.

Clare had known well enough that it was unsafe to take a portion of the dollar that was her weekly wage for the doing of many errands for the dressmaker who lived on the top floor of the building of which Bob Kendry was janitor. But that knowledge had not deterred her. She wanted to go to her Sunday school's picnic, and she had made up her mind to wear a new dress. So, in spite of certain unpleasantness and possible danger, she had taken the money to buy the material for that pathetic little red frock.

There had been, even in those days, nothing sacrificial in Clare Kendry's idea of life, no allegiance beyond her own immediate desire. She was selfish, and cold, and hard. And yet she had, too, a strange capacity of transforming warmth and passion, verging sometimes almost on theatrical heroics.

Irene, who was a year or more older than Clare, remembered the day that Bob Kendry had been brought home dead, killed in a silly saloon fight. Clare, who was at that time a scant fifteen years old, had just stood there with her lips pressed together, her thin arms folded across her narrow chest, staring down at the familiar pasty-white face of her parent with a sort of disdain in her slanting black eyes. For a very long time she had stood like that, silent and staring. Then, quite suddenly, she had given way to a torrent of weeping, swaying her thin body, tearing at her bright hair, and stamping her small feet. The outburst had ceased as suddenly as it had begun. She glanced quickly about the bare room, taking everyone in, even the two policemen, in a sharp look of flashing scorn. And, in the next instant, she had turned and vanished through the door.

Seen across the long stretch of years, the thing had more the appearance of an outpouring of pent-up fury than of an overflow of grief for her dead father; though she had been, Irene admitted, fond enough of him in her own rather catlike way.

Catlike. Certainly that was the word which best described Clare Kendry, if any single word could describe her. Sometimes she was hard and apparently without feeling at all; sometimes she was affectionate and rashly impulsive. And there was about her an amazing soft malice, hidden well away until provoked. Then she was capable of scratching, and very effectively too. Or, driven to anger, she would fight with a ferocity and impetuousness that disregarded or forgot any danger, superior strength, numbers, or other unfavorable circumstances. How savagely she had clawed those boys the day they had hooted her parent and sung a derisive rhyme, of their own composing, which pointed out certain eccentricities in his careening gait! And how deliberately she had—

Irene brought her thoughts back to the present, to the letter from Clare Kendry that she still held unopened in her hand. With a little feeling of apprehension, she very slowly cut the envelope, drew out the folded sheets, spread them, and began to read.

It was, she saw at once, what she had expected since learning from the postmark that Clare was in the city. An extravagantly phrased wish to see her again. Well, she needn't and wouldn't, Irene told herself, accede to that. Nor would she assist Clare to realize her foolish desire to return for a moment to that life which long ago, and of her own choice, she had left behind her.

She ran through the letter, puzzling out, as best she could, the carelessly formed words or making instinctive guesses at them.

". . . For I am lonely, so lonely . . . cannot help longing to be with you again, as I have never longed for anything before; and I have wanted many things in my life. . . . You can't know how in this pale life of mine I am all the time seeing the bright pictures of that other that I once thought I was glad to be free of. . . . It's like an ache, a pain that never ceases. . . ." Sheets upon thin sheets of it. And ending finally with, "and it's your fault, 'Rene dear. At least partly. For I wouldn't now, perhaps, have this terrible, this wild desire if I hadn't seen you that time in Chicago. . . ."

Brilliant red patches flamed in Irene Redfield's warm olive cheeks.

"That time in Chicago." The words stood out from among the many paragraphs of other words, bringing with them a clear, sharp remembrance in which even now, after two years, humiliation, resentment, and rage were mingled.

# T w o

This is what Irene Redfield remembered.

Chicago. August. A brilliant day, hot, with a brutal staring sun pouring down rays that were like molten rain. A day on which the very outlines of the buildings shuddered as if in protest at the heat. Quivering lines sprang up from baked pavements and wriggled along the shining car tracks. The automobiles parked at the curbs were a dancing blaze, and the glass of the shopwindows threw out a blinding radiance. Sharp particles of dust rose from the burning sidewalks, stinging the seared or dripping skins of wilting pedestrians. What small breeze there was seemed like the breath of a flame fanned by slow bellows.

It was on that day of all others that Irene set out to shop for the things which she had promised to take home from Chicago to her two small sons, Brian junior and Theodore. Characteristically, she had put it off until only a few crowded days remained of her long visit. And only this sweltering one was free of engagements till the evening.

Without too much trouble she had got the mechanical airplane for Junior. But the drawing book, for which Ted had so gravely and insistently given her precise directions, had sent her in and out of five shops without success.

It was while she was on her way to a sixth place that right before her smarting eyes a man toppled over and became an inert crumpled heap on the scorching cement. About the lifeless figure a little crowd gathered. Was the man dead or only faint? someone asked her. But Irene didn't know and didn't try to discover. She edged her way out of the increasing crowd, feeling disagreeably damp and sticky and soiled from contact with so many sweating bodies.

For a moment she stood fanning herself and dabbing at her moist face with an inadequate scrap of handkerchief. Suddenly she was aware that the whole street had a wobbly look and realized that she was about to faint. With a quick perception of the need for immediate safety, she lifted a wavering hand in the direction of a cab parked directly in front of her. The perspiring driver jumped out and guided her to his car. He helped, almost lifted her in. She sank down on the hot leather seat.

For a minute her thoughts were nebulous. They cleared.

"I guess," she told her Samaritan, "it's tea I need. On a roof somewhere."

"The Drayton, ma'am?" he suggested. "They do say as how it's always a breeze up there."

"Thank you. I think the Drayton'll do nicely," she told him.

There was that little grating sound of the clutch being slipped in as the man put the car in gear and slid deftly out into the boiling traffic. Reviving under the warm breeze stirred up by the moving cab, Irene made some small attempts to repair the damage that the heat and crowds had done to her appearance.

All too soon the rattling vehicle shot towards the sidewalk and stood still. The driver sprang out and opened the door before the hotel's decorated attendant could reach it. She got out, and thanking him smilingly as well as in a more substantial manner for his kind helpfulness and understanding, went in through the Drayton's wide doors.

Stepping out of the elevator that had brought her to the roof, she was led to a table just in front of a long window whose gently moving curtains suggested a cool breeze. It was, she thought, like being wafted upward on a magic carpet to another world, pleasant, quiet, and strangely remote from the sizzling one that she had left below.

The tea, when it came, was all that she had desired and expected. In fact, so much was it what she had desired and expected that after the first deep cooling drink she was able to forget it, only now and then sipping, a little absently, from the tall green glass, while she surveyed the room about her or looked out over some lower buildings at the bright unstirred blue of the lake reaching away to an undetected horizon.

She had been gazing down for some time at the specks of cars and people creeping about in streets, and thinking how silly they looked, when on taking up her glass she was surprised to find it empty at last. She asked for more tea and, while she waited, began to recall the happenings of the day and to wonder what she was to do about Ted and his book. Why was it that almost invariably he wanted something that was difficult or impossible to get? Like his father. Forever wanting something that he couldn't have.

Presently there were voices, a man's booming one and a woman's slightly husky. A waiter passed her, followed by a sweetly scented woman in a fluttering dress of green chiffon whose mingled pattern of narcissuses, jonquils, and hyacinths was a reminder of pleasantly chill spring days. Behind her there was a man, very red in the face, who was mopping his neck and forehead with a big crumpled handkerchief.

"Oh dear!" Irene groaned, rasped by annoyance, for after a little discussion and commotion they had stopped at the very next table. She had been alone there at the window and it had been so satisfyingly quiet. Now, of course, they would chatter.

But no. Only the woman sat down. The man remained standing, abstractedly pinching the knot of his bright blue tie. Across the small space that separated the two tables his voice carried clearly.

"See you later, then," he declared, looking down at the woman. There was pleasure in his tones and a smile on his face.

His companion's lips parted in some answer, but her words were blurred by the little intervening distance and the medley of noises floating up from the streets below. They didn't reach Irene. But she noted the peculiar caressing smile that accompanied them.

The man said: "Well, I suppose I'd better," and smiled again, and said good-bye, and left.

An attractive-looking woman, was Irene's opinion, with those dark, almost black, eyes and that wide mouth like a scarlet flower against the ivory of her skin. Nice clothes too, just right for the weather, thin and cool without being mussy, as summer things were so apt to be.

A waiter was taking her order. Irene saw her smile up at him as she murmured something—thanks, maybe. It was an odd sort of smile. Irene couldn't quite define it, but she was sure that she would have classed it, coming from another woman, as being just a shade too provocative for a waiter. About this one, however, there was something that made her hesitate to name it that. A certain impression of assurance, perhaps.

The waiter came back with the order. Irene watched her spread out her napkin, saw the silver spoon in the white hand slit the dull gold of the melon. Then, conscious that she had been staring, she looked quickly away.

Her mind returned to her own affairs. She had settled, definitely, the problem of the proper one of two frocks for the bridge party that night, in rooms whose atmosphere would be so thick and hot that every breath would be like breathing soup. The dress decided, her thoughts had gone back to the snag of Ted's book, her unseeing eyes far away on the lake, when by some sixth sense she was acutely aware that someone was watching her.

Very slowly she looked around, and into the dark eyes of the woman in the green frock at the next table. But she evidently failed to realize that such intense interest as she was showing might be embarrassing, and continued to stare. Her demeanor was that of one who with utmost singleness of mind and purpose was determined to impress firmly and accurately each detail of Irene's features upon her memory for all time, nor showed the slightest trace of disconcertment at having been detected in her steady scrutiny.

Instead, it was Irene who was put out. Feeling her color heighten under the continued inspection, she slid her eyes down. What, she wondered, could be the reason for such persistent attention? Had she, in her haste in the taxi, put her hat on backwards? Guardedly she felt at it. No. Perhaps there was a streak of powder somewhere on her face. She made a quick pass over it with her handkerchief. Something wrong with her dress? She shot a glance over it. Perfectly all right. *What* was it?

Again she looked up, and for a moment her brown eyes politely returned the stare of the other's black ones, which never for an instant fell or wavered. Irene made a little mental shrug. Oh well, let her look! She tried to treat the woman and her watching with indifference, but she couldn't. All her efforts to ignore her, it, were futile. She stole another glance. Still looking. What strange languorous eyes she had!

And gradually there rose in Irene a small inner disturbance, odious and hatefully familiar. She laughed softly, but her eyes flashed.

Did that woman, could that woman, somehow know that here before her very eyes on the roof of the Drayton sat a Negro?

Absurd! Impossible! White people were so stupid about such things for all that they usually asserted that they were able to tell; and by the most ridiculous means: fingernails, palms of hands, shapes of ears, teeth, and other equally silly rot. They always took her for an Italian, a Spaniard, a Mexican, or a Gypsy. Never, when she was alone, had they even remotely seemed to suspect that she was a Negro. No, the woman sitting there staring at her couldn't possibly know.

Nevertheless, Irene felt, in turn, anger, scorn, and fear slide over her. It wasn't that she was ashamed of being a Negro, or even of having it declared. It was the idea of being ejected from any place, even in the polite and tactful way in which the Drayton would probably do it, that disturbed her.

But she looked, boldly this time, back into the eyes still frankly intent upon her. They did not seem to her hostile or resentful. Rather, Irene had the feeling that they were ready to smile if she would. Nonsense, of course. The feeling passed, and she turned away with the firm intention of keeping her gaze on the lake, the roofs of the buildings across the way, the sky, anywhere but on that annoying woman. Almost immediately, however, her eyes were back again. In the midst of her fog of uneasiness she had been seized by a desire to outstare the rude observer. Suppose the woman did know or suspect her race. She couldn't prove it.

Suddenly her small fright increased. Her neighbor had risen and was coming towards her. What was going to happen now?

"Pardon me," the woman said pleasantly, "but I think I know you." Her slightly husky voice held a dubious note.

Looking up at her, Irene's suspicions and fears vanished. There was no mistaking the friendliness of that smile or resisting its charm. Instantly she surrendered to it and smiled too, as she said: "I'm afraid you're mistaken."

"Why, of course, I know you!" the other exclaimed. "Don't tell me you're not Irene Westover. Or do they still call you 'Rene?"

In the brief second before her answer, Irene tried vainly to recall where and when this woman could have known her. There, in Chicago. And before her marriage. That much was plain. High school? College? Y.W.C.A. committees? High school, most likely. What white girls had she known well enough to have been familiarly addressed as 'Rene by them? The woman before her didn't fit her memory of any of them. Who was she?

"Yes, I'm Irene Westover. And though nobody calls me 'Rene any more, it's good to hear the name again. And you—" She hesitated, ashamed that she could not remember, and hoping that the sentence would be finished for her.

"Don't you know me? Not really, 'Rene?"

"I'm sorry, but just at the minute I can't seem to place you."

Irene studied the lovely creature standing beside her for some clue to her identity. Who could she be? Where and when had they met? And through her perplexity there came the thought that the trick which her memory had played her was for some reason more gratifying than disappointing to her old acquaintance, that she didn't mind not being recognized.

And, too, Irene felt that she was just about to remember her. For about the woman was some quality, an intangible something, too vague to define, too remote to seize, but which was, to Irene Redfield, very familiar. And that voice. Surely she'd heard those husky tones somewhere before. Perhaps before time, contact, or something had been at them, making them into a voice remotely suggesting England. Ah! Could it have been in Europe that they had met? 'Rene. No.

"Perhaps," Irene began, "you—"

The woman laughed, a lovely laugh, a small sequence of notes that was like a trill and also like the ringing of a delicate bell fashioned of a precious metal, a tinkling.

Irene drew a quick sharp breath. "Clare!" she exclaimed. "Not really Clare Kendry?"

So great was her astonishment that she had started to rise.

"No, no, don't get up," Clare Kendry commanded, and sat down herself. "You've simply got to stay and talk. We'll have something more. Tea? Fancy meeting you here! It's simply too, too lucky!"

"It's awfully surprising," Irene told her, and, seeing the change in Clare's smile, knew that she had revealed a corner of her own thoughts. But she only said: "I'd never in this world have known you if you hadn't laughed. You are changed, you know. And yet, in a way, you're just the same."

"Perhaps," Clare replied. "Oh, just a second."

She gave her attention to the waiter at her side. "M-mm, let's see. Two teas. And bring some cigarettes. Y-es, they'll be all right. Thanks." Again that odd upward smile. Now Irene was sure that it was too provocative for a waiter.

While Clare had been giving the order, Irene made a rapid mental calculation. It must be, she figured, all of twelve years since she, or anybody that she knew, had laid eyes on Clare Kendry.

After her father's death she'd gone to live with some relatives, aunts or cousins two or three times removed, over on the West Side: relatives that nobody had known the Kendrys possessed until they had turned up at the funeral and taken Clare away with them.

For about a year or more afterward she would appear occasionally among her old friends and acquaintances on the South Side for short little visits that were, they understood, always stolen from the endless domestic tasks in her new home. With each succeeding one she was taller, shabbier, and more belligerently sensitive. And each time the look on her face was more resentful and brooding. "I'm worried about Clare, she seems so unhappy," Irene remembered her mother saying. The visits dwindled, becoming shorter, fewer, and further apart until at last they ceased.

Irene's father, who had been fond of Bob Kendry, made a special trip over to the West Side about two months after the last time Clare had been to see them and returned with the bare information that he had seen the relatives and that Clare had disappeared. What else he had confided to her mother, in the privacy of their own room, Irene didn't know.

But she had had something more than a vague suspicion of its nature. For there had been rumors. Rumors that were, to girls of eighteen and nineteen years, interesting and exciting.

There was the one about Clare Kendry's having been seen at the dinner hour in a fashionable hotel in company with another woman and two men, all of them white. And *dressed*! And there was another which told of her driving in Lincoln Park with a man, unmistakably white, and evidently rich. Packard limousine, chauffeur in livery, and all that. There had been others whose context Irene could no longer recollect, but all pointing in the same glamorous direction.

And she could remember quite vividly how, when they used to repeat and discuss these tantalizing stories about Clare, the girls would always look knowingly at one another and then, with little excited giggles, drag away their eager shining eyes and say with lurking undertones of regret or disbelief some such thing as: "Oh, well, maybe she's got a job or something," or "After all, it mayn't have been Clare," or "You can't believe all you hear."

And always some girl, more matter-of-fact or more frankly malicious than the rest, would declare: "Of course it was Clare! Ruth said it was and so did Frank, and they certainly know her when they see her as well as we do." And someone else would say: "Yes, you can bet it was Clare all right." And then they would all join in asserting that there could be no mistake about its having been Clare, and that such circumstances could mean only one thing. Working indeed! People didn't take their servants to the Shelby for dinner. Certainly not all dressed up like that. There would follow insincere regrets, and somebody would say: "Poor girl, I suppose it's true enough, but what can you expect? Look at her father. And her mother, they say, would have run away if she hadn't died. Besides, Clare always had a—a—having way with her."

Precisely that! The words came to Irene as she sat there on the Drayton roof, facing Clare Kendry. "A having way." Well, Irene acknowledged, judging from her appearance and manner, Clare seemed certainly to have succeeded in having a few of the things that she wanted.

It was, Irene repeated, after the interval of the waiter, a great surprise and a very pleasant one to see Clare again after all those years, twelve at least.

"Why, Clare, you're the last person in the world I'd have expected to run into. I guess that's why I didn't know you."

Clare answered gravely: "Yes. It is twelve years. But I'm not surprised to see you, 'Rene. That is, not so very. In fact, ever since I've been here, I've more or less hoped that I should, or someone. Preferably you, though. Still, I imagine that's because I've thought of you often and often, while you—I'll wager you've never given me a thought."

It was true, of course. After the first speculations and indictments, Clare had gone completely from Irene's thoughts. And from the thoughts of others too—if their conversation was any indication of their thoughts.

Besides, Clare had never been exactly one of the group, just as she'd never been merely the janitor's daughter, but the daughter of Mr. Bob Kendry, who, it was true, was a janitor, but who also, it seemed, had been in college with some of their fathers. Just how or why he happened to be a janitor, and a very inefficient one at that, they none of them quite knew. One of Irene's brothers, who had put the question to their father, had been told: "That's something that doesn't concern you," and given him the advice to be careful not to end in the same manner as "poor Bob."

No, Irene hadn't thought of Clare Kendry. Her own life had been too crowded. So, she supposed, had the lives of other people. She defended her—their—forgetfulness. "You know how it is. Everybody's so busy. People leave, drop out, maybe for a little while there's talk about them, or questions; then, gradually they're forgotten."

"Yes, that's natural," Clare agreed. And what, she inquired, had they said of her for that little while at the beginning before they'd forgotten her altogether?

Irene looked away. She felt the telltale color rising in her cheeks. "You can't," she evaded, "expect me to remember trifles like that over twelve years of marriages, births, deaths, and the war."

There followed that trill of notes that was Clare Kendry's laugh, small and clear and the very essence of mockery.

"Oh, 'Rene!" she cried. "Of course you remember! But I won't make you tell me, because I know just as well as if I'd been there and heard every unkind word. Oh, I know, I know. Frank Danton saw me in the Shelby one night. Don't tell me he didn't broadcast that, and with embroidery. Others may have seen me at other times. I don't know. But once I met Margaret Hammer in Marshall Field's. I'd have spoken, was on the very point of doing it, but she cut me dead. My dear 'Rene, I assure you that, from the way she looked through me, even I was uncertain whether I was actually there in the flesh or not. I remember it clearly, too clearly. It was that very thing which, in a way, finally decided me not to go out and see you onc last time before I went away to stay. Somehow, good as all of you, the whole family, had always been to the poor forlorn child that was me, I felt I shouldn't be able to bear that. I mean if any of you, your mother or the boys or— Oh, well, I just felt I'd rather not know it if you did. And so I stayed away. Silly, I suppose. Sometimes I've been sorry I didn't go."

Irene wondered if it was tears that made Clare's eyes so luminous.

"And now, 'Rene, I want to hear all about you and everybody and everything. You're married, I s'pose?"

Irene nodded.

"Yes," Clare said knowingly, "you would be. Tell me about it."

And so for an hour or more they had sat there smoking and drinking tea and filling in the gap of twelve years with talk. That is, Irene did. She told Clare about her marriage and removal to New York, about her husband, and about her two sons, who were having their first experience of being separated from their parents at a summer camp, about her mother's death, about the marriages of her two brothers. She told of the marriages, births, and deaths in other families that Clare had known, opening up, for her, new vistas on the lives of old friends and acquaintances.

Clare drank it all in, these things which for so long she had wanted to know and hadn't been able to learn. She sat motionless, her bright lips slightly parted, her whole face lit by the radiance of her happy eyes. Now and then she put a question, but for the most part she was silent.

Somewhere outside, a clock struck. Brought back to the present, Irene looked down at her watch and exclaimed: "Oh, I must go, Clare!"

A moment passed during which she was the prey of uneasiness. It had suddenly occurred to her that she hadn't asked Clare anything about her own life and that she had a very definite unwillingness to do so. And she was quite well aware of the reason for that reluctance. But, she asked herself, wouldn't it, all things considered, be the kindest thing not to ask? If things with Clare were as she—as they all—had suspected, wouldn't it be more tactful to seem to forget to inquire how she had spent those twelve years?

*If?* It was that "if" which bothered her. It might be, it might just be, in spite of all gossip and even appearances to the contrary, that there was nothing, had been nothing, that couldn't be simply and innocently explained. Appearances, she knew now, had a way some-times of not fitting facts, and if Clare hadn't— Well, if they had all been wrong, then certainly she ought to express some interest in what had happened to her. It would seem queer and rude if she didn't. But how was she to know? There was, she at last decided, no way; so she merely said again, "I must go, Clare."

"Please, not so soon, 'Rene," Clare begged, not moving.

Irene thought: "She's really almost too good-looking. It's hardly any wonder that she—"

"And now, 'Rene dear, that I've found you, I mean to see lots and lots of you. We're here for a month at least. Jack, that's my husband, is here on business. Poor dear! In this heat. Isn't it beastly? Come to dinner with us tonight, won't you?" And she gave Irene a curious little sidelong glance and a sly, ironical smile peeped out on her full red lips, as if she had been in the secret of the other's thoughts and was mocking her.

Irene was conscious of a sharp intake of breath, but whether it was relief or chagrin that she felt, she herself could not have told. She said hastily: "I'm afraid I can't, Clare. I'm filled up. Dinner and bridge. I'm so sorry."

"Come tomorrow instead, to tea," Clare insisted. "Then you'll see Margery—she's just ten—and Jack too, maybe, if he hasn't got an appointment or something."

From Irene came an uneasy little laugh. She had an engagement for tomorrow also and she was afraid that Clare would not believe it. Suddenly, now, that possibility disturbed her. Therefore it was with a half-vexed feeling at the sense of undeserved guilt that had come upon her that she explained that it wouldn't be possible because she wouldn't be free for tea, or for luncheon or dinner either. "And the next day's Friday when I'll be going away for the weekend, Idlewild, you know. It's quite the thing now." And then she had an inspiration.

"Clare!" she exclaimed. "Why don't you come up with me? Our

place is probably full up—Jim's wife has a way of collecting mobs of the most impossible people—but we can always manage to find room for one more. And you'll see absolutely everybody."

In the very moment of giving the invitation she regretted it. What a foolish, what an idiotic impulse to have given way to! She groaned inwardly as she thought of the endless explanations in which it would involve her, of the curiosity, and the talk, and the lifted eyebrows. It wasn't, she assured herself, that she was a snob, that she cared greatly for the petty restrictions and distinctions with which what called itself Negro society chose to hedge itself about; but that she had a natural and deeply rooted aversion to the kind of front-page notoriety that Clare Kendry's presence in Idlewild, as her guest, would expose her to. And here she was, perversely and against all reason, inviting her.

But Clare shook her head. "Really, I'd love to, 'Rene," she said, a little mournfully. "There's nothing I'd like better. But I couldn't. I mustn't, you see. It wouldn't do at all. I'm sure you understand. I'm simply crazy to go, but I can't." The dark eyes glistened and there was a suspicion of a quaver in the husky voice. "And believe me, 'Rene, I do thank you for asking me. Don't think I've entirely forgotten just what it would mean for you if I went. That is, if you still care about such things."

All indication of tears had gone from her eyes and voice, and Irene Redfield, searching her face, had an offended feeling that behind what was now only an ivory mask lurked a scornful amusement. She looked away, at the wall far beyond Clare. Well, she deserved it, for, as she acknowledged to herself, she *was* relieved. And for the very reason at which Clare had hinted. The fact that Clare had guessed her perturbation did not, however, in any degree lessen that relief. She was annoyed at having been detected in what might seem to be an insincerity; but that was all.

The waiter came with Clare's change. Irene reminded herself that she ought immediately to go. But she didn't move.

The truth was, she was curious. There were things that she wanted to ask Clare Kendry. She wished to find out about this hazardous business of "passing," this breaking away from all that was familiar and friendly to take one's chance in another environment, not entirely strange, perhaps, but certainly not entirely friendly. What, for example, one did about background, how one accounted for oneself. And how one felt when one came into contact with other Negroes. But she couldn't. She was unable to think of a single question that in its context or its phrasing was not too frankly curious, if not actually impertinent.

As if aware of her desire and her hesitation, Clare remarked thoughtfully: "You know, 'Rene, I've often wondered why more colored girls, girls like you and Margaret Hammer and Esther Dawson and—oh, lots of others—never 'passed' over. It's such a frightfully easy thing to do. If one's the type, all that's needed is a little nerve."

"What about background? Family, I mean. Surely you can't just drop down on people from nowhere and expect them to receive you with open arms, can you?"

"Almost," Clare asserted. "You'd be surprised, 'Rene, how much easier that is with white people than with us. Maybe because there are so many more of them, or maybe because they are secure and so don't have to bother. I've never quite decided."

Irene was inclined to be incredulous. "You mean that you didn't have to explain where you came from? It seems impossible."

Clare cast a glance of repressed amusement across the table at her. "As a matter of fact, I didn't. Though I suppose under any other circumstances I might have had to provide some plausible tale to account for myself. I've a good imagination, so I'm sure I could have done it quite creditably, and credibly. But it wasn't necessary. There were my aunts, you see, respectable and authentic enough for anything or anybody."

"I see. They were 'passing' too."

"No. They weren't. They were white."

"Oh!" And in the next instant it came back to Irene that she had heard this mentioned before; by her father or, more likely, her mother. They were Bob Kendry's aunts. He had been a son of their brother's, on the left hand. A wild oat.

"They were nice old ladies," Clare explained, "very religious and as poor as church mice. That adored brother of theirs, my grandfather, got through every penny they had after he'd finished his own little bit."

Clare paused in her narrative to light another cigarette. Her smile, her expression, Irene noticed, was faintly resentful.

"Being good Christians," she continued, "when Dad came to his tipsy end, they did their duty and gave me a home of sorts. I was, it was true, expected to earn my keep by doing all the housework and most of the washing. But do you realize, 'Rene, that if it hadn't been for them I shouldn't have had a home in the world?"

Irene's nod and little murmur were comprehensive, understanding.

Clare made a small mischievous grimace and proceeded. "Besides, to their notion, hard labor was good for me. I had Negro blood and they belonged to the generation that had written and read long articles headed: 'Will the Blacks Work?' Too, they weren't quite sure that the good God hadn't intended the sons and daughters of Ham to sweat because he had poked fun at old man Noah once when he had taken a drop too much. I remember the aunts telling me that that old drunkard had cursed Ham and his sons for all time."

Irene laughed. But Clare remained quite serious.

"It was more than a joke, I assure you, 'Rene. It was a hard life for a girl of sixteen. Still, I had a roof over my head, and food, and clothes—such as they were. And there were the Scriptures, and talks on morals and thrift and industry and the loving-kindness of the good Lord."

"Have you ever stopped to think, Clare," Irene demanded, "how much unhappiness and downright cruelty are laid to the loving-kindness of the Lord? And always by His most ardent followers, it seems."

"Have I?" Clare exclaimed. "It, they, made me what I am today. For, of course, I was determined to get away, to be a person and not a charity or a problem, or even a daughter of the indiscreet Ham. Then, too, I wanted things. I knew I wasn't bad-looking and that I could 'pass.' You can't know, 'Rene, how, when I used to go over to the South Side, I used almost to hate all of you. You had all the things I wanted and never had had. It made me all the more determined to get them, and others. Do you, can you understand what I felt?"

She looked up with a pointed and appealing effect, and, evidently finding the sympathetic expression on Irene's face sufficient answer, went on. "The aunts were queer. For all their Bibles and praying and ranting about honesty, they didn't want anyone to know that their darling brother had seduced—ruined, they called it—a Negro girl. They could excuse the ruin, but they couldn't forgive the tar brush. They forbade me to mention Negroes to the neighbors, or even to mention the South Side. You may be sure that I didn't. I'll bet they were good and sorry afterwards."

She laughed and the ringing bells in her laugh had a hard metallic sound.

"When the chance to get away came, that omission was of great value to me. When Jack, a schoolboy acquaintance of some people in the neighborhood, turned up from South America with untold gold, there was no one to tell him that I was colored, and many to tell him about the severity and the religiousness of Aunt Grace and Aunt Edna. You can guess the rest. After he came, I stopped slipping off to the South Side and slipped off to meet him instead. I couldn't manage both. In the end I had no great difficulty in convincing him that it was useless to talk marriage to the aunts. So on the day that I was eighteen we went off and were married. So that's that. Nothing could have been easier."

"Yes, I do see that for you it was easy enough. By the way! I wonder why they didn't tell Father that you were married? He went over to find out about you when you stopped coming over to see us. I'm sure they didn't tell him. Not that you were married."

Clare Kendry's eyes were bright with tears that didn't fall. "Oh, how lovely! To have cared enough about me to do that. The dear sweet man! Well, they couldn't tell him because they didn't know it. I took care of that, for I couldn't be sure that those consciences of theirs wouldn't begin to work on them afterward and make them let the cat out of the bag. The old things probably thought I was living in sin, wherever I was. And it would be about what they expected."

An amused smile lit the lovely face for the smallest fraction of a second. After a little silence she said soberly: "But I'm sorry if they told your father so. That was something I hadn't counted on."

"I'm not sure that they did," Irene told her. "He didn't say so, anyway."

"He wouldn't, 'Rene dear. Not your father."

"Thanks. I'm sure he wouldn't."

"But you've never answered my question. Tell me, honestly, haven't you ever thought of 'passing'?"

Irene answered promptly: "No. Why should I?" And so disdainful was her voice and manner that Clare's face flushed and her eyes glinted. Irene hastened to add: "You see, Clare, I've everything I want. Except, perhaps, a little more money."

At that Clare laughed, her spark of anger vanished as quickly as it had appeared. "Of course," she declared, "that's what everybody wants, just a little more money, even the people who have it. And I must say I don't blame them. Money's awfully nice to have. In fact, all things considered, I think, 'Rene, that it's even worth the price."

Irene could only shrug her shoulders. Her reason partly agreed, her instinct wholly rebelled. And she could not say why. And though conscious that if she didn't hurry away, she was going to be late to dinner, she still lingered. It was as if the woman sitting on the other side of the table, a girl she had known, who had done this rather dangerous and, to Irene Redfield, abhorrent thing successfully and had announced herself well satisfied, had for her a fascination, strange and compelling.

Clare Kendry was still leaning back in the tall chair, her sloping shoulders against the carved top. She sat with an air of indifferent assurance, as if arranged for, desired. About her clung that dim suggestion of polite insolence with which a few women are born and which some acquire with the coming of riches or importance.

Clare, it gave Irene a little prick of satisfaction to recall, hadn't got that by passing herself off as white. She herself had always had it.

Just as she'd always had that pale gold hair, which, unsheared still, was drawn loosely back from a broad brow, partly hidden by the small close hat. Her lips, painted a brilliant geranium red, were sweet and sensitive and a little obstinate. A tempting mouth. The face across the forehead and cheeks was a trifle too wide, but the ivory skin had a peculiar soft luster. And the eyes were magnificent! Dark, sometimes absolutely black, always luminous, and set in long, black lashes. Arresting eyes, slow and mesmeric, and with, for all their warmth, something withdrawn and secret about them.

Ah! Surely! They were Negro eyes! Mysterious and concealing. And set in that ivory face under that bright hair, there was about them something exotic.

Yes, Clare Kendry's loveliness was absolute, beyond challenge, thanks to those eyes which her grandmother and later her mother and father had given her.

Into those eyes there came a smile and over Irene the sense of being petted and caressed. She smiled back.

"Maybe," Clare suggested, "you can come Monday, if you're back. Or, if you're not, then Tuesday."

With a small regretful sigh, Irene informed Clare that she was afraid she wouldn't be back by Monday and that she was sure she had dozens of things for Tuesday, and that she was leaving Wednesday. It might be, however, that she could get out of something Tuesday.

"Oh, do try. Do put somebody else off. The others can see you any time, while I—why, I may never see you again! Think of that, 'Rene! You'll have to come. You'll simply have to! I'll never forgive you if you don't."

At that moment it seemed a dreadful thing to think of never seeing Clare Kendry again. Standing there under the appeal, the caress, of her eyes, Irene had the desire, the hope, that this parting wouldn't be the last.

"I'll try, Clare," she promised gently. "I'll call you—or will you call me?"

"I think, perhaps, I'd better call you. Your father's in the book, I know, and the address is the same. Sixty-four eighteen. Some memory, what? Now remember, I'm going to expect you. You've got to be able to come."

Again that peculiar mellowing smile.

"I'll do my best, Clare."

Irene gathered up her gloves and bag. They stood up. She put out her hand. Clare took and held it.

"It has been nice seeing you again, Clare. How pleased and glad Father'll be to hear about you!"

"Until Tuesday, then," Clare Kendry replied. "I'll spend every minute of the time from now on looking forward to seeing you again. Good-bye, 'Rene dear. My love to your father, and this kiss for him."

The sun had gone from overhead, but the streets were still like fiery furnaces. The languid breeze was still hot. And the scurrying people looked even more wilted than before Irene had fled from their contact.

Crossing the avenue in the heat, far from the coolness of the Drayton's roof, away from the seduction of Clare Kendry's smile, she was aware of a sense of irritation with herself because she had been pleased and a little flattered at the other's obvious gladness at their meeting.

With her perspiring progress homeward this irritation grew, and she began to wonder just what had possessed her to make her promise to find time, in the crowded days that remained of her visit, to spend another afternoon with a woman whose life had so definitely and deliberately diverged from hers; and whom, as had been pointed out, she might never see again.

Why in the world had she made such a promise?

As she went up the steps to her father's house, thinking with what interest and amazement he would listen to her story of the afternoon's encounter, it came to her that Clare had omitted to mention her marriage name. She had referred to her husband as Jack. That was all. Had that, Irene asked herself, been intentional?

Clare had only to pick up the telephone to communicate with her, or to drop her a card, or to jump into a taxi. But she couldn't reach Clare in any way. Nor could anyone else to whom she might speak of their meeting.

"As if I should!"

Her key turned in the lock. She went in. Her father, it seemed, hadn't come in yet.

Irene decided that she wouldn't, after all, say anything to him about Clare Kendry. She had, she told herself, no inclination to speak of a person who held so low an opinion of her loyalty, or her discretion. And certainly she had no desire or intention of making the slightest effort about Tuesday. Nor any other day for that matter.

She was through with Clare Kendry.


# Three


On Tuesday morning a dome of grey sky rose over the parched city, but the stifling air was not relieved by the silvery mist that seemed to hold a promise of rain, which did not fall.

To Irene Redfield this soft foreboding fog was another reason for doing nothing about seeing Clare Kendry that afternoon.

But she did see her.

The telephone. For hours it had rung like something possessed. Since nine o'clock she had been hearing its insistent jangle. Awhile she was resolute, saying firmly each time: "Not in, Liza, take the message." And each time the servant returned with the information: "It's the same lady, ma'am; she says she'll call again."

But at noon, her nerves frayed and her conscience smiting her at the reproachful look on Liza's ebony face as she withdrew for another denial, Irene weakened.

"Oh, never mind. I'll answer this time, Liza."

"It's her again."

"Hello. . . . Yes."

"It's Clare, 'Rene. . . . Where *have* you been? . . . Can you be here around four? . . . What? . . . But, 'Rene, you promised! Just for a little while. . . . You can if you want to. . . . I am *so* disappointed. I had counted so on seeing you. . . . Please be nice and come. Only for a minute. I'm sure you can manage it if you try. . . . I won't beg you to stay. . . . Yes. . . . I'm going to expect you . . . It's the Morgan . . . Oh, yes! The name's Bellew, Mrs. John Bellew. . . . About four, then. . . . I'll be so happy to see you! . . . Good-bye."

"Damn!"

Irene hung up the receiver with an emphatic bang, her thoughts immediately filled with self-reproach. She'd done it again. Allowed Clare Kendry to persuade her into promising to do something for which she had neither time nor any special desire. What was it about Clare's voice that was so appealing, so very seductive?

Clare met her in the hall with a kiss. She said: "You're good to come, 'Rene. But, then, you always were nice to me." And under her potent smile a part of Irene's annoyance with herself fled. She was even a little glad that she had come.

Clare led the way, stepping lightly, towards a room whose door was standing partly open, saying: "There's a surprise. It's a real party. See."

Entering, Irene found herself in a sitting room, large and high, at whose windows hung startling blue draperies which triumphantly dragged attention from the gloomy chocolate-colored furniture. And Clare was wearing a thin floating dress of the same shade of blue, which suited her and the rather difficult room to perfection.

For a minute Irene thought the room was empty, but turning her head, she discovered, sunk deep in the cushions of a huge sofa, a woman staring up at her with such intense concentration that her eyelids were drawn as though the strain of that upward glance had paralyzed them. At first Irene took her to be a stranger, but in the next instant she said in an unsympathetic, almost harsh voice: "And how are you, Gertrude?"

The woman nodded and forced a smile to her pouting lips. "I'm all right," she replied. "And you're just the same, Irene. Not changed a bit."

"Thank you," Irene responded as she chose a seat. She was thinking: "Great goodness! Two of them."

For Gertrude too had married a white man, though it couldn't be truthfully said that she was "passing." Her husband—what was his name?—had been in school with her and had been quite well aware, as had his family and most of his friends, that she was a Negro. It hadn't, Irene knew, seemed to matter to him then. Did it now, she wondered. Had Fred—Fred Martin, that was it—had he ever regretted his marriage because of Gertrude's race? Had Gertrude?

Turning to Gertrude, Irene asked: "And Fred, how is he? It's unmentionable years since I've seen him."

"Oh, he's all right," Gertrude answered briefly.

For a full minute no one spoke. Finally out of the oppressive little silence Clare's voice came pleasantly, conversationally: "We'll have tea right away. I know that you can't stay long, 'Rene. And I'm so sorry you won't see Margery. We went up the lake over the weekend to see some of Jack's people, just out of Milwaukee. Margery wanted to stay with the children. It seemed a shame not to let her, especially since it's so hot in town. But I'm expecting Jack any second."

Irene said briefly: "That's nice."

Gertrude remained silent. She was, it was plain, a little ill at ease. And her presence there annoyed Irene, roused in her a defensive and resentful feeling for which she had at the moment no explanation. But it did seem to her odd that the woman that Clare was now should have invited the woman that Gertrude was. Still, of course, Clare couldn't have known. Twelve years since they had met.

Later, when she examined her feeling of annoyance, Irene admitted, a shade reluctantly, that it arose from a feeling of being outnumbered, a sense of aloneness, in her adherence to her own class and kind; not merely in the great thing of marriage, but in the whole pattern of her life as well.

Clare spoke again, this time at length. Her talk was of the change that Chicago presented to her after her long absence in European cities. Yes, she said in reply to some question from Gertrude, she'd been back to America a time or two, but only as far as New York and Philadelphia, and once she had spent a few days in Washington. John Bellew, who, it appeared, was some sort of international banking agent, hadn't particularly wanted her to come with him on this trip, but as soon as she had learned that it would probably take him as far as Chicago, she made up her mind to come anyway.

"I simply had to. And after I once got here, I was determined to see someone I knew and find out what had happened to everybody. I didn't quite see how I was going to manage it, but I meant to. Somehow. I'd just about decided to take a chance and go out to your house, 'Rene, or call up and arrange a meeting, when I ran into you. What luck!"

Irene agreed that it was luck. "It's the first time I've been home for five years, and now I'm about to leave. A week later and I'd have been gone. And how in the world did you find Gertrude?"

"In the book. I remembered about Fred. His father still has the meat market."

"Oh, yes," said Irene, who had only remembered it as Clare had spoken, "on Cottage Grove near—"

Gertrude broke in. "No. It's moved. We're on Maryland Avenue—used to be Jackson—now. Near Sixty-third Street. And the market's Fred's. His name's the same as his father's."

Gertrude, Irene thought, looked as if her husband might be a butcher. There was left of her youthful prettiness, which had been so much admired in their high school days, no trace. She had grown broad, fat almost, and though there were no lines on her large white face, its very smoothness was somehow prematurely aging. Her black hair was clipped, and by some unfortunate means all the live curliness had gone from it. Her overtrimmed georgette crepe dress was too short and showed an appalling amount of leg, stout legs in sleazy stockings of a vivid rose-beige shade. Her plump hands were newly and not too competently manicured—for the occasion, probably. And she wasn't smoking.

Clare said—and Irene fancied that her husky voice held a slight edge—"Before you came, Irene, Gertrude was telling me about her two boys. Twins. Think of it! Isn't it too marvelous for words?"

Irene felt a warmness creeping into her cheeks. Uncanny, the way Clare could divine what one was thinking. She was a little put out, but her manner was entirely easy as she said: "That is nice. I've two boys myself, Gertrude. Not twins, though. It seems that Clare's rather behind, doesn't it?"

Gertrude, however, wasn't sure that Clare hadn't the best of it. "She's got a girl. I wanted a girl. So did Fred."

"Isn't that a bit unusual?" Irene asked. "Most men want sons. Egotism, I suppose."

"Well, Fred didn't."

The tea things had been placed on a low table at Clare's side. She gave them her attention now, pouring the rich amber fluid from the tall glass pitcher into stately slim glasses, which she handed to her guests, and then offered them lemon or cream and tiny sandwiches or cakes.

After taking up her own glass she informed them: "No, I have no boys and I don't think I'll ever have any. I'm afraid. I nearly died of terror the whole nine months before Margery was born for fear that she might be dark. Thank goodness, she turned out all right. But I'll never risk it again. Never! The strain is simply too—too hellish."

Gertrude Martin nodded in complete comprehension.

This time it was Irene who said nothing.

"You don't have to tell me!" Gertrude said fervently. "I know what it is all right. Maybe you don't think I wasn't scared to death too. Fred said I was silly, and so did his mother. But, of course, they thought it was just a notion I'd gotten into my head and they blamed it on my condition. They don't know like we do, how it might go way back, and turn out dark no matter what color the father and mother are."

Perspiration stood out on her forehead. Her narrow eyes rolled first in Clare's, then in Irene's direction. As she talked she waved her heavy hands about.

"No," she went on, "no more for me either. Not even a girl. It's awful the way it skips generations and then pops out. Why, he actually said he didn't care what color it turned out, if I would only stop worrying about it. But, of course, nobody wants a dark child." Her voice was earnest and she took for granted that her audience was in entire agreement with her.

Irene, whose head had gone up with a quick little jerk, now said in a voice of whose even tones she was proud: "One of my boys is dark."

Gertrude jumped as if she had been shot at. Her eyes goggled. Her mouth flew open. She tried to speak but could not immediately get the words out. Finally she managed to stammer: "Oh! And your husband, is he—is he—er—dark too?"

Irene, who was struggling with a flood of feelings, resentment, anger, and contempt, was, however, still able to answer as coolly as if she had not that sense of not belonging to and of despising the company in which she found herself drinking iced tea from tall amber glasses on that hot August afternoon. Her husband, she informed them quietly, couldn't exactly "pass."

At that reply Clare turned on Irene her seductive caressing smile and remarked a little scoffingly: "I do think that colored people— we—are too silly about some things. After all, the thing's not important to Irene or hundreds of others. Not awfully, even to you, Gertrude. It's only deserters like me who have to be afraid of freaks of nature. As my inestimable dad used to say, 'Everything must be paid for.' Now, please, one of you tell me what ever happened to Claude Jones. You know, the tall, lanky specimen who used to wear that comical little mustache that the girls used to laugh at so. Like a thin streak of soot. The mustache, I mean."

At that Gertrude shrieked with laughter—"Claude Jones!"—and launched into the story of how he was no longer a Negro or a Christian but had become a Jew.

"A Jew!" Clare exclaimed.

"Yes, a Jew. A black Jew, he calls himself. He won't eat ham and goes to the synagogue on Saturday. He's got a beard now as well as a mustache. You'd die laughing if you saw him. He's really too funny for words. Fred says he's crazy and I guess he is. Oh, he's a scream all right, a regular scream!" And she shrieked again.

Clare's laugh tinkled out. "It certainly sounds funny enough. Still, it's his own business. If he gets along better by turning—"

At that, Irene, who was still hugging her unhappy don't-care feeling of rightness, broke in, saying bitingly: "It evidently doesn't occur to either you or Gertrude that he might possibly be sincere in changing his religion. Surely everyone doesn't do everything for gain."

Clare Kendry had no need to search for the full meaning of that utterance. She reddened slightly and retorted seriously: "Yes, I admit that might be possible—his being sincere, I mean. It just didn't happen to occur to me, that's all. I'm surprised," and the seriousness changed to mockery, "that you should have expected it to. Or did you really?"

"You don't, I'm sure, imagine that that is a question that I can answer," Irene told her. "Not here and now."

Gertrude's face expressed complete bewilderment. However, seeing that little smiles had come out on the faces of the two other women and not recognizing them for the smiles of mutual reservations which they were, she smiled too.

Clare began to talk, steering carefully away from anything that might lead towards race or other thorny subjects. It was the most brilliant exhibition of conversational weight lifting that Irene had ever seen. Her words swept over them in charming well-modulated streams. Her laughs tinkled and pealed. Her little stories sparkled.

Irene contributed a bare "Yes" or "No" here and there. Gertrude, a "You don't say!" less frequently.

For a while the illusion of general conversation was nearly perfect. Irene felt her resentment changing gradually to a silent, somewhat grudging admiration.

Clare talked on, her voice, her gestures, coloring all she said of wartime in France, of after-the-wartime in Germany, of the excitement at the time of the general strike in England, of dressmakers' openings in Paris, of the new gaiety of Budapest.

But it couldn't last, this verbal feat. Gertrude shifted in her seat and fell to fidgeting with her fingers. Irene, bored at last by all this repetition of the selfsame things that she had read all too often in papers, magazines, and books, set down her glass and collected her bag and handkerchief. She was smoothing out the tan fingers of her gloves preparatory to putting them on when she heard the sound of the outer door being opened and saw Clare spring up with an expression of relief, saying: "How lovely! Here's Jack at exactly the right minute. You can't go now, 'Rene dear."

John Bellew came into the room. The first thing that Irene noticed about him was that he was not the man that she had seen with Clare Kendry on the Drayton roof. This man, Clare's husband, was a tallish person, broadly made. His age she guessed to be somewhere between thirty-five and forty. His hair was dark brown and waving, and he had a soft mouth, somewhat womanish, set in an unhealthy-looking dough-colored face. His steel-grey opaque eyes were very much alive, moving ceaselessly between thick bluish lids. But there was, Irene decided, nothing unusual about him, unless it was an impression of latent physical power.

"Hello, Nig," was his greeting to Clare.

Gertrude, who had started slightly, settled back and looked covertly towards Irene, who had caught her lip between her teeth and sat gazing at husband and wife. It was hard to believe that even Clare Kendry would permit this ridiculing of her race by an outsider, though he chanced to be her husband. So he knew, then, that Clare was a Negro? From her talk the other day Irene had understood that he didn't. But how rude, how positively insulting, for him to address her in that way in the presence of guests!

In Clare's eyes, as she presented her husband, was a queer gleam, a jeer, it might be. Irene couldn't define it.

The mechanical professions that attend an introduction over, she inquired: "Did you hear what Jack called me?"

"Yes," Gertrude answered, laughing with a dutiful eagerness.

Irene didn't speak. Her gaze remained level on Clare's smiling face.

The black eyes fluttered down. "Tell them, dear, why you call me that."

The man chuckled, crinkling up his eyes, not, Irene was compelled to acknowledge, unpleasantly. He explained: "Well, you see, it's like this. When we were first married, she was as white as—as—well, as white as a lily. But I declare she's gettin' darker and darker. I tell her if she don't look out she'll wake up one of these days and find she's turned into a nigger."

He roared with laughter. Clare's ringing bell-like laugh joined his. Gertrude, after another uneasy shift in her seat, added her shrill one. Irene, who had been sitting with lips tightly compressed, cried out: "That's good!" and gave way to gales of laughter. She laughed and laughed and laughed. Tears ran down her cheeks. Her sides ached. Her throat hurt. She laughed on and on and on, long after the others had subsided. Until, catching sight of Clare's face, the need for a more quiet enjoyment of this priceless joke, and for caution, struck her. At once she stopped.

Clare handed her husband his tea and laid her hand on his arm with an affectionate little gesture. Speaking with confidence as well as with amusement, she said: "My goodness, Jack! What difference would it make if, after all these years, you were to find out that I was one or two percent colored?"

Bellew put out his hand in a repudiating fling, definite and final. "Oh, no, Nig," he declared, "nothing like that with me. I know you're no nigger, so it's all right. You can get as black as you please as far as I'm concerned, since I know you're no nigger. I draw the line at that. No niggers in my family. Never have been and never will be."

Irene's lips trembled almost uncontrollably, but she made a desperate effort to fight back her disastrous desire to laugh again, and succeeded. Carefully selecting a cigarette from the lacquered box on the tea table before her, she turned an oblique look on Clare and encountered her peculiar eyes fixed on her with an expression so dark and deep and unfathomable that she had for a short moment the sensation of gazing into the eyes of some creature utterly strange and apart. A faint sense of danger brushed her, like the breath of a cold fog. Absurd, her reason told her as she accepted Bellew's proffered light for her cigarette. Another glance at Clare showed her smiling. So, as one always ready to oblige, was Gertrude.

An onlooker, Irene reflected, would have thought it a most congenial tea party, all smiles and jokes and hilarious laughter. She said humorously: "So you dislike Negroes, Mr. Bellew?" But her amusement was at her thought, rather than her words.

John Bellew gave a short denying laugh. "You got me wrong there, Mrs. Redfield. Nothing like that at all. I don't dislike them, I hate them. And so does Nig, for all she's trying to turn into one. She wouldn't have a nigger maid around her for love nor money. Not that I'd want her to. They give me the creeps. The black scrimy devils."

This wasn't funny. Had Bellew, Irene inquired, ever known any Negroes? The defensive tone of her voice brought another start from the uncomfortable Gertrude, and, for all her appearance of serenity, a quick apprehensive look from Clare.

Bellew answered: "Thank the Lord, no! And never expect to! But I know people who've known them, better than they know their black selves. And I read in the papers about them. Always robbing and killing people. And," he added darkly, "worse."

From Gertrude's direction came a queer little suppressed sound, a snort or a giggle. Irene couldn't tell which. There was a brief silence, during which she feared that her self-control was about to prove too frail a bridge to support her mounting anger and indignation. She had a leaping desire to shout at the man beside her: "And you're sitting here surrounded by three black devils, drinking tea."

The impulse passed, obliterated by her consciousness of the danger in which such rashness would involve Clare, who remarked with a gentle reprovingness: "Jack dear, I'm sure 'Rene doesn't care to hear all about your pet aversions. Nor Gertrude either. Maybe they read the papers too, you know." She smiled on him, and her smile seemed to transform him, to soften and mellow him, as the rays of the sun does a fruit.

"All right, Nig, old girl. I'm sorry," he apologized. Reaching over, he playfully touched his wife's pale hands, then turned back to Irene. "Didn't mean to bore you, Mrs. Redfield. Hope you'll excuse me," he said sheepishly. "Clare tells me you're living in New York. Great city, New York. The city of the future."

In Irene, rage had not retreated but was held by some dam of caution and allegiance to Clare. So, in the best casual voice she could muster, she agreed with Bellew. Though, she reminded him, it was exactly what Chicagoans were apt to say of their city. And all the while she was speaking, she was thinking how amazing it was that her voice did not tremble, that outwardly she was calm. Only her hands shook slightly. She drew them inward from their rest in her lap and pressed the tips of her fingers together to still them.

"Husband's a doctor, I understand. Manhattan, or one of the other boroughs?"

Manhattan, Irene informed him, and explained the need for Brian to be within easy reach of certain hospitals and clinics.

"Interesting life, a doctor's."

"Ye-es. Hard, though. And, in a way, monotonous. Nerve-racking too."

"Hard on the wife's nerves at least, eh? So many lady patients." He laughed, enjoying, with a boyish heartiness, the hoary joke.

Irene managed a momentary smile, but her voice was sober as she said: "Brian doesn't care for ladies, especially sick ones. I sometimes wish he did. It's South America that attracts him."

"Coming place, South America, if they ever get the niggers out of it. It's run over—"

"Really, Jack!" Clare's voice was on the edge of temper.

"Honestly, Nig, I forgot." To the others he said: "You see how henpecked I am." And to Gertrude: "You're still in Chicago, Mrs. —er—Mrs. Martin?"

He was, it was plain, doing his best to be agreeable to these old friends of Clare's. Irene had to concede that under other conditions she might have liked him. A fairly good-looking man of amiable disposition, evidently, and in easy circumstances. Plain and with no nonsense about him.

Gertrude replied that Chicago was good enough for her. She'd never been out of it and didn't think she ever should. Her husband's business was there.

"Of course, of course. Can't jump up and leave a business."

There followed a smooth surface of talk about Chicago, New York, their differences and their recent spectacular changes.

It was, Irene thought, unbelievable and astonishing that four people could sit so unruffled, so ostensibly friendly, while they were in reality seething with anger, mortification, shame. But no, on second thought she was forced to amend her opinion. John Bellew, most certainly, was as undisturbed within as without. So, perhaps, was Gertrude Martin. At least she hadn't the mortification and shame that Clare Kendry must be feeling, or, in such full measure, the rage and rebellion that she, Irene, was repressing.

"More tea, 'Rene?" Clare offered.

"Thanks, no. And I must be going. I'm leaving tomorrow, you know, and I've still got packing to do."

She stood up. So did Gertrude, and Clare, and John Bellew.

"How do you like the Drayton, Mrs. Redfield?" the latter asked.

"The Drayton? Oh, very much. Very much indeed," Irene answered, her scornful eyes on Clare's unrevealing face.

"Nice place, all right. Stayed there a time or two myself," the man informed her.

"Yes, it is nice," Irene agreed. "Almost as good as our best New York places." She had withdrawn her look from Clare and was searching in her bag for some nonexistent something. Her understanding was rapidly increasing, as were her pity and her contempt. Clare was so daring, so lovely, and so "having."

They gave their hands to Clare with appropriate murmurs. "So good to have seen you." . . . "I do hope I'll see you again soon."

"Good-bye," Clare returned. "It was good of you to come, 'Rene dear. And you too, Gertrude."

"Good-bye, Mr. Bellew." . . . "So glad to have met you." It was Gertrude who had said that. Irene couldn't, she absolutely couldn't bring herself to utter the polite fiction or anything approaching it.

He accompanied them out into the hall, summoned the elevator.

"Good-bye," they said again, stepping in.

Plunging downward, they were silent.

They made their way through the lobby without speaking.

But as soon as they had reached the street Gertrude, in the manner of one unable to keep bottled up for another minute that which for the last hour she had had to retain, burst out: "My God! What an awful chance! She must be plumb crazy."

"Yes, it certainly seems risky," Irene admitted.

"Risky! I should say it was. Risky! My God! What a word! And the mess she's liable to get herself into!"

"Still, I imagine she's pretty safe. They don't live here, you know. And there's a child. That's a certain security."

"It's an awful chance, just the same," Gertrude insisted. "I'd never in the world have married Fred without him knowing. You can't tell what will turn up."

"Yes, I do agree that it's safer to tell. But then Bellew wouldn't have married her. And, after all, that's what she wanted."

Gertrude shook her head. "I wouldn't be in her shoes for all the money she's getting out of it, when he finds out. Not with him feeling the way he does. Gee! Wasn't it awful? For a minute I was so mad I could have slapped him."

It had been, Irene acknowledged, a distinctly trying experience, as well as a very unpleasant one. "I was more than a little angry myself."

"And imagine her not telling us about him feeling that way! Anything might have happened. We might have said something."

That, Irene pointed out, was exactly like Clare Kendry. Taking a chance, and not at all considering anyone else's feelings.

Gertrude said: "Maybe she thought we'd think it a good joke. And I guess you did. The way you laughed. My land! I was scared to death he might catch on."

"Well, it was rather a joke," Irene told her, "on him and us and maybe on her."

"All the same, it's an awful chance. I'd hate to be her."

"She seems satisfied enough. She's got what she wanted, and the other day she told me it was worth it."

But about that Gertrude was skeptical. "She'll find out different," was her verdict. "She'll find out different all right."

Rain had begun to fall, a few scattered large drops.

The end-of-the-day crowds were scurrying in the directions of streetcars and elevated roads.

Irene said: "You're going south? I'm sorry. I've got an errand. If you don't mind, I'll just say good-bye here. It has been nice seeing you, Gertrude. Say hello to Fred for me, and to your mother if she remembers me. Good-bye."

She had wanted to be free of the other woman, to be alone; for she was still sore and angry.

What right, she kept demanding of herself, had Clare Kendry to expose her, or even Gertrude Martin, to such humiliation, such downright insult?

And all the while, on the rushing ride out to her father's house, Irene Redfield was trying to understand the look on Clare's face as she had said good-bye. Partly mocking, it had seemed, and partly menacing. And something else for which she could find no name. For an instant a recrudescence of that sensation of fear which she had had while looking into Clare's eyes that afternoon touched her. A slight shiver ran over her.

"It's nothing," she told herself. "Just somebody walking over my grave, as the children say." She tried a tiny laugh and was annoyed to find that it was close to tears.

What a state she had allowed that horrible Bellew to get her into!

And late that night, even, long after the last guest had gone and the old house was quiet, she stood at her window frowning out into the dark rain and puzzling again over that look on Clare's incredibly beautiful face. She couldn't, however, come to any conclusion about its meaning, try as she might. It was unfathomable, utterly beyond any experience or comprehension of hers.

She turned away from the window at last, with a still deeper frown. Why, after all, worry about Clare Kendry? She was well able to take care of herself, had always been able. And there were, for Irene, other things, more personal and more important to worry about.

Besides, her reason told her, she had only herself to blame for her disagreeable afternoon and its attendant fears and questions. She ought never to have gone.

# Four

The next morning, the day of her departure for New York, had brought a letter, which, at first glance, she had instinctively known came from Clare Kendry, though she couldn't remember ever having had a letter from her before. Ripping it open and looking at the signature, she saw that she had been right in her guess. She wouldn't, she told herself, read it. She hadn't the time. And, besides, she had no wish to be reminded of the afternoon before. As it was, she felt none too fresh for her journey; she had had a wretched night. And all because of Clare's innate lack of consideration for the feelings of others.

But she did read it. After father and friends had waved good-bye, and she was being hurled eastward, she became possessed of an uncontrollable curiosity to see what Clare had said about yesterday. For what, she asked, as she took it out of her bag and opened it, could she, what could anyone, say about a thing like that?

Clare Kendry had said:

> *'Rene dear:*
>
> *However am I to thank you for your visit? I know you are feeling that under the circumstances I ought not to have asked you to come, or, rather, insisted. But if you could know how glad, how excitingly happy, I was to meet you and how I ached to see more of you (to see everybody and couldn't), you would understand my wanting to see you again, and maybe forgive me a little.*
>
> *My love to you always and always and to your dear father, and all my poor thanks.*
>
> *Clare*

And there was a postscript which said:

*It may be, 'Rene dear, it may just be, that, after all, your way may be the wiser and infinitely happier one. I'm not sure just now. At least not so sure as I have been.*

C.

But the letter hadn't conciliated Irene. Her indignation was not lessened by Clare's flattering reference to her wiseness. As if, she thought wrathfully, anything could take away the humiliation, or any part of it, of what she had gone through yesterday afternoon for Clare Kendry.

With an unusual methodicalness she tore the offending letter into tiny ragged squares that fluttered down and made a small heap in her black crepe de chine lap. The destruction completed, she gathered them up, rose, and moved to the train's end. Standing there, she dropped them over the railing and watched them scatter, on tracks, on cinders, on forlorn grass, in rills of dirty water.

And that, she told herself, was that. The chances were one in a million that she would ever again lay eyes on Clare Kendry. If, however, that millionth chance should turn up, she had only to turn away her eyes, to refuse her recognition.

She dropped Clare out of her mind and turned her thoughts to her own affairs. To home, to the boys, to Brian. Brian, who in the morning would be waiting for her in the great clamorous station. She hoped that he had been comfortable and not too lonely without her and the boys. Not so lonely that that old, queer, unhappy restlessness had begun again within him; that craving for some place strange and different, which at the beginning of her marriage she had had to make such strenuous efforts to repress, and which yet faintly alarmed her, though it now sprang up at gradually lessening intervals.

Part Two

# Re-encounter

# One

Such were Irene Redfield's memories as she sat there in her room, a flood of October sunlight streaming in upon her, holding that second letter of Clare Kendry's.

Laying it aside, she regarded with an astonishment that had in it a mild degree of amusement the violence of the feelings which it stirred in her.

It wasn't the great measure of anger that surprised and slightly amused her. That, she was certain, was justified and reasonable, as was the fact that it could hold, still strong and unabated, across the stretch of two years' time entirely removed from any sight or sound of John Bellew or of Clare. That even at this remote date the memory of the man's words and manner had power to set her hands to trembling and to send the blood pounding against her temples did not seem to her extraordinary. But that she should retain that dim sense of fear, of panic, was surprising, silly.

That Clare should have written, should, even all things considered, have expressed a desire to see her again, did not so much amaze her. To count as nothing the annoyances, the bitterness, or the suffering of others, that was Clare.

Well—Irene's shoulders went up—one thing was sure: that she needn't, and didn't intend to, lay herself open to any repetition of a humiliation as galling and outrageous as that which, for Clare Kendry's sake, she had borne "that time in Chicago." Once was enough.

If, at the time of choosing, Clare hadn't precisely reckoned the cost, she had, nevertheless, no right to expect others to help make up the reckoning. The trouble with Clare was not only that she wanted to have her cake and eat it too but that she wanted to nibble at the cakes of other folk as well.

Irene Redfield found it hard to sympathize with this new tenderness, this avowed yearning of Clare's for "my own people."

The letter which she had just put out of her hand was, to her taste, a bit too lavish in its wordiness, a shade too unreserved in the manner of its expression. It roused again that old suspicion that Clare was acting, not consciously, perhaps—that is, not too consciously—but, none the less, acting. Nor was Irene inclined to excuse what she termed Clare's downright selfishness.

And mingled with her disbelief and resentment was another feeling, a question. Why hadn't she spoken that day? Why, in the face of Bellew's ignorant hate and aversion, had she concealed her own origin? Why had she allowed him to make his assertions and express his misconceptions undisputed? Why, simply because of Clare Kendry, who had exposed her to such torment, had she failed to take up the defense of the race to which she belonged?

Irene asked these questions, felt them. They were, however, merely rhetorical, as she herself was well aware. She knew their answers, every one, and it was the same for them all. How sardonic! She

couldn't betray Clare, couldn't even run the risk of appearing to defend a people that were being maligned, for fear that that defense might in some infinitesimal degree lead the way to final discovery of her secret. She had toward Clare Kendry a duty. She was bound to her by those very ties of race which, for all her repudiation of them, Clare had been unable to completely sever.

And it wasn't, as Irene knew, that Clare cared at all about the race or what was to become of it. She didn't. Or that she had for any of its members great, or even real, affection, though she professed undying gratitude for the small kindnesses which the Westover family had shown her when she was a child. Irene doubted the genuineness of it, seeing herself only as a means to an end where Clare was concerned. Nor could it be said that she had even the slight artistic or sociological interest in the race that some members of other races displayed. She hadn't. No, Clare Kendry cared nothing for the race. She only belonged to it.

"Not another damned thing!" Irene declared aloud as she drew a fragile stocking over a pale beige-colored foot.

"Aha! Swearing again, are you, madam? Caught you in the act that time."

Brian Redfield had come into the room in that noiseless way which, in spite, of the years of their life together, still had the power to disconcert her. He stood looking down on her with that amused smile of his, which was just the faintest bit supercilious and yet was somehow very becoming to him.

Hastily Irene pulled on the other stocking and slipped her feet into the slippers beside her chair.

"And what brought on this particular outburst of profanity? That is, if an indulgent but perturbed husband may inquire. The mother of sons, too! The times, alas, the times!"

"I've had this letter," Irene told him. "And I'm sure that anybody'll admit it's enough to make a saint swear. The nerve of her!"

She passed the letter to him, and in the act made a little mental frown. For, with a nicety of perception, she saw that she was doing it instead of answering his question with words, so that he might be

occupied while she hurried through her dressing. For she was late again, and Brian, she well knew, detested that. Why, oh why, couldn't she ever manage to be on time? Brian had been up for ages, had made some calls for all she knew, besides having taken the boys downtown to school. And she wasn't dressed yet; had only begun. Damn Clare! This morning it was her fault.

Brian sat down and bent his head over the letter, puckering his brows slightly in his effort to make out Clare's scrawl.

Irene, who had risen and was standing before the mirror, ran a comb through her black hair, then tossed her head with a light characteristic gesture, in order to disarrange a little the set locks. She touched a powder puff to her warm olive skin and then put on her frock with a motion so hasty that it was with some difficulty properly adjusted. At last she was ready, though she didn't immediately say so, but stood, instead, looking with a sort of curious detachment at her husband across the room.

Brian, she was thinking, was extremely good-looking. Not, of course, pretty or effeminate; the slight irregularity of his nose saved him from the prettiness, and the rather marked heaviness of his chin saved him from the effeminacy. But he was, in a pleasant masculine way, rather handsome. And yet, wouldn't he, perhaps, have been merely ordinarily good-looking but for the richness, the beauty of his skin, which was of an exquisitely fine texture and deep copper color?

He looked up and said: "Clare? That must be the girl you told me about meeting the last time you were out home. The one you went to tea with?"

Irene's answer to that was an inclination of the head.

"I'm ready," she said.

They were going downstairs, Brian deftly, unnecessarily, piloting her round the two short curved steps, just before the center landing.

"You're not," he asked, "going to see her?"

His words, however, were in reality not a question, but, as Irene was aware, an admonition.

Her front teeth just touched. She spoke through them, and her

tones held a thin sarcasm. "Brian darling, I'm really not such an idiot that I don't realize that if a man calls me a nigger it's his fault the first time, but mine if he has the opportunity to do it again."

They went into the dining room. He drew back her chair and she sat down behind the fat-bellied German coffeepot, which sent out its morning fragrance, mingled with the smell of crisp toast and savory bacon, in the distance. With his long, nervous fingers he picked up the morning paper from his own chair and sat down.

Zulena, a small mahogany-colored creature, brought in the grape-fruit.

They took up their spoons.

Out of the silence Brian spoke. Blandly. "My dear, you misunderstand me entirely. I simply meant that I hope you're not going to let her pester you. She will, you know, if you give her half a chance and she's anything at all like your description of her. Anyway, they always do. Besides," he corrected, "the man, her husband, didn't call you a nigger. There's a difference, you know."

"No, certainly he didn't. Not actually. He couldn't, not very well, since he didn't know. But he would have. It amounts to the same thing. And I'm sure it was just as unpleasant."

"U-mm, I don't know. But it seems to me," he pointed out, "that you, my dear, had all the advantage. You knew what his opinion of you was, while he— Well, 'twas ever thus. We know, always have. They don't. Not quite. It has, you will admit, its humorous side, and, sometimes, its conveniences."

She poured the coffee.

"I can't see it. I'm going to write Clare. Today, if I can find a minute. It's a thing we might as well settle definitely, and immediately. Curious, isn't it, that knowing, as she does, his unqualified attitude, she still—"

Brian interrupted: "It's always that way. Never known it to fail. Remember Albert Hammond, how he used to be forever haunting Seventh Avenue, and Lenox Avenue, and the dancing places, until some 'shine' took a shot at him for casting an eye towards his 'sheba'? They always come back. I've seen it happen time and time again."

"But why?" Irene wanted to know. "Why?"

"If I knew that, I'd know what race is."

"But wouldn't you think that, having got the thing, or things, they were after, and at such risk, they'd be satisfied? Or afraid?"

"Yes," Brian agreed, "you certainly would think so. But the fact remains, they aren't. Not satisfied, I mean. I think they're scared enough most of the time, when they give way to the urge and slip back. Not scared enough to stop them, though. Why, the good God only knows."

Irene leaned forward, speaking, she was aware, with a vehemence absolutely unnecessary, but which she could not control.

"Well, Clare can just count me out. I've no intention of being the link between her and her poorer, darker brethren. After that scene in Chicago, too! To calmly expect me—" She stopped short, suddenly too wrathful for words.

"Quite right. The only sensible thing to do. Let her miss you. It's an unhealthy business, the whole affair. Always is."

Irene nodded. "More coffee?" she offered.

"Thanks, no." He took up his paper again, spreading it open with a little rattling noise.

Zulena came in, bringing more toast. Brian took a slice and bit into it with that audible crunching sound that Irene disliked so intensely, and turned back to his paper.

She said: "It's funny about 'passing.' We disapprove of it and at the same time condone it. It excites our contempt and yet we rather admire it. We shy away from it with an odd kind of revulsion, but we protect it."

"Instinct of the race to survive and expand."

"Rot! Everything can't be explained by some general biological phrase."

"Absolutely everything can. Look at the so-called whites, who've left bastards all over the known earth. Same thing in them. Instinct of the race to survive and expand."

With that Irene didn't at all agree, but many arguments in the past had taught her the futility of attempting to combat Brian on ground where he was more nearly at home than she. Ignoring his unqualified assertion, she slid away from the subject entirely.

"I wonder," she asked, "if you'll have time to run me down to the printing office? It's on 116th Street. I've got to see about some handbills and some more tickets for the dance."

"Yes, of course. How's it going? Everything all set?"

"Ye-es. I guess so. The boxes are all sold and nearly all the first batch of tickets. And we expect to take in almost as much again at the door. Then there's all that cake to sell. It's a terrible lot of work, though."

"I'll bet it is. Uplifting the brother's no easy job. I'm as busy as a cat with fleas, myself." And over his face there came a shadow. "Lord! how I hate sick people, and their stupid, meddling families, and smelly, dirty rooms, and climbing filthy steps in dark hallways."

"Surely," Irene began, fighting back the fear and irritation that she felt, "surely—"

Her husband silenced her, saying sharply: "Let's not talk about it, please." And immediately, in his usual slightly mocking tone, he asked: "Are you ready to go now? I haven't a great deal of time to wait."

He got up. She followed him out into the hall without replying. He picked up his soft brown hat from the small table and stood a moment whirling it round on his long tea-colored fingers.

Irene, watching him, was thinking: "It isn't fair, it isn't fair." After all these years to still blame her like this. Hadn't his success proved that she'd been right in insisting that he stick to his profession right there in New York? Couldn't he see, even now, that it *had* been best? Not for her, oh no, not for her—she had never really considered herself—but for him and the boys. Was she never to be free of it, that fear which crouched, always, deep down within her, stealing away the sense of security, the feeling of permanence, from the life which she had so admirably arranged for them all, and desired so ardently to have remain as it was? That strange, and to her fantastic, notion of Brian's of going off to Brazil, which, though unmentioned, yet lived within him; how it frightened her, and—yes, angered her!

"Well?" he asked lightly.

"I'll just get my things. One minute," she promised and turned upstairs.

Her voice had been even and her step was firm, but in her there was no slackening of the agitation, of the alarms, which Brian's expression of discontent had raised. He had never spoken of his desire since that long-ago time of storm and strain, of hateful and nearly disastrous quarreling, when she had so firmly opposed him, so sensibly pointed out its utter impossibility and its probable consequences to her and the boys, and had even hinted at a dissolution of their marriage in the event of his persisting in his idea. No, there had been, in all the years that they had lived together since then, no other talk of it, no more than there had been any other quarreling or any other threats. But because, so she insisted, the bond of flesh and spirit between them was so strong, she knew, had always known, that his dissatisfaction had continued, as had his dislike and disgust for his profession and his country.

A feeling of uneasiness stole upon her at the inconceivable suspicion that she might have been wrong in her estimate of her husband's character. But she squirmed away from it. Impossible! She couldn't have been wrong. Everything proved that she had been right. More than right, if such a thing could be. And all, she assured herself, because she understood him so well, because she had, actually, a special talent for understanding him. It was, as she saw it, the one thing that had been the basis of the success which she had made of a marriage that had threatened to fail. She knew him as well as he knew himself, or better.

Then why worry? The thing, this discontent which had exploded into words, would surely die, flicker out, at last. True, she had in the past often been tempted to believe that it had died, only to become conscious, in some instinctive, subtle way, that she had been merely deceiving herself for a while and that it still lived. But it *would* die. Of that she was certain. She had only to direct and guide her man, to keep him going in the right direction.

She put on her coat and adjusted her hat.

Yes, it would die, as long ago she had made up her mind that it should. But in the meantime, while it was still living and still had the power to flare up and alarm her, it would have to be banked, smothered, and something offered in its stead. She would have to make some plan, some decision, at once. She frowned, for it annoyed her intensely. For, though temporary, it would be important and perhaps disturbing. Irene didn't like changes, particularly changes that affected the smooth routine of her household. Well, it couldn't be helped. Something would have to be done. And immediately.

She took up her purse and, drawing on her gloves, ran down the steps and out through the door which Brian held open for her and stepped into the waiting car.

"You know," she said, settling herself into the seat beside him, "I'm awfully glad to get this minute alone with you. It does seem that we're always so busy—I do hate that—but what can we do? I've had something on my mind for ever so long, something that needs talking over and really serious consideration."

The car's engine rumbled as it moved out from the curb and into the scant traffic of the street under Brian's expert guidance.

She studied his profile.

They turned into Seventh Avenue. Then he said: "Well, let's have it. No time like the present for the settling of weighty matters."

"It's about Junior. I wonder if he isn't going too fast in school? We do forget that he's not eleven yet. Surely it can't be good for him to—well, if he is, I mean. Going too fast, you know. Of course, you know more about these things than I do. You're better able to judge. That is, if you've noticed or thought about it at all."

"I do wish, Irene, you wouldn't be forever fretting about those kids. They're all right. Perfectly all right. Good, strong, healthy boys, especially Junior. Most especially Junior."

"We-ll, I s'pose you're right. You're expected to know about things like that, and I'm sure you wouldn't make a mistake about your own boy." (Now why had she said that?) "But that isn't all. I'm terribly afraid he's picked up some queer ideas about things—some things —from the older boys, you know."

Her manner was consciously light. Apparently she was intent on the maze of traffic, but she was still watching Brian's face closely. On it was a peculiar expression. Was it, could it possibly be, a mixture of scorn and distaste?

"Queer ideas?" he repeated. "D'you mean ideas about sex, Irene?"

"Ye-es. Not quite nice ones. Dreadful jokes, and things like that."

"Oh, I see," he threw at her. For a while there was silence between them. After a moment he demanded bluntly: "Well, what of it? If sex isn't a joke, what is it? And what is a joke?"

"As you please, Brian. He's your son, you know." Her voice was clear, level, disapproving.

"Exactly! And you're trying to make a mollycoddle out of him. Well, just let me tell you, I won't have it. And you needn't think I'm going to let you change him to some nice kindergarten kind of a school because he's getting a little necessary education. I won't! He'll stay right where he is. The sooner and the more he learns about sex, the better for him. And most certainly if he learns that it's a grand joke, the greatest in the world. It'll keep him from lots of disappointments later on."

Irene didn't answer.

They reached the printing shop. She got out, emphatically slamming the car door behind her. There was a piercing agony of misery in her heart. She hadn't intended to behave like this, but her extreme resentment at his attitude, the sense of having been willfully misunderstood and reproved, drove her to fury.

Inside the shop, she stilled the trembling of her lips and drove back her rising anger. Her business transacted, she came back to the car in a chastened mood. But against the armor of Brian's stubborn silence she heard herself saying in a calm, metallic voice: "I don't believe I'll go back just now. I've remembered that I've got to do something about getting something decent to wear. I haven't a rag that's fit to be seen. I'll take the bus downtown."

Brian merely doffed his hat in that maddening polite way which so successfully curbed and yet revealed his temper.

"Good-bye," she said bitingly. "Thanks for the lift," and turned towards the avenue.

What, she wondered contritely, was she to do next? She was vexed with herself for having chosen, as it had turned out, so clumsy an opening for what she had intended to suggest: some European school for Junior next year, and Brian to take him over. If she had been able to present her plan, and he had accepted it, as she was sure that he would have done, with other more favorable opening methods, he would have had that to look forward to as a break in the easy monotony that seemed, for some reason she was wholly unable to grasp, so hateful to him.

She was even more vexed at her own explosion of anger. What could have got into her to give way to it in such a moment?

Gradually her mood passed. She drew back from the failure of her first attempt at substitution, not so much discouraged as disappointed and ashamed. It might be, she reflected, that, in addition to her ill-timed loss of temper, she had been too hasty in her eagerness to distract him, had rushed too closely on the heels of his outburst, and had thus aroused his suspicions and his obstinacy. She had but to wait. Another more appropriate time would come, tomorrow, next week, next month. It wasn't now, as it had been once, that she was afraid that he would throw everything aside and rush off to that remote place of his heart's desire. He wouldn't, she knew. He was fond of her, loved her, in his slightly undemonstrative way.

And there were the boys.

It was only that she wanted him to be happy, resenting, however, his inability to be so with things as they were, and never acknowledging that, though she did want him to be happy, it was only in her own way and by some plan of hers for him that she truly desired him to be so. Nor did she admit that all other plans, all other ways, she regarded as menaces, more or less indirect, to that security of place and substance which she insisted upon for her sons and in a lesser degree for herself.

# Two

Five days had gone by since Clare Kendry's appealing letter. Irene Redfield had not replied to it. Nor had she had any other word from Clare.

She had not carried out her first intention of writing at once because, on going back to the letter for Clare's address, she had come upon something which, in the rigor of her determination to maintain unbroken between them the wall that Clare herself had raised, she had forgotten or not fully noted. It was the fact that Clare had requested her to direct her answer to the post office's general delivery.

That had angered Irene and increased her disdain and contempt for the other.

Tearing the letter across, she had flung it into the scrap basket. It wasn't so much Clare's carefulness and her desire for secrecy in their relations—Irene understood the need for that—as that Clare should have doubted her discretion, implied that she might not be cautious in the wording of her reply and the choice of a posting box. Having always had complete confidence in her own good judgment and tact, Irene couldn't bear to have anyone seem to question them. Certainly not Clare Kendry.

In another, calmer moment she decided that it was, after all, better to answer nothing, to explain nothing, to refuse nothing; to dispose of the matter simply by not writing at all. Clare, of whom it couldn't be said that she was stupid, would not mistake the implication of that silence. She might—and Irene was sure that she would—choose to ignore it and write again, but that didn't matter. The whole thing would be very easy. The basket for all letters, silence for their answers.

Most likely she and Clare would never meet again. Well, she, for one, could endure that. Since childhood their lives had never really touched. Actually they were strangers. Strangers in their ways and means of living. Strangers in their desires and ambitions. Strangers even in their racial consciousness. Between them the barrier was just as high, just as broad, and just as firm as if in Clare did not run that strain of black blood. In truth, it was higher, broader, and firmer; because for her there were perils, not known or imagined by those others who had no such secrets to alarm or endanger them.

The day was getting on toward evening. It was past the middle of October. There had been a week of cold rain, drenching the rotting leaves which had fallen from the poor trees that lined the street on which the Redfields' house was located, and sending a damp air of penetrating chill into the house, with a hint of cold days to come. In Irene's room a low fire was burning. Outside, only a dull grey light was left of the day. Inside, lamps had already been lighted.

From the floor above there was the sound of young voices. Sometimes Junior's serious and positive; again, Ted's deceptively gracious one. Often there was laughter, or the noise of commotion, tussling, or toys being slammed down.

Junior, tall for his age, was almost incredibly like his father in feature and coloring; but his temperament was hers, practical and determined, rather than Brian's. Ted, speculative and withdrawn, was apparently less positive in his ideas and desires. About him there was a deceiving air of candor that was, Irene knew, like his father's show of reasonable acquiescence. If, for the time being, and with a charming appearance of artlessness, he submitted to the force of superior strength, or some other immovable condition or circumstance, it was because of his intense dislike of scenes and unpleasant argument. Brian over again.

Gradually Irene's thought slipped away from Junior and Ted, to become wholly absorbed in their father.

The old fear, with strength increased, the fear for the future, had again laid its hand on her. And, try as she might, she could not shake it off. It was as if she had admitted to herself that against that easy surface of her husband's concordance with her wishes, which had, since the war had given him back to her physically unimpaired, covered an increasing inclination to tear himself and his possessions loose from their proper setting, she was helpless.

The chagrin which she had felt at her first failure to subvert this latest manifestation of his discontent had receded, leaving in its wake an uneasy depression. Were all her efforts, all her labors, to make up to him that one loss, all her silent striving to prove to him that her way had been best, all her ministrations to him, all her outward sinking of self, to count for nothing in some unperceived sudden moment? And if so, what, then, would be the consequences to the boys? To her? To Brian himself? Endless searching had brought no answer to these questions. There was only an intense weariness from their shuttlelike procession in her brain.

The noise and commotion from above grew increasingly louder. Irene was about to go to the stairway and request the boys to be quieter in their play when she heard the doorbell ringing.

Now who was that likely to be? She listened to Zulena's heels, faintly tapping on their way to the door, then to the shifting sound of her feet on the steps, then to her light knock on the bedroom door.

"Yes. Come in," Irene told her.

Zulena stood in the doorway. She said: "Someone to see you, Mrs. Redfield." Her tone was discreetly regretful, as if to convey that she was reluctant to disturb her mistress at that hour, and for a stranger. "A Mrs. Bellew."

Clare!

"Oh dear! Tell her, Zulena," Irene began, "that I can't— No. I'll see her. Please bring her up here."

She heard Zulena pass down the hall, down the stairs, then stood up, smoothing out the tumbled green and ivory draperies of her dress with light stroking pats. At the mirror she dusted a little powder on her nose and brushed out her hair.

She meant to tell Clare Kendry at once, and definitely, that it was of no use, her coming, that she couldn't be responsible, that she'd talked it over with Brian, who had agreed with her that it was wiser, for Clare's own sake, to refrain—

But that was as far as she got in her rehearsal. For Clare had come softly into the room without knocking and, before Irene could greet her, had dropped a kiss on her dark curls.

Looking at the woman before her, Irene Redfield had a sudden inexplicable onrush of affectionate feeling. Reaching out, she grasped Clare's two hands in her own and cried with something like awe in her voice: "Dear God! But aren't you lovely, Clare!"

Clare tossed that aside. Like the furs and small blue hat which she threw on the bed before seating herself slantwise in Irene's favorite chair, with one foot curled under her.

"Didn't you mean to answer my letter, 'Rene?" she asked gravely.

Irene looked away. She had that uncomfortable feeling that one has when one has not been wholly kind or wholly true.

Clare went on: "Every day I went to that nasty little post office place. I'm sure they were all beginning to think that I'd been carrying on an illicit love affair and that the man had thrown me over. Every morning the same answer: 'Nothing for you.' I got into an awful fright, thinking that something might have happened to your letter, or to mine. And half the nights I would lie awake looking out at the watery stars—hopeless things, the stars—worrying and wondering. But at last it soaked in, that you hadn't written and didn't intend to. And then—well, as soon as ever I'd seen Jack off for Florida, I came straight here. And now, 'Rene, please tell me quite frankly why you didn't answer my letter."

"Because, you see—" Irene broke off and kept Clare waiting while she lit a cigarette, blew out the match, and dropped it into a tray. She was trying to collect her arguments, for some sixth sense warned her that it was going to be harder than she thought to convince Clare Kendry of the folly of Harlem for her. Finally she proceeded: "I can't help thinking that you ought not to come up here, ought not to run the risk of knowing Negroes."

"You mean you don't want me, 'Rene?"

Irene hadn't supposed that anyone could look so hurt. She said, quite gently, "No, Clare, it's not that. But even you must see that it's terribly foolish, and not just the right thing."

The tinkle of Clare's laugh rang out, while she passed her hands over the bright sweep of her hair. "Oh, 'Rene," she cried, "you're priceless! And you haven't changed a bit. The right thing!" Leaning forward, she looked curiously into Irene's disapproving brown eyes.

"You don't, you really can't mean exactly that! Nobody could. It's simply unbelievable."

Irene was on her feet before she realized that she had risen. "What I really mean," she retorted, "is that it's dangerous and that you ought not to run such silly risks. No one ought to. You least of all."

Her voice was brittle. For into her mind had come a thought, strange and irrelevant, a suspicion, that had surprised and shocked her and driven her to her feet. It was that in spite of her determined selfishness the woman before her was yet capable of heights and depths of feeling that she, Irene Redfield, had never known. Indeed, never cared to know. The thought, the suspicion, was gone as quickly as it had come.

Clare said: "Oh, me!"

Irene touched her arm caressingly, as if in contrition for that flashing thought. "Yes, Clare, you. It's not safe. Not safe at all."

"Safe!"

It seemed to Irene that Clare had snapped her teeth down on the word and then flung it from her. And for another flying second she had that suspicion of Clare's ability for a quality of feeling that was to her strange and even repugnant. She was aware, too, of a dim premonition of some impending disaster. It was as if Clare Kendry had said to her, for whom safety, security, were all-important: "Safe! Damn being safe!" and meant it.

With a gesture of impatience she sat down. In a voice of cool formality, she said: "Brian and I have talked the whole thing over carefully and decided that it isn't wise. He says it's always a dangerous business, this coming back. He's seen more than one come to grief because of it. And, Clare, considering everything—Mr. Bellew's attitude and all that—don't you think you ought to be as careful as you can?"

Clare's deep voice broke the small silence that had followed Irene's speech. She said, speaking almost plaintively: "I ought to have known. It's Jack. I don't blame you for being angry, though I must say you behaved beautifully that day. But I did think you'd understand, 'Rene. It was that, partly, that has made me want to see other people. It just swooped down and changed everything. If it hadn't been for that, I'd have gone on to the end, never seeing any of you. But that did something to me, and I've been so lonely since! You can't know. Not close to a single soul. Never anyone to really talk to."

Irene pressed out her cigarette. While doing so, she saw again the vision of Clare Kendry staring disdainfully down at the face of her father, and thought that it would be like that that she would look at her husband if he lay dead before her.

Her own resentment was swept aside and her voice held an accent of pity as she exclaimed: "Why, Clare! I didn't know. Forgive me. I feel like seven beasts. It was stupid of me not to realize."

"No. Not at all. You couldn't. Nobody, none of you, could," Clare moaned. The black eyes filled with tears that ran down her cheeks and spilled into her lap, ruining the priceless velvet of her dress. Her long hands were a little uplifted and clasped tightly together. Her effort to speak moderately was obvious but not successful. "How could you know? How could you? You're free. You're happy. And," with faint derision, "safe."

Irene passed over that touch of derision, for the poignant rebellion of the other's words had brought the tears to her own eyes, though she didn't allow them to fall. The truth was that she knew weeping did not become her. Few women, she imagined, wept as attractively as Clare. "I'm beginning to believe," she murmured, "that no one is ever completely happy, or free, or safe."

"Well, then, what does it matter? One risk more or less, if we're not safe anyway, if even you're not, it can't make all the difference in the world. It can't to me. Besides, I'm used to risks. And this isn't such a big one as you're trying to make it."

"Oh, but it is. And it can make all the difference in the world. There's your little girl, Clare. Think of the consequences to her."

Clare's face took on a startled look, as though she were totally unprepared for this new weapon with which Irene had assailed her. Seconds passed, during which she sat with stricken eyes and compressed lips. "I think," she said at last, "that being a mother is the cruelest thing in the world." Her clasped hands swayed forward and back again, and her scarlet mouth trembled irrepressibly.

"Yes," Irene softly agreed. For a moment she was unable to say more, so accurately had Clare put into words that which, not so definitely defined, was so often in her own heart of late. At the same time she was conscious that here to her hand was a reason which could not be lightly brushed aside. "Yes," she repeated, "and the most responsible, Clare. We mothers are all responsible for the security and happiness of our children. Think what it would mean to your Margery if Mr. Bellew should find out. You'd probably lose her. And even if you didn't, nothing that concerned her would ever be the same again. He'd never forget that she had Negro blood. And if she should learn— Well, I believe that after twelve it is too late to learn a thing like that. She'd never forgive you. You may be used to risks, but this is one you mustn't take, Clare. It's a selfish whim, an unnecessary and—"

"Yes, Zulena, what is it?" she inquired, a trifle tartly, of the servant who had silently materialized in the doorway.

"The telephone's for you, Mrs. Redfield. It's Mr. Wentworth."

"All right. Thank you. I'll take it here." And with a muttered apology to Clare she took up the instrument.

"Hello. . . . Yes, Hugh. . . . Oh, quite. . . . And you? . . . I'm sorry, every single thing's gone. . . . Oh, too bad. . . . Ye-es, I s'pose you could. Not very pleasant, though. . . . Yes, of course, in a pinch everything goes. . . . Wait! I've got it! I'll change mine with whoever's next to you, and you can have that. . . . No. . . . I mean it. . . . I'll be so busy I shan't know whether I'm sitting or standing. . . . As long as Brian has a place to drop down now and then. . . . Not a single soul. . . . No, don't. . . . That's nice. . . . My love to Bianca. . . . I'll see to it right away and call you back. . . . Good-bye."

She hung up and turned back to Clare, a little frown on her softly chiselled features. "It's the N. W. L. dance," she explained, "the Negro Welfare League, you know. I'm on the ticket committee, or, rather, I *am* the committee. Thank heaven it comes off tomorrow night and doesn't happen again for a year. I'm about crazy, and now I've got to persuade somebody to change boxes with me."

"That wasn't," Clare asked, "Hugh Wentworth? Not *the* Hugh Wentworth?"

Irene inclined her head. On her face was a tiny triumphant smile. "Yes, *the* Hugh Wentworth. D'you know him?"

"No. How should I? But I do know about him. And I've read a book or two of his."

"Awfully good, aren't they?"

"U-umm, I s'pose so. Sort of contemptuous, I thought. As if he more or less despised everything and everybody."

"I shouldn't be a bit surprised if he did. Still, he's about earned the right to. Lived on the edges of nowhere in at least three continents. Been through every danger in all kinds of savage places. It's no wonder he thinks the rest of us are a lazy self-pampering lot. Hugh's a dear, though, generous as one of the twelve disciples; give you the shirt off his back. Bianca—that's his wife—is nice too."

"And he's coming up here to your dance?"

Irene asked why not.

"It seems rather curious, a man like that, going to a Negro dance."

This, Irene told her, was the year 1927 in the city of New York, and hundreds of white people of Hugh Wentworth's type came to affairs in Harlem, more all the time. So many that Brian had said: "Pretty soon the colored people won't be allowed in at all, or will have to sit in Jim Crowed sections."

"What do they come for?"

"Same reason you're here, to see Negroes."

"But why?"

"Various motives," Irene explained. "A few purely and frankly to enjoy themselves. Others to get material to turn into shekels. More, to gaze on these great and near great while they gaze on the Negroes."

Clare clapped her hand. " 'Rene, suppose I come too! It sounds terribly interesting and amusing. And I don't see why I shouldn't."

Irene, who was regarding her through narrowed eyelids, had the same thought that she had had two years ago on the roof of the Drayton, that Clare Kendry was just a shade too good-looking. Her tone was on the edge of irony as she said: "You mean because so many other white people go?"

A pale rose color came into Clare's ivory cheeks. She lifted a hand in protest. "Don't be silly! Certainly not! I mean that in a crowd of that kind I shouldn't be noticed."

On the contrary, was Irene's opinion. It might be even doubly dangerous. Some friend or acquaintance of John Bellew or herself might see and recognize her.

At that, Clare laughed for a long time, little musical trills following one another in sequence after sequence. It was as if the thought of any friend of John Bellew's going to a Negro dance was to her the most amusing thing in the world.

"I don't think," she said when she had done laughing, "we need worry about that."

Irene, however, wasn't so sure. But all her efforts to dissuade Clare were useless. To her, "You never can tell whom you're likely to meet there," Clare's rejoinder was: "I'll take my chance on getting by."

"Besides, you won't know a soul and I shall be too busy to look after you. You'll be bored stiff."

"I won't, I won't. If nobody asks me to dance, not even Dr. Redfield, I'll just sit and gaze on the great and the near great, too. Do, 'Rene, be polite and invite me."

Irene turned away from the caress of Clare's smile, saying promptly and positively: "I will not."

"I mean to go anyway," Clare retorted, and her voice was no less positive than Irene's.

"Oh, no. You couldn't possibly go there alone. It's a public thing. All sorts of people go, anybody who can pay a dollar, even ladies of easy virtue looking for trade. If you were to go there alone, you might be mistaken for one of them, and that wouldn't be too pleasant."

Clare laughed again. "Thanks. I never have been. It might be amusing. I'm warning you, 'Rene, that if you're not going to be nice and take me I'll still be among those present. I suppose my dollar's as good as anyone's."

"Oh, the dollar! Don't be a fool, Clare. I don't care where you go or what you do. All I'm concerned with is the unpleasantness and possible danger which your going might incur, because of your situation. To put it frankly, I shouldn't like to be mixed up in any row of the kind." She had risen again as she spoke and was standing at the window, lifting and spreading the small yellow chrysanthemums in the grey stone jar on the sill. Her hands shook slightly, for she was in a near rage of impatience and exasperation.

Clare's face looked strange, as if she wanted to cry again. One of her satin-covered feet swung restlessly back and forth. She said vehemently, violently almost: "Damn Jack! He keeps me out of everything. Everything I want. I could kill him! I expect I shall, someday."

"I wouldn't," Irene advised her. "You see, there's still capital punishment, in this state at least. And really, Clare, after everything's said, I can't see that you've a right to put all the blame on him. You've got to admit that there's his side to the thing. You didn't tell him you were colored, so he's got no way of knowing about this hankering of yours after Negroes, or that it galls you to fury to hear them called niggers and black devils. As far as I can see, you'll just have to endure some things and give up others. As we've said before, everything must be paid for. Do, please, be reasonable."

But Clare, it was plain, had shut away reason as well as caution. She shook her head. "I can't, I can't," she said. "I would if I could, but I can't. You don't know, you can't realize how I want to see Negroes, to be with them again, to talk with them, to hear them laugh."

And in the look she gave Irene, there was something groping, and hopeless, and yet so absolutely determined that it was like an image of the futile searching and the firm resolution in Irene's own soul, and increased the feeling of doubt and compunction that had been growing within her about Clare Kendry.

She gave in.

"Oh, come if you want to. I s'pose you're right. Once can't do such a terrible lot of harm."

Pushing aside Clare's extravagant thanks, for immediately she was sorry that she had consented, she said briskly: "Should you like to come up and see my boys?"

"I'd love to."

They went up, Irene thinking that Brian would consider that she'd behaved like a spineless fool. And he would be right. She certainly had.

Clare was smiling. She stood in the doorway of the boys' playroom, her shadowy eyes looking down on Junior and Ted, who had sprung apart from their tussling. Junior's face had a funny little look of resentment. Ted's was blank.

Clare said: "Please don't be cross. Of course, I know I've gone and spoiled everything. But maybe, if I promise not to get too much in the way, you'll let me come in just the same."

"Sure, come in if you want to," Ted told her. "We can't stop you, you know." He smiled and made her a little bow and then turned away to a shelf that held his favorite books. Taking one down, he settled himself in a chair and began to read.

Junior said nothing, did nothing, merely stood there waiting.

"Get up, Ted! That's rude. This is Theodore, Mrs. Bellew. Please excuse his bad manners. He does know better. And this is Brian junior. Mrs. Bellew is an old friend of Mother's. We used to play together when we were little girls."

Clare had gone and Brian had telephoned that he'd been detained and would have his dinner downtown. Irene was a little glad for that. She was going out later herself, and that meant she wouldn't, probably, see Brian until morning and so could put off for a few more hours speaking of Clare and the N. W. L. dance.

She was angry with herself and with Clare. But more with herself, for having permitted Clare to tease her into doing something that Brian had, all but expressly, asked her not to do. She didn't want him ruffled, not just then, not while he was possessed of that unreasonable restless feeling.

She was annoyed, too, because she was aware that she had consented to something which, if it went beyond the dance, would involve her in numerous petty inconveniences and evasions. And not only at home with Brian but outside with friends and acquaintances. The disagreeable possibilities in connection with Clare Kendry's coming among them loomed before her in endless irritating array.

Clare, it seemed, still retained her ability to secure the thing that she wanted in the face of any opposition, and in utter disregard of the convenience and desire of others. About her there was some quality, hard and persistent, with the strength and endurance of rock, that would not be beaten or ignored. She couldn't, Irene thought, have had an entirely serene life. Not with that dark secret forever crouching in the background of her consciousness. And yet she hadn't the air of a woman whose life had been touched by uncertainty or suffering. Pain, fear, and grief were things that left their mark on people. Even love, that exquisite torturing emotion, left its subtle traces on the countenance.

But Clare—she had remained almost what she had always been, an attractive, somewhat lonely child—selfish, willful, and disturbing.

# Three

The things which Irene Redfield remembered afterward about the Negro Welfare League dance seemed, to her, unimportant and unrelated.

She remembered the not quite derisive smile with which Brian had cloaked his vexation when she informed him—oh, so apologetically—that she had promised to take Clare, and related the conversation of her visit.

She remembered her own little choked exclamation of admiration, when, on coming downstairs a few minutes later than she had intended, she had rushed into the living room where Brian was waiting and had found Clare there too. Clare, exquisite, golden, fragrant, flaunting, in a stately gown of shining black taffeta, whose long, full skirt lay in graceful folds about her slim golden feet; her glistening hair drawn smoothly back into a small twist at the nape of her neck; her eyes sparkling like dark jewels. Irene, with her new rose-colored chiffon frock ending at the knees, and her cropped curls, felt dowdy and commonplace. She regretted that she hadn't counseled Clare to wear something ordinary and inconspicuous. What on earth would Brian think of deliberate courting of attention? But if Clare Kendry's appearance had in it anything that was, to Brian Redfield, annoying or displeasing, the fact was not discernible to his wife as, with an uneasy feeling of guilt, she stood there looking into his face while Clare explained that she and he had made their own introductions, accompanying her words with a little deferential smile for Brian, and receiving in return one of his amused, slightly mocking smiles.

She remembered Clare's saying, as they sped northward: "You know, I feel exactly as I used to on the Sunday we went to the Christmas-tree celebration. I knew there was to be a surprise for me and couldn't quite guess what it was to be. I am *so* excited. You can't possibly imagine! It's marvelous to be really on the way! I can hardly believe it!"

At her words and tone a chilly wave of scorn had crept through Irene. All those superlatives! She said, taking care to speak indifferently: "Well, maybe in some ways you will be surprised, more, probably, than you anticipate."

Brian, at the wheel, had thrown back: "And then again, she won't be so very surprised after all, for it'll no doubt be about what she expects. Like the Christmas tree."

She remembered rushing around here and there, consulting with this person and that one, and now and then snatching a part of a dance with some man whose dancing she particularly liked.

She remembered catching glimpses of Clare in the whirling crowd, dancing, sometimes with a white man, more often with a Negro, frequently with Brian. Irene was glad that he was being nice to Clare, and glad that Clare was having the opportunity to discover that some colored men were superior to some white men.

She remembered a conversation she had with Hugh Wentworth in a free half hour when she had dropped into a chair in an emptied box and let her gaze wander over the bright crowd below.

Young men, old men, white men, black men; youthful women,

older women, pink women, golden women; fat men, thin men, tall men, short men; stout women, slim women, stately women, small women moved by. An old nursery rhyme popped into her head. She turned to Wentworth, who had just taken a seat beside her, and recited it:

> *"Rich man, poor man,*
> *Beggar man, thief,*
> *Doctor, lawyer,*
> *Indian chief."*

"Yes," Wentworth said, "that's it. Everybody seems to be here and a few more. But what I'm trying to find out is the name, status, and race of the blond beauty out of the fairy tale. She's dancing with Ralph Hazelton at the moment. Nice study in contrasts, that."

It was. Clare fair and golden, like a sunlit day. Hazelton dark, with gleaming eyes, like a moonlit night.

"She's a girl I used to know a long time ago in Chicago. And she wanted especially to meet you."

" 'S awfully good of her, I'm sure. And now, alas! the usual thing's happened. All these others, these—er—'gentlemen of color' have driven a mere Nordic from her mind."

"Stuff!"

" 'S a fact, and what happens to all the ladies of my superior race who're lured up here? Look at Bianca. Have I laid eyes on her tonight except in spots, here and there, being twirled about by some Ethiopian? I have not."

"But, Hugh, you've got to admit that the average colored man is a better dancer than the average white man—that is, if the celebrities and 'butter and egg' men who find their way up here are fair specimens of white terpsichorean art."

"Not having tripped the light fantastic with any of the males, I'm not in a position to argue the point. But I don't think it's merely that. 'S something else, some other attraction. They're always raving about the good looks of some Negro, preferably an unusually dark one. Take Hazelton there, for example. Dozens of women have declared him to be fascinatingly handsome. How about you, Irene? Do you think he's—er—ravishingly beautiful?"

"I do not! And I don't think the others do either. Not honestly, I mean. I think that what they feel is—well, a kind of emotional excitement. You know, the sort of thing you feel in the presence of something strange, and even, perhaps, a bit repugnant to you; something so different that it's really at the opposite end of the pole from all your accustomed notions of beauty."

"Damned if I don't think you're halfway right!"

"I'm sure I am. Completely. (Except, of course, when it's just patronizing kindness on their part.) And I know colored girls who've experienced the same thing—the other way round, naturally."

"And the men? You don't subscribe to the general opinion about their reason for coming up here? Purely predatory? Or do you?"

"N-no. More curious, I should say."

Wentworth, whose eyes were a clouded amber color, had given her a long, searching look that was really a stare. He said: "All this is awfully interestin', Irene. We've got to have a long talk about it sometime soon. There's your friend from Chicago, first time up here and all that. A case in point."

Irene's smile had only just lifted the corners of her painted lips. A match blazed in Wentworth's broad hands as he lighted her cigarette and his own, and flickered out before he asked: "Or isn't she?"

Her smile changed to a laugh. "Oh, Hugh! You're so clever. You usually know everything. Even how to tell the sheep from the goats. What do you think? Is she?"

He blew a long contemplative wreath of smoke. "Damned if I know! I'll be as sure as anything that I've learned the trick. And then in the next minute I'll find I couldn't pick some of 'em if my life depended on it."

"Well, don't let that worry you. Nobody can. Not by looking."

"Not by looking, eh? Meaning?"

"I'm afraid I can't explain. Not clearly. There are ways. But they're not definite or tangible."

"Feeling of kinship, or something like that?"

"Good heavens, no! Nobody has that, except for their in-laws."

"Right again! But go on about the sheep and the goats."

"Well, take my own experience with Dorothy Thompkins. I'd met her four or five times, in groups and crowds of people, before I knew she wasn't a Negro. One day I went to an awful tea, terribly dicty. Dorothy was there. We got talking. In less than five minutes, I knew she was 'fay.' Not from anything she did or said or anything in her appearance. Just—just something. A thing that couldn't be registered."

"Yes, I understand what you mean. Yet lots of people 'pass' all the time."

"Not on our side, Hugh. It's easy for a Negro to 'pass' for white. But I don't think it would be so simple for a white person to 'pass' for colored."

"Never thought of that."

"No, you wouldn't. Why should you?"

He regarded her critically through mists of smoke. "Slippin' me, Irene?"

She said soberly: "Not you, Hugh. I'm too fond of you. And you're too sincere."

And she remembered that towards the end of the dance Brian had come to her and said: "I'll drop you first and then run Clare down." And that he had been doubtful of her discretion when she had explained to him that he wouldn't have to bother because she had asked Bianca Wentworth to take her down with them. Did she, he had asked, think it had been wise to tell them about Clare?

"I told them nothing," she said sharply, for she was unbearably tired, "except that she was at the Walsingham. It's on their way. And, really, I haven't thought anything about the wisdom of it, but now that I do, I'd say it's much better for them to take her than you."

"As you please. She's your friend, you know," he had answered, with a disclaiming shrug of his shoulders.

Except for these few unconnected things the dance faded to a blurred memory, its outlines mingling with those of other dances of its kind that she had attended in the past and would attend in the future.

# Four

But undistinctive as the dance had seemed, it was, nevertheless, important. For it marked the beginning of a new factor in Irene Redfield's life, something that left its trace on all the future years of her existence. It was the beginning of a new friendship with Clare Kendry.

She came to them frequently after that. Always with a touching gladness that welled up and overflowed on all the Redfield household. Yet Irene could never be sure whether her comings were a joy or a vexation.

Certainly she was no trouble. She had not to be entertained, or even noticed—if anyone could ever avoid noticing Clare. If Irene happened to be out or occupied, Clare could very happily amuse herself with Ted and Junior, who had conceived for her an admiration that verged on adoration, especially Ted. Or, lacking the boys, she would descend to the kitchen and with—to Irene—an exasperating childlike lack of perception spend her visit in talk and merriment with Zulena and Sadie.

Irene, while secretly resenting these visits to the playroom and kitchen, for some obscure reason which she shied away from putting into words, never requested that Clare make an end of them, or hinted that she wouldn't have spoiled her own Margery so outrageously, nor been so friendly with white servants.

Brian looked on these things with the same tolerant amusement that marked his entire attitude toward Clare. Never since his faintly derisive surprise at Irene's information that she was to go with them the night of the dance had he shown any disapproval of Clare's presence. On the other hand, it couldn't be said that her presence seemed to please him. It didn't annoy or disturb him, so far as Irene could judge. That was all.

Didn't he, she once asked him, think Clare was extraordinarily beautiful?

"No," he had answered. "That is, not particularly."

"Brian, you're fooling!"

"No, honestly. Maybe I'm fussy. I s'pose she'd be an unusually good-looking white woman. I like my ladies darker. Beside an A-number-one sheba, she simply hasn't got 'em."

Clare went, sometimes with Irene and Brian, to parties and dances, and on a few occasions when Irene hadn't been able or inclined to go out, she had gone alone with Brian to some bridge party or benefit dance.

Once in a while she came formally to dine with them. She wasn't, however, in spite of her poise and air of worldliness, the ideal dinner-party guest. Beyond the aesthetic pleasure one got from watching her, she contributed little, sitting for the most part silent, an odd dreaming look in her hypnotic eyes. Though she could for some purpose of her own—the desire to be included in some party being made up to go cabareting, or an invitation to a dance or a tea—talk fluently and entertainingly.

She was generally liked. She was so friendly and responsive, and so ready to press the sweet food of flattery on all. Nor did she object to appearing a bit pathetic and ill used, so that people could feel sorry for her. And, no matter how often she came among them, she still remained someone apart, a little mysterious and strange, someone to wonder about and to admire and to pity.

Her visits were undecided and uncertain, being, as they were, dependent on the presence or absence of John Bellew in the city. But she did, once in a while, manage to steal uptown for an afternoon even when he was not away. As time went on without any apparent danger of discovery, even Irene ceased to be perturbed about the possibility of Clare's husband's stumbling on her racial identity.

The daughter, Margery, had been left in Switzerland in school, for

Clare and Bellew would be going back in the early spring. In March, Clare thought. "And how I do hate to think of it!" she would say, always with a suggestion of leashed rebellion. "But I can't see how I'm going to get out of it. Jack won't hear of my staying behind. If I could have just a couple of months more in New York, alone, I mean, I'd be the happiest thing in the world."

"I imagine you'll be happy enough, once you get away," Irene told her one day when she was bewailing her approaching departure. "Remember, there's Margery. Think how glad you'll be to see her after all this time."

"Children aren't everything," was Clare Kendry's answer to that. "There are other things in the world, though I admit some people don't seem to suspect it." And she laughed, more, it seemed, at some secret joke of her own than at her words.

Irene replied: "You know you don't mean that, Clare. You're only trying to tease me. I know very well that I take being a mother rather seriously. I *am* wrapped up in my boys and the running of my house. I can't help it. And, really, I don't think it's anything to laugh at." And though she was aware of the slight primness in her words and attitude, she had neither power nor wish to efface it.

Clare, suddenly very sober and sweet, said: "You're right. It's no laughing matter. It's shameful of me to tease you, 'Rene. You are so good." And she reached out and gave Irene's hand an affectionate little squeeze. "Don't think," she added, "whatever happens, that I'll ever forget how good you've been to me."

"Nonsense!"

"Oh, but you have, you have. It's just that I haven't any proper morals or sense of duty, as you have, that makes me act as I do."

"Now you are talking nonsense."

"But it's true, 'Rene. Can't you realize that I'm not like you a bit? Why, to get the things I want badly enough, I'd do anything, hurt anybody, throw anything away. Really, 'Rene, I'm not safe." Her voice as well as the look on her face had a beseeching earnestness that made Irene vaguely uncomfortable.

She said: "I don't believe it. In the first place what you're saying

is so utterly, so wickedly wrong. And as for your giving up things—"
She stopped, at a loss for an acceptable term to express her opinion
of Clare's "having" nature.

But Clare Kendry had begun to cry, audibly, with no effort at
restraint, and for no reason that Irene could discover.

## Part Three

# Finale

# One

The year was getting on towards its end. October, November had gone. December had come and brought with it a little snow and then a freeze and after that a thaw and some soft pleasant days that had in them a feeling of spring.

It wasn't, this mild weather, a bit Christmasy, Irene Redfield was thinking as she turned out of Seventh Avenue into her own street. She didn't like it to be warm and springy when it should have been cold and crisp, or grey and cloudy as if snow was about to fall. The weather, like people, ought to enter into the spirit of the season. Here the holidays were almost upon them, and the streets through which she had come were streaked with rills of muddy water and the sun shone so warmly that children had taken off their hats and scarfs. It was all as soft, as like April, as possible. The kind of weather for Easter. Certainly not for Christmas.

Though, she admitted reluctantly, she herself didn't feel the proper Christmas spirit this year either. But that couldn't be helped, it seemed, any more than the weather. She was weary and depressed. And for all her trying, she couldn't be free of that dull, indefinite misery which with increasing tenaciousness had laid hold of her. The morning's aimless wandering through the teeming Harlem streets, long after she had ordered the flowers which had been her excuse for setting out, was but another effort to tear herself loose from it.

She went up the cream stone steps, into the house, and down to the kitchen. There were to be people in to tea. But that, she found, after a few words with Sadie and Zulena, need give her no concern. She was thankful. She didn't want to be bothered. She went upstairs and took off her things and got into bed.

She thought: "Bother those people coming to tea!"

She thought: "If I could only be sure that at bottom it's just Brazil."

She thought: "Whatever it is, if I only knew what it was, I could manage it."

Brian again. Unhappy, restless, withdrawn. And she, who had prided herself on knowing his moods, their causes and their remedies, had found it first unthinkable, and then intolerable, that this, so like and yet so unlike those other spasmodic restlessnesses of his, should be to her incomprehensible and elusive.

He was restless and he was not restless. He was discontented, yet there were times when she felt he was possessed of some intense secret satisfaction, like a cat who had stolen the cream. He was irritable with the boys, especially Junior, for Ted, who seemed to have an uncanny knowledge of his father's periods of off moods, kept out of his way when possible. They got on his nerves, drove him to violent outbursts of temper, very different from his usual gently sarcastic remarks that constituted his idea of discipline for them. On the other hand, with her he was more than customarily considerate and abstemious. And it had been weeks since she had felt the keen edge of his irony.

He was like a man marking time, waiting. But what was he waiting for? It was extraordinary that, after all these years of accurate perception, she now lacked the talent to discover what that appearance of waiting meant. It was the knowledge that, for all her watching, all her patient study, the reason for his humor still eluded her which filled her with foreboding dread. That guarded reserve of his seemed to her unjust, inconsiderate, and alarming. It was as if he had stepped out beyond her reach into some section, strange and walled, where she could not get at him.

She closed her eyes, thinking what a blessing it would be if she could get a little sleep before the boys came in from school. She couldn't, of course, though she was so tired, having had, of late, so many sleepless nights. Nights filled with questionings and premonitions.

But she did sleep—several hours.

She wakened to find Brian standing at her bedside looking down at her, an unfathomable expression in his eyes.

She said: "I must have dropped off to sleep," and watched a slender ghost of his old amused smile pass over his face.

"It's getting on to four," he told her, meaning, she knew, that she was going to be late again.

She fought back the quick answer that rose to her lips and said instead: "I'm getting right up. It was good of you to think to call me." She sat up.

He bowed. "Always the attentive husband, you see."

"Yes indeed. Thank goodness, everything's ready."

"Except you. Oh, and Clare's downstairs."

"Clare! What a nuisance! I didn't ask her. Purposely."

"I see. Might a mere man ask why? Or is the reason so subtly feminine that it wouldn't be understood by him?"

A little of his smile had come back. Irene, who was beginning to shake off some of her depression under his familiar banter, said, almost gaily: "Not at all. It just happens that this party happens to be for Hugh, and that Hugh happens not to care a great deal for Clare; therefore I, who happen to be giving the party, didn't happen to ask her. Nothing could be simpler. Could it?"

"Nothing. It's so simple that I can easily see beyond your simple explanation and surmise that Clare, probably, just never happened to pay Hugh the admiring attention that he happens to consider no more than his just due. Simplest thing in the world."

Irene exclaimed in amazement: "Why, I thought you liked Hugh! You don't, you can't, believe anything so idiotic!"

"Well, Hugh does think he's God, you know."

"That," Irene declared, getting out of bed, "is absolutely not true. He thinks ever so much better of himself than that, as you, who know and have read him, ought to be able to guess. If you remember what a low opinion he has of God, you won't make such a silly mistake."

She went into the closet for her things and, coming back, hung her frock over the back of a chair and placed her shoes on the floor beside it. Then she sat down before her dressing table.

Brian didn't speak. He continued to stand beside the bed, seeming to look at nothing in particular. Certainly not at her. True, his gaze was on her, but in it there was some quality that made her feel that at that moment she was no more to him than a pane of glass through which he stared. At what? She didn't know, couldn't guess. And this made her uncomfortable. Piqued her.

She said: "It just happens that Hugh prefers intelligent women."

Plainly he was startled. "D'you mean that you think Clare is stupid?" he asked, regarding her with lifted eyebrows, which emphasized the disbelief of his voice.

She wiped the cold cream from her face before she said: "No, I don't. She isn't stupid. She's intelligent enough in a purely feminine way. Eighteenth-century France would have been a marvelous setting for her, or the old South if she hadn't made the mistake of being born a Negro."

"I see. Intelligent enough to wear a tight bodice and keep bowing swains whispering compliments and retrieving dropped fans. Rather a pretty picture. I take it, though, as slightly feline in its implication."

"Well, then, all I can say is that you take it wrongly. Nobody admires Clare more than I do, for the kind of intelligence she has, as well as for her decorative qualities. But she's not— She isn't— She hasn't— Oh, I can't explain it. Take Bianca, for example, or, to keep to the race, Felise Freeland. Looks *and* brains. Real brains that can hold their own with anybody. Clare has got brains of a sort, the kind that are useful too. Acquisitive, you know. But she'd bore a man like Hugh to suicide. Still, I never thought that even Clare would come to a private party to which she hadn't been asked. But it's like her."

For a minute there was silence. She completed the bright red arch of her full lips. Brian moved towards the door. His hand was on the knob. He said: "I'm sorry, Irene. It's my fault entirely. She seemed so hurt at being left out that I told her I was sure you'd forgotten and to just come along."

Irene cried out: "But, Brian, I—" and stopped, amazed at the fierce anger that had blazed up in her.

Brian's head came round with a jerk. His brows lifted in an odd surprise.

Her voice, she realized, *had* gone queer. But she had an instinctive feeling that it hadn't been the whole cause of his attitude. And that little straightening motion of the shoulders. Hadn't it been like that of a man drawing himself up to receive a blow? Her fright was like a scarlet spear of terror leaping at her heart.

Clare Kendry! So that was it! Impossible. It couldn't be.

In the mirror before her she saw that he was still regarding her with that air of slight amazement. She dropped her eyes to the jars and bottles on the table and began to fumble among them with hands whose fingers shook slightly.

"Of course," she said carefully, "I'm glad you did. And in spite of my recent remarks, Clare does add to any party. She's so easy on the eyes."

When she looked again, the surprise had gone from his face and the expectancy from his bearing.

"Yes," he agreed. "Well, I guess I'll run along. One of us ought to be down, I s'pose."

"You're right. One of us ought to." She was surprised that it was in her normal tones she spoke, caught as she was by the heart since that dull indefinite fear had grown suddenly into sharp panic. "I'll be down before you know it," she promised.

"All right." But he still lingered. "You're quite certain? You don't mind my asking her? Not awfully, I mean? I see now that I ought to have spoken to you. Trust women to have their reasons for everything."

She made a little pretense at looking at him, managed a tiny smile, and turned away. Clare! How sickening!

"Yes, don't they?" she said, striving to keep her voice casual. Within her she felt a hardness from feeling, not absent, but repressed. And that hardness was rising, swelling. Why didn't he go? Why didn't he?

He had opened the door at last. "You won't be long?" he asked, admonished.

She shook her head, unable to speak, for there was a choking in her throat, and the confusion in her mind was like the beating of wings. Behind her she heard the gentle impact of the door as it closed behind him, and knew that he had gone. Down to Clare.

For a long minute she sat in strained stiffness. The face in the mirror vanished from her sight, blotted out by this thing which had so suddenly flashed across her groping mind. Impossible for her to put it immediately into words or give it outline, for, prompted by some impulse of self-protection, she recoiled from exact expression.

She closed her unseeing eyes and clenched her fists. She tried not to cry. But her lips tightened and no effort could check the hot tears of rage and shame that sprang into her eyes and flowed down her cheeks; so she laid her face in her arms and wept silently.

When she was sure that she had done crying, she wiped away the warm remaining tears and got up. After bathing her swollen face in cold, refreshing water and carefully applying a stinging splash of toilet water, she went back to the mirror and regarded herself gravely. Satisfied that there lingered no betraying evidence of weeping, she dusted a little powder on her dark-white face and again examined it carefully, and with a kind of ridiculing contempt.

"I do think," she confided to it, "that you've been something—oh, very much—of a damned fool."

Downstairs the ritual of tea gave her some busy moments, and that, she decided, was a blessing. She wanted no empty spaces of time in which her mind would immediately return to that horror which she had not yet gathered sufficient courage to face. Pouring tea properly and nicely was an occupation that required a kind of well-balanced attention.

In the room beyond, a clock chimed. A single sound. Fifteen minutes past five o'clock. That was all! And yet in the short space of half an hour all of life had changed, lost its color, its vividness, its whole meaning. No, she reflected, it wasn't that that had happened. Life about her, apparently, went on exactly as before.

"Oh, Mrs. Runyon. . . . So nice to see you. . . . Two? . . . Really? . . . How exciting! . . . Yes, I think Tuesday's all right. . . ."

Yes, life went on precisely as before. It was only she that had changed. Knowing, stumbling on this thing, had changed her. It was as if in a house long dim a match had been struck, showing ghastly shapes where had been only blurred shadows.

Chatter, chatter, chatter. Someone asked her a question. She glanced up with what she felt was a rigid smile.

"Yes . . . Brian picked it up last winter in Haiti. Terribly weird, isn't it? . . . It *is* rather marvelous in its own hideous way. . . . Practically nothing, I believe. A few cents. . . ."

Hideous. A great weariness came over her. Even the small exertion of pouring golden tea into thin old cups seemed almost too much for her. She went on pouring. Made repetitions of her smile. Answered questions. Manufactured conversation. She thought: "I feel like the oldest person in the world with the longest stretch of life before me."

"Josephine Baker? . . . No. I've never seen her. . . . Well, she might have been in *Shuffle Along* when I saw it, but if she was, I don't remember her. . . . Oh, but you're wrong! . . . I do think Ethel Waters is awfully good. . . ."

There were the familiar little tinkling sounds of spoons striking against frail cups, the soft running sounds of inconsequential talk, punctuated now and then with laughter. In irregular small groups, disintegrating, coalescing, striking just the right note of disharmony, disorder in the big room, which Irene had furnished with a sparingness that was almost chaste, moved the guests with that slight familiarity that makes a party a success. On the floor and the walls the sinking sun threw long, fantastic shadows.

So like many other tea parties she had had. So unlike any of those others. But she mustn't think yet. Time enough for that after. All the time in the world. She had a second's flashing knowledge of what those words might portend. Time with Brian. Time without him. It was gone, leaving in its place an almost uncontrollable impulse to laugh, to scream, to hurl things about. She wanted, suddenly, to shock people, to hurt them, to make them notice her, to be aware of her suffering.

"Hello, Dave. . . . Felise. . . . Really, your clothes are the despair of half the women in Harlem. . . . How do you do it? . . . Lovely, is it Worth or Lanvin? . . . Oh, a mere Babani. . . ."

"Merely that," Felise Freeland acknowledged. "Come out of it, Irene, whatever it is. You look like the second gravedigger."

"Thanks for the hint, Felise. I'm not feeling quite up to par. The weather, I guess."

"Buy yourself an expensive new frock, child. It always helps. Any time this child gets the blues, it means money out of Dave's pocket. How're those boys of yours?"

The boys! For once she'd forgotten them.

They were, she told Felise, very well. Felise mumbled something about that being awfully nice and said she'd have to fly, because for a wonder she saw Mrs. Bellew sitting by herself, "and I've been trying to get her alone all afternoon. I want her for a party. Isn't she stunning today?"

Clare was. Irene couldn't remember ever having seen her look better. She was wearing a superlatively simple cinnamon-brown frock which brought out all her vivid beauty, and a little golden bowl of a hat. Around her neck hung a string of amber beads that would easily have made six or eight like one Irene owned. Yes, she was stunning.

The ripple of talk flowed on. The fire roared. The shadows stretched longer.

Across the room was Hugh. He wasn't, Irene hoped, being too bored. He seemed as he always did, a bit aloof, a little amused, and somewhat weary. And as usual he was hovering before the book-shelves. But he was not, she noticed, looking at the book he had taken down. Instead, his dull amber eyes were held by something across the room. They were a little scornful. Well, Hugh had never cared for Clare Kendry. For a minute Irene hesitated, then turned her head, though she knew what it was that held Hugh's gaze. Clare, who had suddenly clouded all her days. Brian, the father of Ted and Junior.

Clare's ivory face was what it always was, beautiful and caressing. Or maybe today a little masked. Unrevealing. Unaltered and undisturbed by any emotion within or without. Brian's seemed to Irene to be pitiably bare. Or was it too as it always was? That half-effaced seeking look, did he always have that? Queer that now she didn't know, couldn't recall. Then she saw him smile, and the smile made his face all eager and shining. Impelled by some inner urge of loyalty to herself, she glanced away. But only for a moment. And when she turned towards them again, she thought that the look on his face was the most melancholy and yet the most scoffing that she had ever seen upon it.

In the next quarter of an hour she promised herself to Bianca Wentworth in Sixty-second Street, Jane Tenant at Seventh Avenue and 150th Street, and the Dashields in Brooklyn for dinner all on the same evening and at almost the same hour.

Oh, well, what did it matter? She had no thoughts at all now, and all she felt was a great fatigue. Before her tired eyes Clare Kendry was talking to Dave Freeland. Scraps of their conversation, in Clare's husky voice, floated over to her: ". . . always admired you . . . so much about you long ago . . . everybody says so . . . no one but you . . ." And more of the same. The man hung rapt on her words, though he was the husband of Felise Freeland, and the author of novels that revealed a man of perception and a devastating irony. And he fell for such pishposh! And all because Clare had a trick of sliding down ivory lids over astonishing black eyes and then lifting them suddenly and turning on a caressing smile. Men like Dave Freeland fell for it. And Brian.

Her mental and physical languor receded. Brian. What did it mean? How would it affect her and the boys? The boys! She had a surge of relief. It ebbed, vanished. A feeling of absolute unimportance followed. Actually, she didn't count. She was, to him, only the mother of his sons. That was all. Alone she was nothing. Worse. An obstacle.

Rage boiled up in her.

There was a slight crash. On the floor at her feet lay the shattered cup. Dark stains dotted the bright rug. Spread. The chatter stopped. Went on. Before her, Zulena gathered up the white fragments.

As from a distance Hugh Wentworth's clipped voice came to her, though he was, she was aware, somehow miraculously at her side. "Sorry," he apologized. "Must have pushed you. Clumsy of me. Don't tell me it's priceless and irreplaceable."

It hurt. Dear God! How the thing hurt! But she couldn't think of that now. Not with Hugh sitting there mumbling apologies and lies. The significance of his words, the power of his discernment, stirred in her a sense of caution. Her pride revolted. Damn Hugh! Something would have to be done about him. Now. She couldn't, it seemed, help his knowing. It was too late for that. But she could and would keep him from knowing that she knew. She could, she would bear it. She'd have to. There were the boys. Her whole body went taut. In that second she saw that she could bear anything, but only if no one knew that she had anything to bear. It hurt. It frightened her, but she could bear it.

She turned to Hugh. Shook her head. Raised innocent dark eyes to his concerned pale ones. "Oh, no," she protested, "you didn't push me. Cross your heart, hope to die, and I'll tell you how it happened."

"Done!"

"Did you notice that cup? Well, you're lucky. It was the ugliest thing that your ancestors, the charming Confederates, ever owned. I've forgotten how many thousands of years ago it was that Brian's great-great-granduncle owned it. But it has, or had, a good old hoary history. It was brought North by way of the subway. Oh, all right! Be English if you want to and call it the underground. What I'm coming to is the fact that I've never figured out a way of getting rid of it until about five minutes ago. I had an inspiration. I had only to break it, and I was rid of it forever. So simple! And I'd never thought of it before."

Hugh nodded and his frosty smile spread over his features. Had she convinced him?

"Still," she went on with a little laugh that didn't, she was sure, sound the least bit forced, "I'm perfectly willing for you to take the blame and admit that you pushed me at the wrong moment. What are friends for, if not to help bear our sins? Brian will certainly be told that it was your fault.

"More tea, Clare? . . . I haven't had a minute with you. . . . Yes, it is a nice party. . . . You'll stay to dinner, I hope. . . . Oh, too bad! . . . I'll be alone with the boys. . . . They'll be sorry. Brian's got a medical meeting, or something. . . . Nice frock you're wearing. . . . Thanks. . . . Well, good-bye; see you soon, I hope."

The clock chimed. One. Two. Three. Four. Five. Six. Was it, could it be, only a little over an hour since she had come down to tea? One little hour.

"Must you go? . . . Good-bye. . . . Thank you so much. . . . So nice to see you. . . . Yes, Wednesday. . . . My love to Madge. . . . Sorry, but I'm filled up for Tuesday. . . . Oh, really? . . . Yes. . . . Good-bye. . . . Good-bye. . . ."

It hurt. It hurt like hell. But it didn't matter, if no one knew. If everything could go on as before. If the boys were safe.

It did hurt.

But it didn't matter.

# Two

But it did matter. It mattered more than anything had ever mattered before.

What bitterness! That the one fear, the one uncertainty, that she had felt, Brian's ache to go somewhere else, should have dwindled to a childish triviality! And with it the quality of the courage and resolution with which she had met it. From the visions and dangers which she now perceived she shrank away. For them she had no remedy or courage. Desperately she tried to shut out the knowledge from which had risen this turmoil, which she had no power to moderate or still, within her. And half succeeded.

For, she reasoned, what was there, what had there been, to show that she was even half correct in her tormenting notion? Nothing. She had seen nothing, heard nothing. She had no facts or proofs. She was only making herself unutterably wretched by an unfounded suspicion. It had been a case of looking for trouble and finding it in good measure. Merely that.

With this self-assurance that she had no real knowledge, she redoubled her efforts to drive out of her mind the distressing thought of faiths broken and trusts betrayed which every mental vision of Clare, of Brian, brought with them. She could not, she would not, go again through the tearing agony that lay just behind her.

She must, she told herself, be fair. In all their married life she had had no slightest cause to suspect her husband of any infidelity, of any serious flirtation even. If—and she doubted it—he had had his hours of outside erratic conduct, they were unknown to her. Why begin now to assume them? And on nothing more concrete than an idea that had leapt into her mind because he had told her that he had invited a friend, a friend of hers, to a party in his own house. And at a time when she had been, it was likely, more asleep than awake. How could she without anything done or said, or left undone or unsaid, so easily believe him guilty? How be so ready to renounce all confidence in the worth of their life together?

And if, perchance, there were some small something—well, what could it mean? Nothing. There were the boys. There was John Bellew. The thought of these three gave her some slight relief. But she did not look the future in the face. She wanted to feel nothing, to think nothing; simply to believe that it was all silly invention on her part. Yet she could not. Not quite.

Christmas, with its unreality, its hectic rush, its false gaiety, came and went. Irene was thankful for the confused unrest of the season. Its irksomeness, its crowds, its inane and insincere repetitions of genialities, pushed between her and the contemplation of her growing unhappiness.

She was thankful, too, for the continued absence of Clare, who, John Bellew having returned from a long stay in Canada, had withdrawn to that other life of hers, remote and inaccessible. But beating against the walled prison of Irene's thoughts was the shunned fancy that, though absent, Clare Kendry was still present, that she was close.

Brian, too, had withdrawn. The house contained his outward self and his belongings. He came and went with his usual noiseless irregularity. He sat across from her at table. He slept in his room next to hers at night. But he was remote and inaccessible. No use pretending that he was happy, that things were the same as they had always been. He wasn't and they weren't. However, she assured herself, it needn't necessarily be because of anything that involved Clare. It was, it must be, another manifestation of the old longing.

But she did wish it were spring, March, so that Clare would be sailing, out of her life and Brian's. Though she had come almost to believe that there was nothing but generous friendship between those two, she was very tired of Clare Kendry. She wanted to be free of her, and of her furtive comings and goings. If something would only happen, something that would make John Bellew decide on an earlier departure, or that would remove Clare. Anything. She didn't care what. Not even if it were that Clare's Margery were ill, or dying. Not even if Bellew should discover—

She drew a quick, sharp breath. And for a long time sat staring down at the hands in her lap. Strange, she had not before realized how easily she could put Clare out of her life! She had only to tell John Bellew that his wife— No. Not that! But if he should somehow learn of these Harlem visits— Why should she hesitate? Why spare Clare?

But she shrank away from the idea of telling that man, Clare Kendry's white husband, anything that would lead him to suspect that his wife was a Negro. Nor could she write it, or telephone it, or tell it to someone else who would tell him.

She was caught between two allegiances, different, yet the same. Herself. Her race. Race! The thing that bound and suffocated her. Whatever steps she took, or if she took none at all, something would be crushed. A person or the race. Clare, herself, or the race. Or, it might be, all three. Nothing, she imagined, was ever more completely sardonic.

Sitting alone in the quiet living room in the pleasant firelight, Irene Redfield wished, for the first time in her life that she had not been born a Negro. For the first time she suffered and rebelled because she was unable to disregard the burden of race. It was, she cried silently, enough to suffer as a woman, an individual, on one's own account, without having to suffer for the race as well. It was a brutality, and undeserved. Surely no other people so cursed as Ham's dark children.

Nevertheless, her weakness, her shrinking, her own inability to compass the thing, did not prevent her from wishing fervently that, in some way with which she had no concern, John Bellew would discover, not that his wife had a touch of the tar brush—Irene didn't want that—but that she was spending all the time that he was out of the city in black Harlem. Only that. It would be enough to rid her forever of Clare Kendry.

# Three

As if in answer to her wish, the very next day Irene came face to face with Bellew.

She had gone downtown with Felise Freeland to shop. The day was an exceptionally cold one, with a strong wind that had whipped a dusky red into Felise's smooth golden cheeks and driven moisture into Irene's soft brown eyes.

Clinging to each other, with heads bent against the wind, they turned out of the Avenue into Fifty-seventh Street. A sudden bluster flung them around the corner with unexpected quickness and they collided with a man.

"Pardon," Irene begged laughingly, and looked up into the face of Clare Kendry's husband.

"Mrs. Redfield!"

His hat came off. He held out his hand, smiling genially.

But the smile faded at once. Surprise, incredulity, and—was it understanding?—passed over his features.

He had, Irene knew, become conscious of Felise, golden, with curly black Negro hair, whose arm was still linked in her own. She was sure, now, of the understanding in his face, as he looked at her again and then back at Felise. And displeasure.

He didn't, however, withdraw his outstretched hand. Not at once.

But Irene didn't take it. Instinctively, in the first glance of recognition, her face had become a mask. Now she turned on him a totally uncomprehending look, a bit questioning. Seeing that he still stood with hand outstretched, she gave him the cool appraising stare which she reserved for mashers, and drew Felise on.

Felise drawled: "Aha! Been 'passing,' have you? Well, I've queered that."

"Yes, I'm afraid you have."

"Why, Irene Redfield! You sound as if you cared terribly. I'm sorry."

"I do, but not for the reason you think. I don't believe I've ever gone native in my life except for the sake of convenience, restaurants, theater tickets, and things like that. Never socially I mean, except once. You've just passed the only person that I've ever met disguised as a white woman."

"Awfully sorry. Be sure your sin will find you out and all that. Tell me about it."

"I'd like to. It would amuse you. But I can't."

Felise's laughter was as languidly nonchalant as her cool voice. "Can it be possible that the honest Irene has— Oh, do look at that coat! There. The red one. Isn't it a dream?"

Irene was thinking: "I had my chance and didn't take it. I had only to speak and to introduce him to Felise with the casual remark that he was Clare's husband. Only that. Fool. Fool." That instinctive loyalty to a race. Why couldn't she get free of it? Why should it include Clare? Clare, who'd shown little enough consideration for her and hers. What she felt was not so much resentment as a dull despair because she could not change herself in this respect, could not separate individuals from the race, herself from Clare Kendry.

"Let's go home, Felise. I'm so tired I could drop."

"Why, we haven't done half the things we planned."

"I know, but it's too cold to be running all over town. But you stay down if you want to."

"I think I'll do that, if you don't mind."


And now another problem confronted Irene. She must tell Clare of this meeting. Warn her. But how? She hadn't seen her for days. Writing and telephoning were equally unsafe. And even if it was possible to get in touch with her, what good would it do? If Bellew hadn't concluded that he'd made a mistake, if he was certain of her identity—and he was nobody's fool—telling Clare wouldn't avert the results of the encounter. Besides, it was too late. Whatever was in store for Clare Kendry had already overtaken her.

Irene was conscious of a feeling of relieved thankfulness at the thought that she was probably rid of Clare, and without having lifted a finger or uttered one word.

But she did mean to tell Brian about meeting John Bellew.

But that, it seemed, was impossible. Strange. Something held her back. Each time she was on the verge of saying: "I ran into Clare's husband on the street downtown today. I'm sure he recognized me, and Felise was with me," she failed to speak. It sounded too much like the warning she wanted it to be. Not even in the presence of the boys at dinner could she make the bare statement.

The evening dragged. At last she said good night and went upstairs, the words unsaid.

She thought: "Why didn't I tell him? Why didn't I? If trouble comes from this, I'll never forgive myself. I'll tell him when he comes up."

She took up a book, but she could not read, so oppressed was she by a nameless foreboding.

What if Bellew should divorce Clare? Could he? There was the Rhinelander case. But in France, in Paris, such things were very easy. If he divorced her— If Clare were free— But of all the things that could happen, that was the one she did not want. She must get her mind away from that possibility. She must.

Then came a thought which she tried to drive away. If Clare should die! Then— Oh, it was vile! To think, yes, to wish that! She felt faint and sick. But the thought stayed with her. She could not get rid of it.

She heard the outer door open. Close. Brian had gone out. She turned her face into her pillow to cry. But no tears came.

She lay there awake, thinking of things past. Of her courtship and marriage and Junior's birth. Of the time they had bought the house in which they had lived so long and so happily. Of the time Ted had passed his pneumonia crisis and they knew he would live. And of other sweet painful memories that would never come again.

Above everything else she had wanted, had striven, to keep undisturbed the pleasant routine of her life. And now Clare Kendry had come into it, and with her the menace of impermanence.

"Dear God," she prayed, "make March come quickly."

By and by she slept.

# Four

The next morning brought with it a snowstorm that lasted throughout the day.

After a breakfast which had been eaten almost in silence and which she was relieved to have done with, Irene Redfield lingered for a little while in the downstairs hall, looking out at the soft flakes fluttering down. She was watching them immediately fill some ugly irregular gaps left by the feet of hurrying pedestrians when Zulena came to her, saying: "The telephone, Mrs. Redfield. It's Mrs. Bellew."

"Take the message, Zulena, please."

Though she continued to stare out of the window, Irene saw nothing now, stabbed as she was by fear—and hope. Had anything happened between Clare and Bellew? And if so, what? And was she to be freed at last from the aching anxiety of the past weeks? Or was there to be more, and worse? She had a wrestling moment in which it seemed that she must rush after Zulena and hear for herself what it was that Clare had to say. But she waited.

Zulena, when she came back, said: "She says, ma'am, that she'll be able to go to Mrs. Freeland's tonight. She'll be here sometime between eight and nine."

"Thank you, Zulena."

The day dragged on to its end.

At dinner Brian spoke bitterly of a lynching that he had been reading about in the evening paper.

"Dad, why is it that they only lynch colored people?" Ted asked.

"Because they hate 'em, son."

"Brian!" Irene's voice was a plea and a rebuke.

Ted said: "Oh! And why do they hate 'em?"

"Because they are afraid of them."

"But what makes them afraid of 'em?"

"Because—"

"Brian!"

"It seems, son, that is a subject we can't go into at the moment without distressing the ladies of our family," he told the boy with mock seriousness, "but we'll take it up sometime when we're alone together."

Ted nodded in his engaging grave way. "I see. Maybe we can talk about it tomorrow on the way to school."

"That'll be fine."

"Brian!"

"Mother," Junior remarked, "that's the third time you've said 'Brian' like that."

"But not the last, Junior, never you fear," his father told him.

After the boys had gone up to their own floor, Irene said suavely: "I do wish, Brian, that you wouldn't talk about lynching before Ted and Junior. It was really inexcusable for you to bring up a thing like that at dinner. There'll be time enough for them to learn about such horrible things when they're older."

"You're absolutely wrong! If, as you're so determined, they've got to live in this damned country, they'd better find out what sort of thing they're up against as soon as possible. The earlier they learn it, the better prepared they'll be."

"I don't agree. I want their childhood to be happy and as free from the knowledge of such things as it possibly can be."

"Very laudable," was Brian's sarcastic answer. "Very laudable indeed, all things considered. But can it?"

"Certainly it can. If you'll only do your part."

"Stuff! You know as well as I do, Irene, that it can't. What was the use of our trying to keep them from learning the word 'nigger' and its connotation? They found out, didn't they? And how? Because somebody called Junior a dirty nigger."

"Just the same, you're not to talk to them about the race problem. I won't have it."

They glared at each other.

"I tell you, Irene, they've got to know these things, and it might as well be now as later."

"They do not!" she insisted, forcing back the tears of anger that were threatening to fall.

Brian growled: "I can't understand how anybody as intelligent as you like to think you are can show evidences of such stupidity." He looked at her in a puzzled harassed way.

"Stupid!" she cried. "Is it stupid to want my children to be happy?" Her lips were quivering.

"At the expense of proper preparation for life and their future happiness, yes. And I'd feel I hadn't done my duty by them if I didn't give them some inkling of what's before them. It's the least I can do. I wanted to get them out of this hellish place years ago. You wouldn't let me. I gave up the idea, because you objected. Don't expect me to give up everything."

Under the lash of his words she was silent. Before any answer came to her, he had turned and gone from the room.

Sitting there alone in the forsaken dining room, unconsciously pressing the hands lying in her lap tightly together, she was seized by a convulsion of shivering. For, to her, there had been something ominous in the scene that she had just had with her husband. Over and over in her mind his last words: "Don't expect me to give up everything," repeated themselves. What had they meant? What could they mean? Clare Kendry?

Surely she was going mad with fear and suspicion. She must not work herself up. She must not! Where were all the self-control, the common sense, that she was so proud of? Now, if ever, was the time for it.

Clare would soon be there. She must hurry or she would be late again, and those two would wait for her downstairs together, as they had done so often since that first time, which now seemed so long ago. Had it been really only last October? Why, she felt years, not months, older.

Drearily she rose from her chair and went upstairs to set about the business of dressing to go out when she would far rather have remained at home. During the process she wondered, for the hundredth time, why she hadn't told Brian about herself and Felise running into Bellew the day before, and for the hundredth time she turned away from acknowledging to herself the real reason for keeping back the information.

When Clare arrived, radiant in a shining red gown, Irene had not finished dressing. But her smile scarcely hesitated as she greeted her, saying: "I always seem to keep C. P. time, don't I? We hardly ex-

pected you to be able to come. Felise will be pleased. How nice you look."

Clare kissed a bare shoulder, seeming not to notice a slight shrinking.

"I hadn't an idea in the world, myself, that I'd be able to make it; but Jack had to run down to Philadelphia unexpectedly. So here I am."

Irene looked up, a flood of speech on her lips. "Philadelphia. That's not very far, is it? Clare, I—?"

She stopped, one of her hands clutching the side of her stool, the other lying clenched on the dressing table. Why didn't she go on and tell Clare about meeting Bellew? Why couldn't she?

But Clare didn't notice the unfinished sentence. She laughed and said lightly: "It's far enough for me. Anywhere, away from me, is far enough. I'm not particular."

Irene passed a hand over her eyes to shut out the accusing face in the glass before her. With one corner of her mind she wondered how long she had looked like that, drawn and haggard and—yes, frightened. Or was it only imagination?

"Clare," she asked, "have you ever seriously thought what it would mean if he should find you out?"

"Yes."

"Oh! You have! And what you'd do in that case?"

"Yes." And having said it, Clare Kendry smiled quickly, a smile that came and went like a flash, leaving untouched the gravity of her face.

That smile and the quiet resolution of that one word, "Yes," filled

Irene with a primitive paralyzing dread. Her hands were numb, her feet like ice, her heart like a stone weight. Even her tongue was like a heavy dying thing. There were long spaces between the words as she asked: "And what should you do?"

Clare, who was sunk in a deep chair, her eyes far away, seemed wrapped in some pleasant impenetrable reflection. To Irene, sitting expectantly upright, it was an interminable time before she dragged herself back to the present to say calmly: "I'd do what I want to do more than anything else right now. I'd come up here to live. Harlem, I mean. Then I'd be able to do as I please, when I please."

Irene leaned forward, cold and tense. "And what about Margery?" Her voice was a strained whisper.

"Margery?" Clare repeated, letting her eyes flutter over Irene's concerned face. "Just this, 'Rene. If it wasn't for her, I'd do it anyway. She's all that holds me back. But if Jack finds out, if our marriage is broken, that lets me out. Doesn't it?"

Her gentle resigned tone, her air of innocent candor, appeared, to her listener, spurious. A conviction that the words were intended as a warning took possession of Irene. She remembered that Clare Kendry had always seemed to know what other people were thinking. Her compressed lips grew firm and obdurate. Well, she wouldn't know this time.

She said: "Do go downstairs and talk to Brian. He's got a mad on."

Though she had determined that Clare should not get at her thoughts and fears, the words had sprung, unthought of, to her lips. It was as if they had come from some outer layer of callousness that had no relation to her tortured heart. And they had been, she realized, precisely the right words for her purpose.

For as Clare got up and went out she saw that that arrangement was as good as her first plan of keeping her waiting up there while she dressed—or better. She would only have hindered and rasped her. And what matter if those two spent one hour, more or less, alone together, one or many, now that everything had happened between them?

Ah! The first time that she had allowed herself to admit to herself that everything had happened, had not forced herself to believe, to hope, that nothing irrevocable had been consummated! Well, it had happened. She knew it, and knew that she knew it.

She was surprised that, having thought the thought, conceded the fact, she was no more hurt, cared no more, than during her previous frenzied endeavors to escape it. And this absence of acute, unbearable pain seemed to her unjust, as if she had been denied some exquisite solace of suffering which the full acknowledgment should have given her.

Was it, perhaps, that she had endured all that a woman could endure of tormenting humiliation and fear? Or was it that she lacked the capacity for the acme of suffering? "No, no!" she denied fiercely. "I'm human like everybody else. It's just that I'm so tired, so worn out, I can't feel any more." But she did not really believe that.

Security. Was it just a word? If not, then was it only by the sacrifice of other things, happiness, love, or some wild ecstasy that she had never known, that it could be obtained? And did too much striving, too much faith in safety and permanence, unfit one for these other things?

Irene didn't know, couldn't decide, though for a long time she sat questioning and trying to understand. Yet all the while, in spite of her searchings and feeling of frustration, she was aware that, to her, security was the most important and desired thing in life. Not for any of the others, or for all of them, would she exchange it. She wanted only to be tranquil. Only, unmolested, to be allowed to direct for their own best good the lives of her sons and her husband.

Now that she had relieved herself of what was almost like a guilty knowledge, admitted that which by some sixth sense she had long known, she could again reach out for plans. Could think again of ways to keep Brian by her side, and in New York. For she would not go to Brazil. She belonged in this land of rising towers. She was an American. She grew from this soil, and she would not be uprooted. Not even because of Clare Kendry, or a hundred Clare Kendrys.

Brian, too, belonged here. His duty was to her and to his boys.

Strange that she couldn't now be sure that she had ever truly known love. Not even for Brian. He was her husband and the father of her sons. But was he anything more? Had she ever wanted or tried for more? In that hour she thought not.

Nevertheless, she meant to keep him. Her freshly painted lips narrowed to a thin straight line. True, she had left off trying to believe that he and Clare loved and yet did not love, but she still intended to hold fast to the outer shell of her marriage, to keep her life fixed, certain. Brought to the edge of distasteful reality, her fastidious nature did not recoil. Better, far better, to share him than to lose him completely. Oh, she could close her eyes, if need be. She could bear it. She could bear anything. And there was March ahead. March and the departure of Clare.

Horribly clear, she could now see the reason for her instinct to withhold—omit, rather—her news of the encounter with Bellew. If Clare was freed, anything might happen.

She paused in her dressing, seeing with perfect clearness that dark truth which she had from that first October afternoon felt about Clare Kendry and of which Clare herself had once warned her—that she got the things she wanted because she met the great condition of conquest, sacrifice. If she wanted Brian, Clare wouldn't revolt from the lack of money or place. It was as she had said, only Margery kept her from throwing all that away. And if things were taken out of her hands— Even if she was only alarmed, only suspected that such a thing was about to occur, anything might happen. Anything.

No! At all costs, Clare was not to know of that meeting with Bellew. Nor was Brian. It would only weaken her own power to keep him.

They would never know from her that he was on his way to suspecting the truth about his wife. And she would do anything, risk anything, to prevent him from finding out that truth. How fortunate that she had obeyed her instinct and omitted to recognize Bellew!

. . .

"Ever go up to the sixth floor, Clare?" Brian asked as he stopped the car and got out to open the door for them.

"Why, of course! We're on the seventeenth."

"I mean, did you ever go up by nigger power?"

"That's good!" Clare laughed. "Ask 'Rene. My father was a janitor, you know, in the good old days before every ramshackle flat had its elevator. But you can't mean we've got to walk up? Not here!"

"Yes, here. And Felise lives at the very top," Irene told her.

"What on earth for?"

"I believe she claims it discourages the casual visitor."

"And she's probably right. Hard on herself, though."

Brian said, "Yes, a bit. But she says she'd rather be dead than bored."

"Oh, a garden! And how lovely with that undisturbed snow!"

"Yes, isn't it? But keep to the walk with those foolish thin shoes. You too, Irene."

Irene walked beside them on the cleared cement path that split the whiteness of the courtyard garden. She felt a something in the air, something that had been between those two and would be again. It was like a live thing pressing against her. In a quick furtive glance she saw Clare clinging to Brian's other arm. She was looking at him with that provocative upward glance of hers, and his eyes were fastened on her face with what seemed to Irene an expression of wistful eagerness.

"It's this entrance, I believe," she informed them in quite her ordinary voice.

"Mind," Brian told Clare, "you don't fall by the wayside before the fourth floor. They absolutely refuse to carry anyone up more than the last two flights."

"Don't be silly!" Irene snapped.


The party began gaily.

Dave Freeland was at his best, brilliant, crystal clear, and sparkling. Felise, too, was amusing, and not so sarcastic as usual, because she liked the dozen or so guests who dotted the long, untidy living room.

Brian was witty, though, Irene noted, his remarks were somewhat more barbed than was customary even with him. And there was Ralph Hazelton, throwing nonsensical shining things into the pool of talk, which the others, even Clare, picked up and flung back with fresh adornment.

Only Irene wasn't merry. She sat almost silent, smiling now and then, that she might appear amused.

"What's the matter, Irene?" someone asked. "Taken a vow never to laugh or something? You're as sober as a judge."

"No. It's simply that the rest of you are so clever that I'm speechless, absolutely stunned."

"No wonder," Dave Freeland remarked, "that you're on the verge of tears. You haven't a drink. What'll you take?"

"Thanks. If I must take something, make it a glass of ginger ale and three drops of Scotch. The Scotch first, please. Then the ice, then the ginger ale."

"Heavens! Don't attempt to mix that yourself, Dave darling. Have the butler in," Felise mocked.

"Yes, do. And the footman." Irene laughed a little, then said: "It seems dreadfully warm in here. Mind if I open this window?" With that she pushed open one of the long casement windows of which the Freelands were so proud.

It had stopped snowing some two or three hours back. The moon was just rising, and far behind the tall buildings a few stars were creeping out. Irene finished her cigarette and threw it out, watching the tiny spark drop slowly down to the white ground below.

Someone in the room had turned on the phonograph. Or was it the radio? She didn't know which she disliked more. And nobody was listening to its blare. The talking, the laughter never for a minute ceased. Why must they have more noise?

Dave came with her drink. "You ought not," he told her, "to stand there like that. You'll take cold. Come along and talk to me, or listen to me gabble." Taking her arm, he led her across the room. They had just found seats when the doorbell rang and Felise called over to him to go and answer it.

In the next moment Irene heard his voice in the hall, carelessly polite: "Your wife? Sorry. I'm afraid you're wrong. Perhaps next—"

Then the roar of John Bellew's voice above all the other noises of the room: "I'm *not* wrong! I've been to the Redfields' and I know she's with them. You'd better stand out of my way and save yourself trouble in the end."

"What is it, Dave?" Felise ran out to the door.

And so did Brian. Irene heard him saying: "I'm Redfield. What the devil's the matter with you?"

But Bellew didn't heed him. He pushed past them all into the room and strode towards Clare. They all looked at her as she got up from her chair, backing a little from his approach.

"So you're a nigger, a damned dirty nigger!" His voice was a snarl and a moan, an expression of rage and of pain.

Everything was in confusion. The men had sprung forward. Felise had leapt between them and Bellew. She said quickly: "Careful. You're the only white man here." And the silver chill of her voice, as well as her words, was a warning.

Clare stood at the window, as composed as if everyone were not staring at her in curiosity and wonder, as if the whole structure of her life were not lying in fragments before her. She seemed unaware of any danger or uncaring. There was even a faint smile on her full red lips and in her shining eyes.

It was that smile that maddened Irene. She ran across the room, her terror tinged with ferocity, and laid a hand on Clare's bare arm. One thought possessed her. She couldn't have Clare Kendry cast aside by Bellew. She couldn't have her free.

Before them stood John Bellew, speechless now in his hurt and anger. Beyond them the little huddle of other people, and Brian stepping out from among them.

What happened next, Irene Redfield never afterwards allowed herself to remember. Never clearly.

One moment Clare had been there, a vital glowing thing, like a flame of red and gold. The next she was gone.

There was a gasp of horror, and above it a sound not quite human, like a beast in agony. "Nig! My God! Nig!"

A frenzied rush of feet down long flights of stairs. The slamming of distant doors. Voices.

Irene stayed behind. She sat down and remained quite still, staring at a ridiculous Japanese print on the wall across the room.

Gone! The soft white face, the bright hair, the disturbing scarlet mouth, the dreaming eyes, the caressing smile, the whole torturing loveliness that had been Clare Kendry. That beauty that had torn at Irene's placid life. Gone! The mocking daring, the gallantry of her pose, the ringing bells of her laughter.

Irene wasn't sorry. She was amazed, incredulous almost.

What would the others think? That Clare had fallen? That she had deliberately leaned backward? Certainly one or the other. Not—

But she mustn't, she warned herself, think of that. She was too tired, and too shocked. And, indeed, both were true. She was utterly weary, and she was violently staggered. But her thoughts reeled on. If only she could be as free of mental as she was of bodily vigor; could only put from her memory the vision of her hand on Clare's arm!

"It was an accident, a terrible accident," she muttered fiercely. "It *was*."

People were coming up the stairs. Through the still open door their steps and talk sounded nearer, nearer.

Quickly she stood up and went noiselessly into the bedroom and closed the door softly behind her.

Her thoughts raced. Ought she to have stayed? Should she go back out there to them? But there would be questions. She hadn't thought of them, of afterwards, of this. She had thought of nothing in that sudden moment of action.

It was cold. Icy chills ran up her spine and over her bare neck and shoulders.

In the room outside there were voices. Dave Freeland's and others that she did not recognize.

Should she put on her coat? Felise had rushed down without any wrap. So had all the others. So had Brian. Brian! He mustn't take cold. She took up his coat and left her own. At the door she paused for a moment, listening fearfully. She heard nothing. No voices. No footsteps. Very slowly she opened the door. The room was empty. She went out.

In the hall below she heard dimly the sound of feet going down the steps, of a door being opened and closed, and of voices far away.

Down, down, down, she went, Brian's great coat clutched in her shivering arms and trailing a little on each step behind her.

What was she to say to them when at last she had finished going down those endless stairs? She should have rushed out when they did. What reason could she give for her dallying behind? Even she didn't know why she had done that. And what else would she be asked? There had been her hand reaching out towards Clare. What about that?

In the midst of her wonderings and questionings came a thought so terrifying, so horrible, that she had had to grasp hold of the banister to save herself from pitching downwards. A cold perspiration drenched her shaking body. Her breath came short in sharp and painful gasps.

What if Clare was not dead?

She felt nauseated, as much at the idea of the glorious body mutilated as from fear.

How she managed to make the rest of the journey without fainting she never knew. But at last she was down. Just at the bottom she came on the others, surrounded by a little circle of strangers. They were all speaking in whispers, or in the awed, discreetly lowered tones adapted to the presence of disaster. In the first instant she wanted to turn and rush back up the way she had come. Then a calm desperation came over her. She braced herself, physically and mentally.

"Here's Irene now," Dave Freeland announced, and told her that, having only just missed her, they had concluded that she had fainted or something like that, and were on the way to find out about her. Felise, she saw, was holding on to his arm, all the insolent nonchalance gone out of her, and the golden brown of her handsome face changed to a queer mauve color.

Irene made no indication that she had heard Freeland but went straight to Brian. His face looked aged and altered, and his lips were purple and trembling. She had a great longing to comfort him, to charm away his suffering and horror. But she was helpless, having so completely lost control of his mind and heart.

She stammered: "Is she—is she—?"

It was Felise who answered. "Instantly, we think."

Irene struggled against the sob of thankfulness that rose in her throat. Choked down, it turned to a whimper, like a hurt child's. Someone laid a hand on her shoulder in a soothing gesture. Brian wrapped his coat about her. She began to cry rackingly, her entire body heaving with convulsive sobs. He made a slight perfunctory attempt to comfort her.

"There, there, Irene. You mustn't. You'll make yourself sick. She's—" His voice broke suddenly.

As from a long distance she heard Ralph Hazelton's voice saying: "I was looking right at her. She just tumbled over and was gone before you could say 'Jack Robinson.' Fainted, I guess. Lord! It was quick. Quickest thing I ever saw in all my life."

"It's impossible, I tell you! Absolutely impossible!"

It was Brian who spoke in that frenzied hoarse voice, which Irene had never heard before. Her knees quaked under her.

Dave Freeland said: "Just a minute, Brian. Irene was there beside her. Let's hear what she has to say."

She had a moment of stark craven fear. "Oh, God," she thought, prayed, "help me."

A strange man, official and authoritative, addressed her. "You're sure she fell? Her husband didn't give her a shove or anything like that, as Dr. Redfield seems to think?"

For the first time she was aware that Bellew was not in the little group shivering in the small hallway. What did that mean? As she began to work it out in her numbed mind, she was shaken with another hideous trembling. Not that! Oh, not that!

"No, no!" she protested. "I'm quite certain that he didn't. I was there, too. As close as he was. She just fell, before anybody could stop her. I—"

Her quaking knees gave way under her. She moaned and sank down, moaned again. Through the great heaviness that submerged and drowned her she was dimly conscious of strong arms lifting her up. Then everything was dark.

Centuries after, she heard the strange man saying: "Death by misadventure, I'm inclined to believe. Let's go up and have another look at that window."

# Nella Larsen—
# A Chronology

| | |
|---|---|
| April 13, 1891 | Born. New York (?) |
| 1912–1915 | Nursing Degree, Lincoln Hospital and Home |
| 1915–1917 | Works as nurse at Tuskegee Normal and Industrial Institute, Tuskegee, Alabama |
| 1918 | New York City Department of Health |
| May 3, 1919 | Marries Elmer S. Imes |
| 1920 | "Three Scandinavian Games," *The Brownies' Book* (June)<br>"Danish Fun," *The Brownies' Book* (July) Published under name Nella Larsen Imes |

| | |
|---|---|
| 1921–1926 | Works as a librarian for the New York City Public Library (Harlem Branch) |
| 1926 | "The Wrong Man," *Young's Magazine* (January); "Freedom," *Young's Magazine* (April) Published under pseudonym: Allen Semi |
| 1928 | *Quicksand* Awarded Bronze Award for Literature (Harmon Foundation) |
| 1929 | *Passing* |
| 1930 | "Sanctuary," *Forum* (January) Accused of plagiarism |
| 1930–1931 | Guggenheim Fellow in Europe Working on *Mirage* |
| 1932 | Nashville, with Elmer |
| August 30, 1933 | Divorces Elmer Imes |
| September 11, 1941 | Elmer Imes dies |
| February 14, 1944 | Appointed Chief Nurse at Gouverneur Hospital, New York City |
| September 1954 | Night Supervisor at Gouverneur Hospital |
| 1962 | Supervisor of Nurses, Metropolitan Hospital, New York City |
| September 12, 1963 | Retires from nursing |
| March 30, 1964 | Discovered dead in her apartment |

CHARLES R. LARSON is Professor of Literature at American University in Washington, D.C. He is the author of three critical works on Third World literature: *The Emergence of African Fiction* (1972), *The Novel in the Third World* (1976), and *American Indian Fiction* (1978). He has also published three novels: *Academia Nuts* (1977), *The Insect Colony* (1978), and *Arthur Dimmesdale* (1983). Previously, he was a general editor of Collier Books' African-American Library.

MARITA GOLDEN is the author of *Migrations of the Heart*, *A Woman's Place*, and *Long Distance Life*. Her writing has appeared in *Ms.*, *Essence*, the *New York Times*, the *Washington Post*, and many other publications. She is a founding member of the African American Writers' Guild. Ms. Golden lives in Washington, D.C., where she teaches in the MFA Creative Writing Program at George Mason University.